THE ACTOR'S
WORKBOOK

THE ACTOR'S WORKBOOK

A Practical Guide to Training, Rehearsing and Devising + Video

ALEX CLIFTON

Bloomsbury Methuen Drama
An imprint of Bloomsbury Publishing Plc

B L O O M S B U R Y
LONDON · OXFORD · NEW YORK · NEW DELHI · SYDNEY

Bloomsbury Methuen Drama

An imprint of Bloomsbury Publishing Plc

50 Bedford Square	1385 Broadway
London	New York
WC1B 3DP	NY 10018
UK	USA

www.bloomsbury.com

Bloomsbury is a registered trade mark of Bloomsbury Publishing Plc

First published 2016

Copyright © Alex Clifton 2016

British Library Cataloguing in Publication Data

A catalogue record for this book is available from the British Library.

ISBN: PB: 978-1-4725-3004-2
epDF: 978-1-4725-2326-6
ePub: 978-1-4725-3180-3

Library of Congress Cataloging-in-Publication Data

A catalog record for this book is available from the Library of Congress.

Typeset by Fakenham Prepress Solutions, Fakenham, Norfolk NR21 8NN
Printed and bound in India

For Holly, Nathaniel and Joseph

CONTENTS

PART THREE THE STORY 245

ACKNOWLEDGEMENTS

Many thanks to David and Rebecca Carey for the opportunity, guidance and support.

Particular thanks to Mike Caemmerer, whose sharp eye and whip-hand were most welcome.

Thanks to Glyn Maxwell for inspiration and better words, and to trusted adviser and collaborator Jess Curtis.

Above all, thanks to the many brilliant teachers and actors I've had the good fortune to teach and learn alongside at RADA.

INTRODUCTION

I must Create a System or be enslav'd by another Man's.
WILLIAM BLAKE, *Jerusalem: The Emanation of the Giant Albion*

People need to share stories. Through stories we rehearse our lives and build communities, together asking, 'How shall we live?' Stories train us as rule-breakers and agents of change, and allow us to rehearse possible futures. Through stories we examine who we are, and explore who we could be. We employ a remarkable human superpower to do so: imagination.

There are things in your brain called 'mirror neurones'. These are cells that fire when you do something, but also when you watch someone else do something. They mirror other people's behaviours. Whether you do a star jump or watch your friend do one, your brain's mirror neurones will behave in exactly the same way. No-one is yet sure what exact function they serve.

It might be that these neurones are the reason why if I yawn, you want to yawn. It might be how babies instinctively mimic their parents. It might be that these neurone systems are the basis of how we observe other people's actions and infer their intentions. It might even be that these ignite our capacity for empathy, helping us imagine other lives.

What does this mean for an actor? As you howl to heaven's vault and carry the body of your dead daughter Cordelia on stage, a part of your audience's brain exactly mimics your action. Because the audience offers its full attention to what you have seen and done, a little bit of them is King Lear too. Eight hundred people watching, all carry Cordelia together: they achieve a kind of shared consciousness. This, I suppose, is how storytelling can affect people so deeply and build community: people share a profound neurological ability to make themselves affected.

This capacity for empathetic role-play is a basic human reflex and a condition of human physiology. Role-play need not be taught, but it can be trained.

*

This workbook offers a comprehensive collection of acting exercises for training, rehearsing and devising role-play. Use it to build your own systems for acting and theatre-making.

Throughout the workbook I refer to *Macbeth*, *Romeo and Juliet* and *A Doll's House*. They are three of the most staged plays in the world, so I hope at least one of them will be a clear reference point for you. My choices reflect the book's cultural bias: it has grown out of European traditions of practice and reflects the values of that culture. Each practitioner will need to be creative in making this work available to anyone who seeks to participate in its learning.

This is as much cookbook as workbook. In your kitchen you take recipes and adapt them to your cupboard's resources, your oven's oddities, your family's tastes. While the book is written to be progressive, dip into different sections and reimagine these exercises in ways that suit your resources and needs.

*

As you read, keep William Blake's challenge in mind: create your own system, don't be enslaved by those outlined here. Reading and writing about acting is intoxicating, but like any intoxicant too much of it can become deadly. Develop your own practical system for each production you work on: adapt don't adopt.

None of the exercises has primacy over that which you are building: great stories that move audiences. Whenever you find yourself talking about a system for acting more than you talk about the society acting serves, throw that system out the window and start again.

The value of what we do is in the audience's reception of what we do. It doesn't much matter what your journey is, or where it takes you; it matters where it takes the audience. Process is not our main focal point, it is our pragmatic and playful means to reach a glorious destination for our audience.

First, learn to play. Next, take a role in a play. Then, make a play. This is the course of the workbook. Play is the common thread. It is a mad privilege to make play your work – it is probably what you dreamed of doing as a child and is why our work feels like an extension of childhood. Bring joy to it. Go on a child-like adventure, take wrong turns and discover unexpected treasures – then share those treasures with everyone you can.

ON REFLECTION

As you work, keep a journal. Get a book and write, draw, stick stuff into it. You might write reminders to your future self – notes you think you might need in time to come. You might write to yourself as you are now – noting your tensions, habitual behaviours, thought patterns. You might write to your past self, observing previous behaviours and choices. Write for and to yourself in any case.

You might do drawings and sketches. Stick in images from books, magazines, newspapers that you find stimulating. Make lists. I always find it helpful to have a few pages covered in about twenty big squares that I can challenge myself to fill with ideas on a single subject in a fixed time. (What are twenty things you could do today? Fill all the squares in three minutes.)

I will ask you to use this journal often over the course of the book. Action is the life of play, but we don't learn from experience; we learn from reflecting on experience.

Reflection comes with rest. Rest is not a wasted opportunity for productivity and it isn't idleness. In rest brains build connections. We embed experiences as learning, by linking them to other experiences, filing away their images for future reference. A journal is somewhere to help your brain make connections. Reflection is interpretation and integration.

Narcissus showed us what happens when reflection is self-absorbed: in love with his own image, he fell into the water which held his reflection and drowned. Reflection is not introspection. Understand yourself in relation to the world; reflection's rhythm is attentive.

Use your journal as somewhere to wander. Sometimes we cling too tightly to our dreams – we long for Narnia, and weep as we find only old coats and mothballs. Make time to let go, and imagine the games you could play with all those old coats.

PART ONE

THE ACTOR

Train the skills of role-play: release, imagination, presence, transformation, play.

Training makes your talent more resilient. It makes what is private become public, what is personal become political, the sudden burst of talent sustain. It makes the spirit of play the subject of serious work. Training's destination is public, sustainable free play.

There is a journey an actor makes to reach free play. It takes you from person, to actor, to role. It is the course an actor learns over several years of training: it is the path we lay in rehearsals; it is the route that an actor walks every night in order to step on stage.

First, take the decision that you are willing to travel. Believe in something bigger than you, and fuel a desire to serve that.

- *Relinquish* those things of your person which will inhibit or burden you on your journey to a new world; take only what the actor needs for the adventures ahead.

- *Imagine* the new world. Fly towards your goal transported by the mind's eye.

- *Arrive,* here and now, step into the new world: recognize, sense, breathe in your environment.

- *Adapt* to a new role and habitat. Chime with the rhythm of the world – its time, its climate and horizon; its language, culture and politics. Make yourself more than a tourist if you are to truthfully live here.

- *Play*. Pursue desires, break rules, explore freely. Take daring adventures fuelled by curiosity's hunger.

Acting is learning and preparing to play. Perhaps we should still call actors 'players', as we did 400 years ago. Play is where we will begin the story, since it is where we will end our journey.

*

The foundation stones of play are curiosity and exploration. These send us out into the world. Do you remember a time when you played more with the cardboard boxes than with the presents inside them? Play seeks to be *transformational*: asking not just 'What is it?', but 'What else can it be?' Transformation is at the heart of all play.

Our culture asserts that play's opposite is work. It is not. Work will have more ease, more flow and find creativity if it involves play. Play fires up the brain, helps memory and energizes the brain into free flow – that state of involved focus when you're 'on-your-game'. The opposite of play is not work, it is depression.

Our culture urges play to be fun – full of laughter and giggles. Ease away this assumption: it may become an unwelcome pressure on your work as an actor. Much play will find its greatest value when it moves *beyond* fun. You need playmates, not necessarily friends. Play can be deliciously serious.

Play is more than a spirit. It follows a universal code of trust:

- Ask first
- Be honest
- Follow the rules
- Admit when you're wrong.

When the code is violated, fairness breaks down and so does play.

Ask first means do not begin without the permission of all involved: this blocks bullying and delivers complicity.

Be honest means speak only for yourself and be specific and passionate in your actions.

Follow the rules means own your responsibilities as well as your rights.

Admit when you're wrong means respect the ensemble's needs over those of the individual.

This code roots collaboration. Actors cannot play alone – at the very least we require an audience to join us in making the work. The success of our venture is bound to the success of our collaboration. Make yourself a welcome playmate.

The greatest obstacle to the life of play is fear. Fear in the past, present and future expresses itself through guilt, control and anxiety. These are the demons which will oppose free play: the thresholds of play mark boundaries beyond which guilt, control and anxiety cannot be welcomed. This is rough-and-tumble play: fear will make us uncover our claws.

The parable of the rats

Let me digress, to show the true worth of play.

A group of scientists ran an experiment on two nests of rats. They set up one nest (the control group), which they allowed to get on with life as normal. They also had another nest of rats, which was denied play. Whenever these rats performed any non-utilitarian activity – chasing tails or bouncing around with each other – they were separated. They were fed separately, and at night they were kept in solitary confinement.

All rats are hardwired to flee from the scent of a cat: it's just part of being a rat. The scientists dropped a cat-collar into the two nests. All the rats fled, just as they must. Both nests of rats waited. The control group (who had been allowed to play) eventually came out to check whether it was really a cat they could smell or just some cat's collar. The rats who had been denied play, never came out from hiding to look. They waited.

The rats who had never played, died.

Play is an evolutionary requisite. In play, potential behaviours for survival are rehearsed. Play is a theatre for transgression (rats can chase cats) and evolution. It has a biological function like sleep and dreams: we need play, just as we need shelter and warmth.

Don't learn to act, learn to play. Don't act a character, play a role: explore with curiosity and open presence, ready to transform and be transformed by all that is around you. Explore the world and use your work to ask 'How shall we live?'

1
RELINQUISH

Learn to recognize and relinquish unnecessary tension and make yourself available to fulfilled and truthful transformation.

Framework

Training begins as you acknowledge and relinquish your own habitual tensions and behaviours, in order to absorb the affective tensions of each new role. Tension itself is no bad thing – obviously muscular tensions are how we hold ourselves upright or make ourselves move – but tension is a behaviour; it is something you do, not part of who you are. What the actor requires is an active awareness of physical and psychological tension, in order to release, at will, tensions which inhibit transformative play.

*

I have recently been working with an actor with very pronounced jaw tension – a tension many young actors carry. He habitually clamps his mouth shut: you can see the jaw muscles at work, even when he is at rest. This behaviour is so engrained, it is now unconscious. No matter what he does, his jaw is bound tightly shut – and by association his brow slightly furrowed, his neck tense. His speech is accordingly limited: he never softens his jaw and releases a large, open sound; his teeth are clamped together as he speaks.

This has consequences for his ability to fulfil the depth of his talent. Any role he plays will communicate that tension to the audience, from which they will infer character anxiety or inner life he may not intend.

So we work together to build an awareness of this tension and develop an understanding of how it feels to let it go. At first it will feel strange for him, as the tension drops away: he will have to get used to a new sound that he will make, a lighter neck and a less penetrative brow through which to see. But if he can release this tension, he will be able to choose whether or not to employ it in the story of each role.

Any habitual tension denies free transformation and communicates powerfully to an audience: on stage or under the fierce gaze of a camera, tensions take on great meaning. They come to stand for psychological conditions and problems, as every physical act will on screen or stage. Because it is the actor's job to *make the psychological physical*, we must become acutely aware of what psychology our physicality communicates.

*

Psychological tensions are equally inhibiting. I think of one fiercely talented actor I trained, who, playing the role of the strongest of Greek warriors, found her body unwittingly creeping back from confrontation – something she feared. While this is a valid – even appealing – human trait, it isn't one that sits well on the broad shoulders of Ajax preparing for battle: this actor did not believe that her body was capable of provoking the fear in others that the role demanded. This psychological doubt fled into tension throughout her body, as she retreated from confrontation. Empower yourself.

I often find myself working with actors to achieve disempowerment – typically young men who have been cultured never to back down or make themselves vulnerable. Our received role in culture and society affects our ability to handle power and effect change. The world tells us stories about what we are capable of achieving, dependent upon race, class, gender. You must become aware of your social inheritance and be ready to release it in role-play: to grow beyond that inheritance. It is at this point that release becomes a political act: it asks you to deconstruct social roles into which you have been born. Discovering that the world of play can allow you to be utterly but safely disempowered or empowered can be a profound revelation for many young actors: rats can chase cats. Enter into role-play ready to break the rules of the world into which you were born.

From all I have said so far, there is a danger of treating your body as a problem to be solved, so that you can work. Please don't think for a second that I want you to start thinking of your body as a problem to solve: it is the solution. Release into the rich, vivid potential of your body. Don't wish to change your body: work to inhabit it, accepting that it is honest, active and responsive. Enfranchise yourself.

*

The mind and body are not separate. As soon as you have a thought, muscles are activated: your breath changes, your body's chemical balance alters and readies muscular tension. Thoughts of being late, of not being good enough, of not getting something done will perhaps cause tension in your neck, shoulders and arms, make your stomach muscles tighten and interfere with your breathing. Thoughts of sunny beaches, an evening with friends, a quiet walk through a park on a beautiful day will have another effect; a lighter, more released state both mentally and physically. Recognize this link between thought and tension. Through focused awareness and imagination, as well as physical exercises, the body can achieve readiness and freedom.

This helps us understand what we mean by *psychophysical*: that psychology and physicality are intertwined. The Greek word *psyche* meant 'mind', but also 'breath' and 'blood'.

There is one other tension I want to address, before outlining exercises. Pretending an audience or camera is not there is an active tension: it involves blocking and denying. Doing so makes the vital witness some sort of Medusa whose eyes will petrify the actor. Accept the audience. To deny them is a futile, expensive effort of tension and at worst a vanity. Our generous permission to the audience to be there enfranchises everyone's clear sight and vivid response. Being 'present' or 'in the moment' is not selective: there is only the here and now, and that must include the audience or camera; drama is never blind. Release of tension is also about allowing yourself to be seen.

Release is necessary to play a role freely, but also to relinquish that role once the play is over. The exercises in this chapter will be as necessary after work as before it. Release helps the transition in and out of role-play. This is the crucial importance of a bow after performance: it marks a public release from the play after all is said and done.

The physical act of the complete bow – a spine roll down and back up again, releasing breath out as you go down and inhaling as you come up – is perhaps the most important release exercise of all.

Exploration

These exploratory exercises can be done as pre-class work, or as starters to a session. They establish an awareness of psychophysical connection and flow. Acting is a study in human psychology as physical behaviour.

- Develop a habit of awareness. As you watch a television programme or read a book, be aware of your own body. What connection is there between what you are seeing or reading and your muscles? Notice your jaw, your shoulders, your brow, your neck and spine and how they are changed by the story. Write/draw these tensions in your journal and how they relate to what you read, heard, saw.

- Build this habit of awareness. As you sit and watch your colleagues at work in class, notice your body as you react to what you are seeing. Notice if you have breath patterns and tensions which respond to or mirror those of the actor you are observing. Notice what feelings these evoke in you. Write/draw these tensions and feelings in your journal. Notice how what you see affects the rhythm of your body, thought and behaviour.

- Stand with your feet about hip width apart and at a gentle, open angle. Allow yourself to have soft (not bent, just soft) knees. Let your arms hang at your sides. Centre your weight by evenly spreading your weight through the balls and heels of your feet. Gently rock forwards and backwards between your heel and toes, to explore the journey from balance to off-balance, from centre to off-centre. Don't just push your shoulders forwards and backwards – gently rock through your feet. Try letting the movement slowly grow until you need to take a step to stop yourself falling. Try lessening the movement until it is almost imperceptible; the smallest journey from centre to off-centre that you can find. What is the sensation? How does it make you feel? This simple unbalancing is evocative and very strange; the sensation of being off-centre for a sustained period like this can evoke strong reactions. The physical is psychological.

- Do not try this exercise if you have a bad back or are protecting another injury. Do two clean press-ups, with your body straight – clench your buttocks and squeeze your abdominals to be sure of not lifting your bottom up and putting strain on your back. Now hold your body in position in a plank (the top position of a press-up). Breathe. Imagine the smell of hot chocolate or the taste of an orange. Release from the plank. Now lie supine – on your back, legs stretched out, toes falling away from each other with your arms at your sides and palms open to the ceiling. Find a calm, simple breath pattern, as you notice your breath coming in and out of your body. Release. Now imagine the smell of hot chocolate. Now imagine the taste of an orange. Notice how release frees the imagination: physical tension binds the mind as well as the body.

- Within Western culture, we value independence very highly. But we must build a healthy relationship to our dependence on others. We rely on others for our psychological well-being: one certain way to drive someone mad is to leave them on their own for a long time. People need people; we are fundamentally social. Accepting this is a crucial phase of release. Who do you depend on? How do they depend on you? Draw a spider's web of people to whom you are connected, with yourself at the centre. Draw lines linking you to everyone in that network. Draw lines between others in the web who depend on each other. I've done a version to show you what I mean, using a few people from my own life. Let yours – as it is more private than mine is here – grow. If I lost any of the people in this network I would be very sad. The sadder I think I would be to lose them, the more lucky I feel to have them in my life.

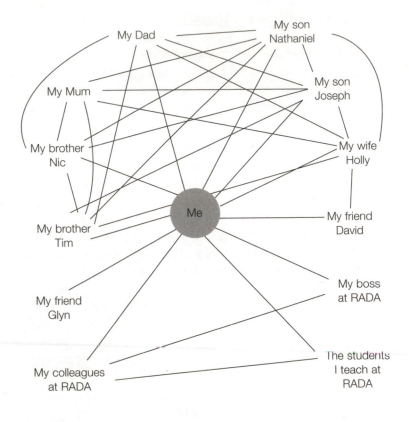

Exercises

As with all the chapters, lots of the exercises in this section are physical in nature. Wear loose, comfortable clothing. Always have a pencil and your journal to hand.

I have broken these exercises into three sections: 'Basic psychophysical release', which includes simple exercises to develop an awareness of habitual tension and the sensation of release; 'Relinquish through imagination', which includes exercises training imagination as a tool for individual or partnered release; and 'Relinquish through play', which includes exercises using play as a tool to achieve social release.

Basic psychophysical release

A working contract (30–40 minutes)

Establish the rules of play which provide a structure for trust within an ensemble. Trust makes release possible.

I

- Break into groups of five or six.
- On large sheets of paper, write out three things:
  1 What you are working to achieve in this class.
  2 What your rights will be as you work towards this objective.
  3 What your responsibilities will be as you work towards this objective.
- Your rights and responsibilities relate to yourself, your colleagues (including teachers), your space and your objective. These documents can be as long or as short as you like. At the very least, they should include the four rules of play: ask first, be honest, follow the rules, admit when you're wrong.
- Take your time and allow the discussion to flow freely: this is a crucial document to develop together. Everyone should have a say here.

II

I work as a full group and share your documents. Together, build a single document. Everyone sign their names on this document. Pin this document to a wall of your classroom. Revisit it later in the process to reconsider what you have agreed. Remember, like any contract, every signatory has agreed to its terms. But also like any contract, the terms can be renegotiated and the document can evolve and change as you work.

Centre and align (2 minutes)

Provide focus before an exercise, or release tension after an exercise.

- Work individually.
- Stand with your feet about hip-width apart and at a gentle, open angle. Allow yourself to have soft (not bent, just soft) knees. Let your arms hang at your sides. Centre your weight by evenly spreading your weight through the balls and the heels of your feet.
- Find a target on the other side of the room and put your attention onto it. This might be a mark on a wall, a light switch, a point out of a window … anything specific and at a reasonable distance from you: something 'there' not 'here'.
- Be aware of your own width, length and depth. Don't stretch your spine to impress with your height, don't pull back your shoulders and heave out your chest to create artificial depth, don't move your legs apart to seem wider; simply think long, wide and deep. Be aware of your three dimensions.
- Think this – don't do it at all – 'let my neck be free, so that my head can go forward and up, so that my back can lengthen and widen'.
- As you settle with this thought, breathe in through your nose over a count of three, let your breath rest for a moment (not the same as holding your breath) and release that breath through your mouth over a steady count of eight. Don't rush this. Don't heave air in, don't hold your breath, don't force the air out; this is about finding a simple, cleansing breath pattern.
- Repeat this breath pattern five times. When you first begin, you may only manage an out breath of five counts. As you develop control you may move to an out breath over a count of twelve. The goal is measured, controlled breathing.
- See the object you are looking at and its specific shape, colour, form and function: move from the state of concentration to put your attention onto the object. Broaden your focus to include

the room and the context of that object – see where and when you are here and now. Move away from the spot you are in, ready to begin a new exercise or rejoin the class.

Progressive relaxation (10 minutes)

Achieve basic psychophysical release and train yourself to recognize habitual tension and the sensation of release.

- Work individually.

- Lie supine – on your back, legs stretched out, toes falling away from each other with your arms at your sides, your shoulders falling into the floor and your palms open to the ceiling. Alternatively lie semi-supine – on your back, knees drawn up towards the sky so your feet rest flat on the floor, your arms at your sides with your shoulders falling into the floor and palms open and up.

- You will be lying here for a while, so be sure you are comfortable and warm enough. Perhaps rest your head on a book or jumper to align your neck.

- Think of your length, width and depth. Find a calm, simple breath pattern by becoming aware of your breathing. Where do you feel your body responding to your breath? What do you feel in your ribs? Your abdomen? Your pelvis? Focus on the lowest point in your torso where you feel a response.

- The class leader speaks through the following progressive relaxation, slowly and clearly:

    I'm relaxing my feet, my feet are completely relaxed
    I'm relaxing my ankles, my ankles are completely relaxed
    I'm relaxing my knees, my knees are completely relaxed
    I'm relaxing thighs, my thighs are completely relaxed
    I'm relaxing my pelvis, my pelvis is completely relaxed
    I'm relaxing my buttocks, my buttocks are completely relaxed
    I'm relaxing my lower back, my lower back is completely relaxed
    I'm relaxing my abdominal muscles, my abdominal muscles are completely relaxed
    I'm relaxing my upper back, my upper back is completely relaxed

I'm relaxing my chest, my chest is completely relaxed
I'm relaxing my shoulders, my shoulders are completely relaxed
I'm relaxing my neck, my neck is completely relaxed
I'm relaxing my jaw, my jaw is completely relaxed
I'm relaxing my eyes, my eyes are completely relaxed
I'm relaxing my forehead, my forehead is completely relaxed
I'm relaxing my mind, my mind is completely relaxed.

- Even writing these words is relaxing.

- Now open your eyes and focus on what you see above you.
  From memory, locate your current given circumstances (the
  environmental and situational conditions, which affect your
  behaviour) – don't look. What day is it? What time is it? Who is
  near to you? Where is the door? What is the floor beneath you
  like? This is not a test. This is about locating where and when
  you are *now*; don't locate where you have come from or are
  going to, as this may introduce anxiety. After exploring these
  given circumstances from memory, look around and see where
  and when you in fact are.

- Get up slowly. Rock your knees to one side and follow them
  into a foetal position, before moving onto all fours and then to
  kneeling. Finally, stand.

Teaching Tip: Do vary your pitch and tone so the class don't fall
asleep. Walking around the room, coming close to people, helps
keep them awake. If someone does drift off – inevitably it will
happen sometimes – then a silent hand on a shoulder is usually
enough to bring them back. If this doesn't do it, perhaps let them
have 5 minutes restorative sleep.

Once you have completed this exercise, perhaps move straight
into an imagination or memory exercise (see Chapter 2 for
examples). It can also lead beautifully into Meisner repetition work
and other communion exercises requiring situational concentration,
detailed in Chapter 3 (see pages 68–74). Or you might like to reflect
on this exercise by discussing the sensation of relaxation and how it
affects the quality of situational awareness.

Brasso (20 minutes)

Find release with a partner. Make release a shared and social act, not just a private one. Develop trust and openness.

I learned this exercise from two people: the wonderful movement specialist and educator Ruth Spencer, and my nan. Whenever my nan came round to our house as kids, she would polish our brass. With a flat hand holding a cloth dipped in Brasso, she would vigorously but gently rub our brass door knobs and surfaces with a quick, small circular motion of her hand and arm. It looked exhausting, and her whole body was involved in the activity. Her focus on the brass was absolute and her whole body would judder in time with the polishing. By the end of the morning, our house shone. So did my nan.

- Split into pairs, labelling yourselves A and B.
- Agree on which body parts are 'made of brass' and which are not. Anything brass will be polished; anything else will be left alone. Anywhere you would normally cover with a swimming costume is not made of brass. There may be other sensitive areas which are not 'brass' – particularly if you are carrying injuries which you want to protect.
- This exercise will be done in silence.
- Partner A, align and centre yourself. Stand with your feet about hip-width apart and at a gentle, open angle. Allow yourself to have soft (not bent, just soft) knees. Let your arms hang at your sides. Centre your weight by evenly spreading your weight through the balls and the heels of your feet.
- Think of your length, width and depth. Find a calm, simple breath pattern by becoming aware of your breathing, with particular awareness of the deepest point this breath reaches in your body. Allow your eyes to close.
- Partner B, gently place your flat hands onto your partner's back. Slowly begin to polish. Keep it soft and light, but thorough and quick. Remember your objective: to make your partner shine. Shift the quality of your action to achieve

the intended outcome. Receive information back from your partner's body: you are in a silent dialogue here.

- Be precise: you do not want to make your partner glow (or wobble), so don't use too much force; you do not want to make your partner tingle (or giggle), so don't use your fingers too much; you singularly want to make them *shine*. Achieve your objective.

- Be really thorough. Make sure every area of 'brass' has definitely been brought to the light. Be particularly careful where you are polishing directly onto skin: this is obviously the most sensitive area and here the contact will need to be especially responsive. For Partner B this is a focused listening exercise and requires great generosity and sensitivity.

- Once you have finished polishing, silently communicate that to Partner A with your hands and move away. Partner A, slowly open your eyes.

- When you are ready, change places and Partner A now take responsibility for shining Partner B.

- Once you have experienced both roles, take time to discuss the exchange. How do you feel? How was your breathing changed in each role? How did you 'listen' and receive information from your partner? How did you shift the quality of your action to ensure you were achieving your objective? How did your awareness of your body, space and time change during the process? Is the person being polished passive? Reflect on this in your journal.

Teaching Tip: Assign partners for this exercise if there are class members who might feel vulnerable or uncomfortable with its physical contact.

If you have already done several exercises involving alignment and centring, you might ask students to lead each other in aligning and centring themselves (so partner B would talk partner A through the process and then vice versa). This helps both students focus and empowers them as peer educators.

Relinquish through imagination

Visualized release (10–15 minutes)

Train psychophysical release and connection led by the imagination.

- Work individually.

- Lie supine or semi-supine (see page 19 for a description of these positions). You will be lying here for a while, so be sure you are comfortable and warm enough. Perhaps rest your head on a book.

- Think of your length, width and depth. Find a calm, simple breath pattern by becoming aware of your breathing, with particular awareness of the deepest point you can feel this breath in your torso. Centre and align yourself with your breath. Allow your eyes to close.

- Imagine a ball of glowing light at your feet. Its size means you could cup it in your hands. Think of it as a small sun. Feel its warmth as it floats over your feet.

- Imagine it splits into two and moves into your feet. Feel it warming and bringing light to your toes, slowly moving into the souls of your feet and on into your heels, carrying tension away. It travels through your ankles, softening and relaxing this joint. Up your calves it goes and progressively on up your body – your knees, thighs, buttocks and hips, meeting to become one again at your pelvis.

- At every stage tension will release and you will feel your body sink further into the ground.

- Now it moves slowly up through your spine, warming and relaxing, softening and opening, lightening and easing all the way. As it goes through your spine it passes your stomach, chest, heart and reaches your shoulders. Its warmth and light soften these and they fall further into the floor. It continues up your neck, and into your mind before passing out through the top of your head, carrying tension out and away from you. It flies off into the stars.

- Rest.
- Get up slowly, beginning with a roll to the side and then onto all fours and slowly to kneeling. Do not rise up quickly or you will fall over even quicker.

Teaching Tip: This exercise leads brilliantly into rich visualization work, as you've already opened your body and mind up to imaginative suggestion.

A safe place (20–25 minutes)

Train memory and imagination as a basis for release. Make release personal and train psychophysical connection.

- Work individually.
- Align and centre yourself. Stand with your feet about hip-width apart and at a gentle, open angle. Allow yourself to have soft (not bent, just soft) knees. Let your arms hang at your sides, like wet dishcloths. Centre your weight by evenly spreading your weight through the balls and the heels of your feet.
- Think of your length, width and depth. Find a calm, simple breath pattern by becoming aware of your breathing, with particular awareness of the deepest point you feel this breath reach in your torso. Allow your eyes to close.
- Be ready to imagine or think of somewhere you feel safe. It is of crucial importance that if you choose somewhere real, it feels completely safe for you. If you are uncertain, build somewhere new with your imagination.
- You do not need to know any more than the answer to each question as it is asked.
- Are you standing or sitting in this place? Stand or sit now as if you were in that place. What are you sitting on? If all you are

aware of initially is that this is something warm and soft, that is enough – we will find out later if it is grass or a sofa or sand.

- How warm is it here? That sensation should make you feel safer.

- How light is it here? Where is the threshold to the space? Each answer should help you feel safer. Perhaps you are in a bedroom, perhaps a cave; perhaps you are on an empty beach, or in a room you once visited as a child.

- Notice the threshold to the space in more detail. Notice the walls and their colour or texture, or the shore or sky if you can see it. Notice the source of light, if there is one; notice what blocks out the light if there is very little. This is a safe space.

- What are you sitting on? Perhaps you can notice in more detail what it is now. Are there any other objects in the space? There is nothing here that you do not choose to be here, but perhaps there is something that makes you feel safer, more at ease.

- Allow yourself to look around this safe space in your imagination and find details you have not yet noticed – other things you have not yet seen which contribute to your ease and contentment in this space. There are no unpleasant surprises.

- The space is yours to control and nothing will be here that you do not choose to be here, as it exists only in your imagination and no-one else can access it.

- Allow yourself to settle into this space and allow the sensation of being here to settle into your body.

- Rest with this sensation for a while: be aware of your own body and how it feels.

- Allow yourself to be aware of where you are now – of what the classroom you are a part of feels like, sounds like, looks like – and slowly open your eyes when you are ready.

- You might write or draw this imagined space in your reflective journal. Consider why this environment, this sort of space, made you safe. As a class, perhaps discuss the effect it has on your body.

> *Teaching Tip:* You might use this imagined space as a point of
> departure and return for other imaginative exercises described in
> later chapters.

Imagination warm-up (30 minutes)

*Warm up the mind's eye. Extended use of this trains stamina of
concentrated release and imagination.*

I

- Work individually.
- Lie supine or semi-supine. You will be lying here for a while, so
  be sure you are comfortable and warm enough. Perhaps rest
  your head on a book.
- Think of your length, width and depth. Find a calm, simple
  breath pattern by becoming aware of your breathing, with
  particular awareness of the deepest point you feel this breath
  reach in your torso.
- Allow your weight to be taken from you by the floor as you
  release your weight into it, and allow your body to warm the
  floor. Be aware of your own breath.
- Hear the breath coming in and out of your body. Hear how
  deep it goes into your body. Hear the unconscious sounds of
  your body at work: allow your mind's ear to hear your heartbeat
  – its pace, its rhythm. Hear your blood pulsing round your body
  and your guts at work. Hear your body relaxing as it releases
  unnecessary tension into the floor.
- Hear the sounds of the room. Hear the voice of your teacher
  and their footsteps.
- Hear sounds that come into the room from outside – though
  don't distinguish these from those made within the room. They
  are all heard here. Allow yourself to listen.

- Allow your ear to hear more. Hear sounds that *were once* made in this room: the sounds of your class coming in to the room today; your bodies moving in the space; interactions between you; moments of contact between bodies as you came into class.

- Imagine or remember a moment in this room when there has been contact between two people which has inspired *joy*. Hear that moment, witness that moment.

- Slow it down in your mind's eye so you can witness it in slow motion. How does that contact affect the two bodies? How are they changed by joy? What muscles are newly engaged? How are their breath patterns changed?

- Leave that moment.

- Imagine or remember a moment of contact between two people in this room, which has inspired *anger*. Hear that moment, witness that moment. How are the bodies, breaths and rhythms of the two bodies changed?

- Leave that moment.

- Find a moment of *fear*. Perhaps it is a flash of anxiety, perhaps it is full-blown terror.

- Witness its detailed effect on the bodies and breaths of those involved as you slow it down. Imagine a context for this moment. Even if it is only a detail, discover an insight into what caused this moment of fear.

- Leave that moment.

- Find a moment of contact characterized by *sadness*. Witness it.

- Find a moment of contact characterized by *desire*. Witness it.

- Find a moment of contact producing *surprise*. Witness it.

- Find a moment of contact producing *disgust*. Witness it.

- Come back to the room as you hear it now. Notice what you can hear here and now. You may wish to end the exercise here, moving into another exercise with your imagination opened.

II

- Notice what you can hear outside of the room. Can you hear other classes? Can you hear streets outside? Allow your imagination to follow those sounds and discover images attached to them.

- Slowly imagine moments of human contact outside your classroom, characterized by any of the seven universal emotions: *joy, fear, anger, sadness, arousal, surprise, disgust.* Witness these moments in increasing detail; imagine contexts for these fragments.

- Finally, return to listening to the room as it is now. Hear the sound of your own breath, visualizing it coming in to its deepest point, and slowly open your eyes.

- You will need to sit up slowly, rolling onto your side first to avoid getting dizzy as you lift yourself up again.

- Share some of the images and stories you witnessed. Draw or write these in your reflective journal.

Teaching Tip: It is valuable to allow students not to speak as well as to speak after an exercise like this. Some students will be enthusiastic to share their imagined experiences, others will want to keep them private. It is worth validating the right to silence by restating that students do have the right not to speak too, so long as they are using the private space of their reflective journal to evaluate and assess their experiences.

This can be a great basis for creative devising – see Part Three for more.

Learn to walk (15 minutes)

Explore release as forgetting. Learning to forget is a crucial quality of release: put that forgetting into your body.

- Work with a partner, with whom you have not yet had much opportunity to work.

- Partner A, stand centred and aligned. If you are confident in this work, Partner B might guide Partner A into this place of readiness, talking them through the simple process of release, focus and alignment (see page 18).

- Partner A, you do not know how to walk. Partner B, your task is to teach your partner to walk.

- Partner B, explore different ways to teach Partner A. Try words, try physically guiding their body, try demonstration. Use all of yourself and all the means at your disposal to achieve your objective.

- Partner A, the challenge here is not to know something which you already know with unconscious ease. Try not to impersonate ignorance or demonstrate it by being slow to pick up new information. Let this be as honest a process of present-tense discovery as you can.

- Reflect on this exercise in your journal, with your partner or as a group, depending on the time available. How possible is it to release unconscious physical knowledge? What tactics did you employ as a teacher? In what different ways did you learn? How did it feel to put trust into your partner as a teacher/learner?

> **Teaching Tip:** Once you have got your partner walking, you might turn this into Finger Following (page 60) or a Shared Walk (the next exercise), or take yourselves into work on rhythm and tempo (see Chapter 4). You could even begin to feed in an inner monologue or desires relevant to a character you are working on (see Chapter 8). From this state of playful, open discovery, you can build new rhythms of thought, action and will.

Relinquish through play

Shared walk (20 minutes)

Take release into group work. Train yourself to relinquish ego and absorb an ensemble objective.

- Work in silence, as a full group.

- Begin to walk around the room. Be conscious of using the whole room. Balance your bodies through the space as you move, so the whole room is active.

- Let your arms swing loosely from your shoulders. Use the whole of your foot as you walk: roll through from your heel to your toes, which push you on as you walk. Let your comfortable, open stride take you forwards. Let your neck be free, so that your head can go forwards and up, so that your back can lengthen and widen.

- Walk with ease and flow.

- Become aware of the shared rhythm of the ensemble as you walk through the space together. Hear it, see it, feel your part in it.

- Altogether and without leaders, go from this pace to the fastest walking tempo the group can manage. No-one will reach their top speed – this will be as fast as the group can safely walk within this room without causing collisions and accidents.

- From this top speed, gradually decelerate as one until you are moving in slow motion and, eventually, come to stillness. When you are all still, all sit in unison. Then stand as one and accelerate back to the natural rhythm of the walk you currently share.

- The challenge here is to work without one person taking charge. The transitions between tempi, even between stillness, sitting and standing, should not be conducted by individuals. Let them be discovered by the group in a shared and unspoken will to action.

- After completing this exercise, discuss the state of group awareness you found. Discuss awareness: how did you relate to time, space, your body and other people? How did you feel? Where were you looking? How were you sensing other people's rhythms and movements? How did the group breathe? How might this relate to an actor's work and play?

- Extend this exercise by moving between different types of movement – a skip, a jump or a dance – without planning or discussion.

- Extend it further by adding sound. The group might all start to hum, sing a song, speak a speech, laugh, without discussion or planning.

Yes and (20 minutes)

Explore how language can inhibit or release play. Establish the different functions of 'yes' and 'no', as a basis for considering language and release.

- Work with a partner.

I

- Partner A will make a simple, imagined verbal offer to Partner B (e.g. 'Would you like a glass of orange juice?'). Partner B will simply say 'No' to reject this offer. It doesn't matter how tempting the offers become, or how alluringly they are presented, Partner B will simply say 'No'. Partner A make it as difficult as possible for B to say 'No' and mean it. Partner B, dare to mean it.

- Keep going for long enough that Partner A is forced to become really imaginative with the offers. Be disciplined; Partner B just say 'No', nothing more.

- Try switching around so you both get a turn to say 'No'. It can be rather empowering if you're not used to it. 'No' is a valuable word – enjoy it. Allow your bodies to move as you work: don't get stuck in one shape or place.

II

- Now change the language. This time, Partner A will make an offer and Partner B will say 'Yes, but …', offering an excuse – or even a reason – why they can't take up the offer. Be disciplined; stick to the phrase 'Yes, but'. So Partner A might ask 'Would you like a back massage?' to which the response could be 'Yes, but I've been advised against massages since I injured my lower back.'

- This will be more demanding, as you will need to invent a lot of excuses, but don't inhibit yourself with too much logic. Play need not be restricted by reality; it is only restricted by the agreed rules. Use the language, work fairly with your partner and dare to mean it.

- Try switching around so you both get a turn to say 'Yes, but'. It feels very different to saying 'No'. Allow your bodies to move with the language. Allow this to continue until you are really finding imaginative, creative flow.

III

- Now change the language. This time, Partner A will make an offer and Partner B will say 'Yes, and', building on the offer made and extending it. Be disciplined; stick to the phrase 'Yes, and'. So Partner A might ask 'Would you like to go for a picnic?' to which Partner B might say 'Yes, and let's take it down to the river', to which Partner A might respond 'Yes, and let's take our wet suits', to which B might respond 'Yes, and let's hire a boat' and so on and so on and so on. Unleash your imaginations.

- In this final iteration, you will not need to take it in turns to have a go: you will play together. Allow your bodies to move with the ideas. Allow this to continue on into the moon and the stars.

IV

- Take time for reflection. Discuss the language. What did each prefix (No/Yes but/Yes and) release and permit? How did each make you feel? How might the 'Yes, and' approach be a useful principle for a creative ensemble? Discuss the body language of each stage: how did the language affect your body?

Teaching Tip: If the group is an odd number and one person cannot have a partner, this person could draw the room: the bodies, tensions and dances between people. Draw quickly and without inhibition: draw crude outlines of people, to show shapes and forms. This will form an excellent tool for later reflection on the exercise.

Follow-up

Embed and extend your habit of awareness. These can be done after class/between classes as work on release grows and develops.

- Build your habit of awareness. Notice tension in people sitting in a cafe or waiting for a train; notice especially unnecessary tension: it will be especially easy to observe in the lips, jaw, brow and shoulders. Turn this attention on yourself. When you are carrying out a task that requires particular focus – working at a computer, hurrying to get somewhere, reading – take a moment to be aware of unnecessary shoulder, brow, abdominal or jaw tension. Try releasing this tension and continuing the activity with more flow and ease. Write/draw about this in your journal to evaluate and embed the learning.

- Use your journal to reflect on language we regularly use which relates to tension and release. Consider in what circumstances we use this language and what its imagery suggests: chill out, ease up, cool it, lay off, let go; hold it, hang on, seize the moment, grab your chance and so on. Consider the implications of this language and its use.

- Find still images of elite athletes in action. Observe tension and release in their bodies and how this focused physical action is manifest. Colour in the athlete to indicate degrees of tension and release throughout their body.

- Consider the story you tell of your own body. Do you tell a story of yourself as tall, skinny, weak, strong, fat, short? How does this affect how you carry your own body? How does it condition and inhibit your behaviour? Make a self-portrait in your journal. Colour in the areas of habitual tension as you become aware of them. As with everything in your journal, remember this is a private drawing.

- Is there a private inner monologue you step into – a little phrase you find plays on loop through your head? Notice as you sit in class or walk through your town, what your inner monologue is. Note it down into your reflective journal verbatim, there and then. You may be asking yourself why you aren't as clever as others in the class, you may be telling yourself everyone else is stupid, you may be hoping you don't get picked, you may be hoping the teacher is pleased with you, you may be trying not to be seen … Build a habit of awareness of your inner life and the story you are telling yourself about the world around you and your place in it. Do not worry to judge this; simply become aware of it. If you feel strongly that the inner monologue is limiting you in a way you don't like, then try rewriting it and changing what you say to yourself. See how this feels and alters your behaviour. Consider how this thought pattern affects your physicality and becomes a tension. Reflect on this in your journal.

Further reading

Carey, David and Rebecca Carey (2010), *Vocal Arts Workbook*, Methuen. Chapter 1, 'Relaxation, Release and Alignment'.
Chekhov, Michael (2002), *To the Actor,* Routledge. Chapter 1, 'The Actor's Body and Psychology'.
McEvenue, Kelly (2001), *The Alexander Technique for Actors,* Methuen. Part 1, 'The Alexander Technique in the Theatre'.
Stanislavski, Konstantin, trans. Jean Benedetti (2008), *An Actor's Work,* Routledge. Chapter 6, 'Muscular Release'.

2
IMAGINE

Train your imagination as a trigger for psychophysical transformation and dramatic play.

Framework

The imagination is your most important tool. It is the most powerful, immediate stimulant for transformation. It forms a bridge between you and a new world.

Imagination reforms the world around you. Its materials are the pictures you hold in your memory. Memory is imagination's arts-and-crafts box, out of which you build new collages of possible lives to live. Much of the work in this chapter trains you to have free access to your memory; this is only ever in the service of your acting super-power: visceral imagination.

Memory coordinates our present and conceives our future. Memories give us patterns, and patterns give us meaning. I know who I am, by the repeating pattern of effects I have on the world. A story of 'me' emerges from my life's patterns: I'm lucky or clumsy or likeable or not. These patterns make my world. I can't remember this group of letters:

I	P	D	N	A	D
T	W	E	O	M	E
A	O	V	S	I	N
H	N	O	A	E	I
W	S	R	W	C	G

But I can remember this sentence by William Blake: 'What is now proved was once imagined.' Once I find a way to connect all those random letters (read up from the bottom-left corner), they become easy to carry in my mind. They are connected, they carry meaning and images. Biographical memories do the same: from them we create meaningful patterns out of life's random events.

*

Memory is vast. The capacity of long-term memory – as far as we know – is limitless. We have a lifelong bank of experiences to access in the service of imagination. Out of the story of your life, you can construct limitless others. For an actor, this implies a practical process: draw on the endless resources of memory to fuel a limitless imagination.

Imagination and memory are linked. But let's go further than that: *they are neurologically indistinguishable from each other*. They reside in the same place in the brain; to a brain scan, an imagined event looks identical to a remembered one. Think of your own experience of this: it is often impossible to tell whether an event you recall is a real memory or an imagined one.

Look at a photo of yourself from your childhood and you may not be sure if you really remember the moment it captures. Maybe you have just seen the photo so many times you *think* you remember it. Dreams fill your body with sensation. Meet a friend in the street and your heart leaps, as images from last night's dream flood in to your mind: for a moment you can't be sure – did that really happen? The feelings are real, though the experience was imagined.

For the actor, this is vital. If we submit to the active imagination, events can come to life in the mind and body, which are neurologically indistinguishable from reality.

Witnesses are how humans keep the boundary clear between the real and the imagined. We can only be sure that a memory was a dream, because the person we meet doesn't acknowledge the event occurred. Witnesses to our lives prove our lives. Shared memories build your life story.

For the actor, this provides the key to making the imagined real: *if two of us say together that it happened, then it did*. If we imagine an event vividly and confirm its occurrence together, then we make it as truthful as any memory. Add to that, this reassurance: like two witnesses on the stand in court, we can have divergent accounts of these shared memories. If we each own our account as truth, there is nothing any lawyer can do to disprove it.

*

Everything you imagine could be true. Everything on stage is a lie, until you bring it to truth through your imagination. A moment may not be real, but imagination can make it true.

Exploration

Develop a basic awareness of how memory and imagination operate, and encourage imaginative, creative thought and action. These exercises could be done as pre-class work, or as a starter exercise to a session.

- A 'flashbulb memory' is one of which you can give a vivid and detailed account as if it were lit up by a flashbulb. A neural mechanism is triggered by events that are emotionally significant and unexpected, with the result that the whole scene becomes imprinted on the memory. This is still no guarantee of the accuracy of the memory, but the sensory recall is full and vivid. Locate a flashbulb memory from your own life. This doesn't have to be a negative memory: it could be when you were told you had won a competition, got into a sports team or were cast in a play. If you are unsure, or working as a large class, use a major public event – the death of a public figure, the victory of a national sports team or another major international event. Either tell a partner, or write notes on the memory in your journal. Where were you? Who else was there? What were you doing? How did you feel? What physical sensations do you recall? What was the emotional impact on others (describe their physical behaviours)? What did you do afterwards? Allow the sensations of that moment into your body here and now.

- The following comes from Lewis Carroll's *Through the Looking-Glass*:

  'How old are you?'

  'I'm seven and a half, exactly.'

  'You needn't say "exactly"', the Queen remarked. 'I can believe it without that. Now I'll give you something to believe. I'm just one hundred and one, five months and a day.'

  'I can't believe that!' said Alice. 'Can't you?' the Queen said in a pitying tone. 'Try again: draw a long breath and shut your eyes.' Alice laughed. 'There's no use trying,' she said: 'one can't believe impossible things.' 'I daresay you haven't had much practice,' said the Queen. 'When I was your age, I always did it for half-an-hour a day. Why, sometimes, I've believed as many as six impossible things before breakfast.'

Try it: take a deep, settling breath, shut your eyes and imagine and believe something impossible (do breathe out too, or you won't imagine a thing). Steal disparate, seemingly unrelated images from your memory and connect them up in new ways to forge an impossible event. A green and yellow stripy elephant overtakes the Statue of Liberty in a flying race in the Hogwarts Quidditch arena. Either share these with a partner or write/draw them in your journal. Ideally six before breakfast.

- Metaphors make sensations and experiences come alive in imaginative, non-literal language. They are wonderful tools to trigger imagination and access sensation. Come up with three original metaphors for the experience of seeing someone you love ('He's Sunrise', says Emily Dickinson or 'Juliet is the sun', says Shakespeare's Romeo). Test your metaphor. Look at someone and let your imagination make the metaphor real in them – for example, see them as the sun rising. Is this love?

- Train yourself to have free, uninhibited imagination. Draw circles all over a page of blank paper – so you have 30 or so circles. Now give yourself 1 minute and make each one something different: a football, a happy face, a sad face, a balloon, an open mouth. Anything you like. Don't self-edit ('that idea's not creative enough … I can't do a football since he suggested it …'); go for quantity not quality. This is a good principle: design many prototypes at speed and then see which one you like. As the director John Wright puts it, 'You can talk about one idea for five minutes, or try five different ideas in those five minutes'.

- Learn to make creative thought creative action. List twenty things you could do with a satsuma. Do five of them.

Exercises

I've divided the exercises in this chapter into two groups. The first group of exercises explores and trains active imagination. The second group of exercises explores and trains sense memory as a tool of active imagination.

Active imagination

Two truths and a lie (5–10 minutes)

Playfully explore and blur the boundary between memory and imagination, making the imagined as if real. This is one of many exercises in this book which I learned from Jennie Buckman, Head of Acting at RADA for many years and the source of endless inspiration.

- Work as a full group or in pairs.
- Share three unrelated, perhaps improbable, things that have happened to you. Two will be truths and one will be a lie. These are two remarkable memories and one utterly imagined, remarkable event. Blur them and try to deceive your classmates. See if your colleagues can spot the lie.

Teaching Tip: The first time you do this, forewarn the students you are going to do it so they can prepare events and lies. As you repeat it, allow less and less time for preparation so the students are accessing memories and forging imagined events with greater speed.

Passive vs active imagination (15 minutes)

Explore the difference between passive and active imagination.
Develop a habit of employing active imagination.

- Work with a partner.
- Imagine and describe a short but sensorily rich walk someone might take. Describe it in the third person and the dramatic present tense (i.e. 'a woman walks down a beach. She's barefoot. The sun is shining and the sea is lapping at the shoreline ...').
- Now your partner will describe the same journey to you, but in the second person and the dramatic present tense, adding more detailed sensory description (i.e. 'you are walking down a beach; you can feel the warm sun on you. You're barefoot. The warm sand under your feet is slowing your walk, and the waves occasionally reach your feet ...').
- Now you will describe the journey again, but in the first person and present continuous tense, adding more sensory detail (i.e. 'I am walking down a beach; the sun is warm on my body and my shoulders are starting to burn. I've got no shoes on and my ankles are slightly straining as the sand falls away from me as I walk. The warm water is making sand stick to my feet ...').
- Discuss this journey from passive imagination (observer's) to active imagination (from within the events): How does it feel to tell the story from the different viewpoints? How does it change the story? How does it change the audience's relationship to the story?

A window on your world (15–20 minutes)

Explore psychological boundaries between the past, the
present and the future. Consider your relationship to time.

Our sense that we exist in time – that we have a past and a future – separates us from those animals which exist only in space. A frog has a here and a there and a now, but no 'then'. You have one vital extra dimension that a frog simply isn't aware of: a recalled past and an imagined future. Time burdens you with biography and ambition.

- Work individually.
- You will need colouring pens and pencils for this exercise.
- In your journal, draw a door that leads into your life at this exact moment.
- On another page, draw a door that opens into your past.
- On another page, draw a window that allows you to see into the future.
- Do not draw anything on the other side of the doors or anything you might be able to see through the window, just draw the thresholds to those times.
- How big are they? What are they made of? What colour are they? Do they have handles or knobs to open them? Do they have locks? If so, how elaborate are they? What are the frames to those doors and windows like? Are they elaborate frames, or simple frames, colourful or sparse?
- Allow time and space to achieve this exercise; do not rush it.
- Reflect on this exercise as a class. You might share these either with the group or in pairs; you could even create an anonymous gallery of these images. Sharing and comparing helps you learn about your own choices – however, they could simply be kept private and taken home. How did you feel drawing these pictures? How do you feel about what you have drawn? If you are sharing these with the rest of the class, consider what these other drawings can teach you about yourself (not about the artists whose work you are observing). What time does your drawing suggest surrounds you?

> ***Teaching Tip***: This can be a powerful exercise for a class, and the period of both private and shared reflection is vital. It can be worth scheduling time to check in with students about this a couple of days later, to help them process what they have learned.

Musical visualization (15–20 minutes)

Train the art of listening and responding with the imagination.
Train your imagination to follow music – a skill linked to
following the moods, rhythms and tempi of scenes.

- Work individually. You will need a sound system for this.

- The exercise requires a rich and evocative piece of music.
  It works best with something instrumental. Vitezslav
  Novak's *Eternal Longing* offers an appropriately expansive,
  transformational journey. Other suggestions for music are
  below in 'Suggested material'. The longer the piece of music,
  the more you are training your imagination's stamina.

- Lie semi-supine or supine. Focus, centre and align yourself.
  Close your eyes.

- Listen to the music. Allow the gathering instruments to form
  images in your mind's eye. Begin seeing colours and abstract
  shapes; let them swirl around you and form patterns with the
  rhythm, pitch and force of the music. Do they form into objects,
  animals, faces? Allow the music to guide your imagination.

- Fall into a dream led by the music. Visualize the journey of the
  music; discover landscapes. Put yourself at the centre of the
  journey, whatever, whenever and wherever you find yourself.

- The music will surprise you. Let the dream change direction
  as suddenly as the music may do; don't edit your imagination:
  if something new arrives very suddenly which is apparently
  unconnected to what has gone before, don't dismiss it, follow
  it. Let yourself be carried along by the swell of the music and
  the flow of your subconscious as acted upon by the music.
  Follow this journey until its musical resolution.

- Once the music ends, carefully and slowly bring yourself
  upright – unless you wish to dovetail this exercise into other
  visualization/imagination work.

- Reflect on this exercise. Either with a partner or in a group or in
  your reflective journal, share as much as you can of what you

saw in your dream. How easy is it to remember the dream? How do the skills employed here have value for an actor?

Teaching Tip: This exercise is another candidate for sleeping students. Keep moving through the space and speaking at irregular intervals. Guide the students away from inner editing and encourage them to keep imagination active – to put themselves at the centre of the journey, seeing through the eyes of someone on the journey, not having the passive outsider's eye.

What are you doing? (5–35 minutes depending on how far you develop)

Train your imagination to follow your body.

Part of your skill is an openness to being taken by surprise by your own body, recognizing its unconscious offers and suggestions. This exercise was taught to me by the brilliant writer and educator Tom Green.

- Work as a full group.

- Everyone move freely around the room. Use lots of different levels, roll around, stretch limbs out at random. Allow your body to make unusual shapes.

- It can be liberating to do this to music – but avoid any dance music if you do (even ballet), or the shapes become quotes of social dance. If you feel self-conscious doing this at first, everyone should do it with their eyes closed.

- Either when the music stops or the exercise leader calls, everyone freeze in your random position.

- Find an imaginative answer to the basic question: What are you doing? Let your imagination find a context that makes this odd shape necessary.

- Continue. Remember, this unlocks doors when it moves beyond fun, into that delicious territory of serious play. Repeat it several times.

II

- Link your discoveries with someone else: as you freeze, notice the person nearest to you. What are you doing together?

- You might even connect freezes into a scene. After a count of three, bring your frozen scene to life. This can contribute to a devising process, as outlined in Part Three.

- Reflect on this exercise and on the nature of creativity and its relationship to discovery: make a choice and see what it offers and stimulates. How is this relevant to your work as an actor?

Magic if (30 minutes)

Train your active imagination to work on someone else's life.

- Work in pairs.

- Take the given circumstances of a key moment in history, or a scene you are working on, or a moment in a novel you are studying, and ask 'What if I were there?'

- You might imagine you are a Thane at Macbeth's banquet when Macbeth sees the ghost of Banquo. You might imagine you are sitting on the bus when Rosa Parks refuses to move to the back of the bus. You might imagine you are sitting at a table when Oliver Twist asks the Beadle for more to eat.

- Where and when is it? Who is there? What has just happened? What do the people involved want?

- Having established the circumstances, make it active. Answer these three questions, as if you were in these circumstances:

1   What could I want?

2   What obstacles might be in the way of fulfilling that want?

3   What could I do to overcome those obstacles?

- Avoid answering questions which falsely limit your imagination. Don't ask the limiting 'What *would* I want, what *would* I do?' Certainly don't translate it into the obligated 'What *should* I want, what *should* I do?' Operate within the widest range of possibility: 'What *could* I want, what *could* I do?' Give your vivid imagination free reign to play.

- Tell the story of the event to the group or your partner in the first person (from your point of view – 'I was sitting on the back row of the bus, when …'), with an imagined 'what happened next'. How did you affect the events? How were you changed by them? If you are working alone, write/draw it in your journal.

- Reflect on this exercise. How do the skills it develops support the actor's work?

This exercise can grow easily into 'Storyretelling' (page 284) and exercises outlined in Chapter 10.

Shared endowments (about 20–25 minutes, depending on group size)

Train seeing and sensing, as against showing or demonstrating. Learn to see clearly and sense richly, rather than demonstrating experiences to an audience.

- Define a performance space for this exercise. You might use masking tape to mark a square on the floor, lay out a large rug or use four chairs to define the boundaries of the space.

|

- Move into groups of about five people.
- Each group secretly agrees on a location and an event to witness through a window, e.g. visiting a friend's new-born

child in hospital or looking down on the earth from a spaceship. Be as specific as you can when defining what you are seeing.

- Work without words (though not necessarily in silence). Each group does this in front of the rest of the class. One by one, each group member steps into the space and looks through that imagined window.

- Allow what you see to affect and move you – to change your breath pattern and your body. Do not try and show the audience what you are seeing or demonstrate its effects on you. Trust that seeing it is enough and that your body will follow where your mind's eye leads.

- Do not allow this to last long – 30 seconds per group will be plenty.

- Ask the observers what they saw happening to the actors (the chorus of their bodies and breath patterns). What might they have been seeing? Discuss how the audience's breath patterns and bodies were changed.

II

- In the same groups, decide on a location and something specific to which you can listen. For example, you might hear the padding of heavy paws and snuffling breath outside your tent on a safari, or the voice of Winston Churchill declaring war over your wireless.

- One group presents at a time. Step into the space and listen. Again, this is done without language. Allow the sounds to affect you, to condition your breath and therefore your body. Allow 20–30 seconds for each group.

- Ask the audience what they saw happening to the actors' bodies and breath patterns, what their imagination heard and how their own bodies and breath patterns were altered.

III

- In the same groups, decide on a location through which to pass. This might be a graveyard at night or a sunny beach in Rio. Define its unique temperature, weather, atmosphere, noises, smells and horizon.

- Each group presents to the rest of the class, without words. One by one or in pairs move through the imagined space with a simple, defined purpose. Don't feel you have to help the audience understand where you are or what your relationship to the space is, instead simply move through the imagined space, not the square on the floor of your classroom.

- Reflect on this exercise and the difference between playing and showing.

Sense memory

Basic sense memory (10–15 minutes)

Train your ability to access and enliven imagined or remembered experiences.

- Work individually.

- If you find this exercise uncomfortable, simply open your eyes and focus on the experience the rest of the class is having. Return to the exercise when you are ready.

- Allow each memory to naturally release/engage the tension that comes from that sensation. Everyone in the room has their eyes closed, so you are not showing this to anyone. Simply receive the sensations into your body.

- Stand. Focus, centre and align yourself. Close your eyes.

- Remember the taste of warm chocolate.

- Release that. Notice the sounds of the room you are in.

- Now remember the smell of rain on the streets.

- Release that. Notice the sounds of the room you are in.

- Now remember the sound of the sea.

- Release that. Notice the sounds of the room you are in.

- Now remember the feeling of standing in a warm shower.

- Release that. Notice the sounds of the room you are in.

- Now remember the physical sensation of having your hand held by someone you love and with whom you feel safe.

- Release that. Softly open your eyes and take in where and when you are now.

- Reflect on this exercise. How vividly did these sense memories come back to you? What associations did they stir for you? How did your body respond in holding tension and an altered breath pattern? Specifically, where did each sense memory take you? Perhaps share these with your group/a partner.

Teaching Tip: This can easily be extended by working with different experiences and sensations. It can easily become an exercise for character development, to build new character memories out of specific sensations.

Sense memory: Falling (10 minutes)

Use memory to bring life to imagined sensations.

- Work individually.

- Stand. Focus, centre and align yourself.

- See a table or chair in front of you. Visualize falling from it face first.

- Allow the sensation in – that lurching panic, sickness and fear. Now release that image and centre yourself again.

- See that table or chair and visualize falling again. As you do so, tip yourself gently forwards off-balance, as if you were on that chair or table.

- Release that image and centre yourself again. Expand that sensation. What if you were stepping out of a plane with a parachute on your back? Try falling into a simple step forward with this thought.

- Release and centre yourself again. Expand that sensation. What if you were falling out of a plane without a parachute on your back? Try falling into a simple step forward with this thought.

- Reflect on the power of the imagination over your body. How were you changed by this simple idea and expanding on it? How available was your body to the suggestion of an image which you inhabited? How is this relevant to the actor?

Teaching Tip: This simple exercise can be a delicious stimulus into text. Use this image and the step forward at the beginning of a scene or speech (or adapt it and use another physical image/memory). Take this falling, lurching energy as the opening impulse. It can drive your body into text. Try it.

Sense memory: Finding hands (15 minutes)

Train sensual alertness and short-term sense memory. Discover the intensity and specificity of sensual connection, and build trust within an ensemble.

- Work as a full group.
- You will need a clear room for this exercise, free of trip hazards.
- Find a partner with whom you have not worked much. Take off any rings, watches or bracelets.
- Stand facing your partner, close enough to touch. Focus, centre and align yourself. Close your eyes and acknowledge and accept the proximity of your partner.

- Work in silence. Take each other's hands. Gently and softly, explore each other's hands. Do not reach the wrist and pulse; just explore the hand.

- Discover the length of the fingernails, the rough and the smooth, the creases and the bumps. Take your time.

- Open your eyes and everyone move across the space and away from each other.

- Close your eyes. Very slowly and carefully move through the space, using small steps and with your hands out in front of you. Do not open your eyes and continue to work in silence. Only by touching hands, find your partner.

- When you have found your partner, open your eyes and watch the rest of the group in silence.

- Reflect and evaluate. How did it feel to hold hands like this? How did you feel when searching? How did you recognize your partner's hands? How did you feel when you found them again? How is this relevant to an actor's work?

Teaching Tip: Guide people away from walls as they move. If the group is larger than around seven, then ask for one or two people to stand out as privileged observers to the exercise. They will help you guide people away from hazards and provide feedback to the group on what they saw happening as people sought their partners, and how their bodies changed once they found them.

The quality of intense connection this creates is a good platform for other partnering work. Mirroring, communion or repetition work (all in Chapter 3) each follow well from this exercise.

Memory and imagination: A commuter (10–12 minutes)

Use memory as a springboard for rich imaginative leaps – in this case, specifically for character work.

- Work individually.

- Focus, centre and align yourself. You can do this exercise either standing or supine, depending on what you plan to follow it.

- Remember someone whom you noticed on your journey in to class today – someone you do not know, but who caught your attention. Notice them again now. What were they wearing? What rhythm did they carry? What tensions were they holding? What was the pattern of their breathing? How did they appear to feel? What did they make you feel? Remember them and their context in detail.

- Now allow your imagination to fill in gaps. Where do you think they were going? Where were they coming from? What did they want and for what reason? Who were they afraid they might be in that moment and who were they trying to be?

- Extend your imagination to build a tiny story around this person and their single journey. In the middle of what drama did you find them?

- Share this, or write/storyboard it into your journal.

Teaching Tip: This exercise could contribute to a devising process, as in Part 3.

Objects of value (30 minutes)

Work with real relationships (in this case, a relationship with an object, though later in the process you will use relationships with people in the same way), and train the safe use of these relationships within your work.

Your own life and relationships are the inevitable references and resources of your work. You will need to prepare this exercise in advance of a class.

- Everyone will need to bring in an object of rich personal value. It would greatly upset you to lose this object. It may have little or no monetary worth; this is about its personal value.

- The crucial rule, which helps protect you from anything too upsetting, is that you should be happy for the rest of the group to hear about this object and inspect it. Do not bring in an object which relates to an open grief or unresolved trauma.

I

- Sit comfortably, with the object in front of you. Close your eyes. Focus, centre and align yourself.

- With your eyes still closed, bring your attention to the object. Imagine it. Remember how it feels to touch it – its weight, its texture, its shape and form. Remember its smell if you know it well, and allow these memories to affect you.

- With your eyes still closed, reach forward and touch the object. Take it into your hands and explore it. What can you discover about this object that you had forgotten or not previously noticed? Notice its scent and what this evokes and stimulates within you.

- Now open your eyes and look at the object. See it and the associated memories of people and places. When did you receive or get this object? Notice this moment in great sensory detail. Where were you? What could you see, smell, hear? Who else was there and how were they affected in that moment? How did you feel? Allow your body and breath to be affected.

- Release these tensions and breath patterns by focusing again on the object's shape and form and by locating it in your classroom here and now.

II

- Come into a large circle to work as a full group, or break into pairs, and share the object.

- Share what you have noticed about its form, its value to you, the story of the moment you got it. Where do you keep it now? What would its loss mean? Allow your partner or the group to hold the object and ask questions about it. Allow yourself to be affected by the telling: make yourself open.

- Reflect on this exercise. What does it reveal about our relationship to memory? What does it suggest about how an actor might relate to their imagined or actual playing space? What was the storytelling experience like, when you shared your objects?

Follow-up

Embed your awareness and understanding of memory and imagination, continuing the training away from class.

- Consider your use of sense memory throughout your day: when you choose between meals in a cafe, you are using sense memory and your imagination (what would a cheese and satsuma sandwich taste like? I bet you can imagine, by combining sense memories); when you notice a smell and it reminds you of another place and time; when a stranger you see reminds you of a friend and you feel unexpectedly connected to that person, and so on.

- Last thing before you go to sleep at night – just before you drift off – tell yourself 'I remember my dreams'. When you wake up, recall them in as much detail as you can before you get out of bed and write them down in your private reflective journal.

- At the end of your day, remember what you did today, moment by moment. Try and trace through your whole day, using your active memory to visualize your journey and remember what you felt.

- At the end of your day, notice what you did *not* do today. Trace through your day and notice choices you could have made or things that could have happened that would have taken your day somewhere else. What if I'd missed that train? What if I'd grown wings this morning? What if I'd woken up invisible? Follow a flight of fancy like the beginning of a dream, exploring fully what might have happened today. Use your active imagination and sense memory to discover detail.

Suggested material

Other possible music for visualization exercises:
Benjamin Britten, *Sea Interludes* from *Peter Grimes*
Benjamin Britten, *Phantasy Quartet*
Antonin Dvorak, *Symphony No. 6 in D*
Leos Janacek, *Sinfonietta,* Movements 1 and 2
Arvo Part, *Fratres*

Further reading

See a remarkable example of the power of memory as Clive Wearing and his
    wife speak in a documentary, *Life without Memory*, on *youtube.com*
Damasio, Antonio (2000), *The Feeling of What Happens*. Vintage Books.
Damasio, Antonio (2003), *Looking for Spinoza*. Vintage Books.
Hagen, Uta (1973), *Respect for Acting*. Wiley Publishing Inc. Chapters 4, 5
    and 6, 'Emotional Memory', 'Sense Memory', 'The Five Senses'.
Marshall, Lorna (2008), *The Body Speaks*. Methuen Drama. Chapter 3,
    'Emotion'.
Stanislavski, Konstantin, trans. Jean Benedetti (2008), *An Actor's Work*.
    Routledge. Chapter 4, 'Imagination' and Chapter 9, 'Emotion Memory'.

3
ARRIVE

Train a quality of presence and immediacy, in which you are connected and responsive to your environment, situation and other people.

Framework

Acting demands that you commit utterly to the imagined 'here and now' in which you place yourself. This is often called *being present*. An actor's quality of presence is utterly immediate, engaged and active, and is what the exercises in this chapter will train you to use.

You have worked to train your memory, in the service of imagination. Memory and imagination propel you into the new world, but you will now train another human super-power: forgetting. Forgetting keeps you present: how else do you make something you've already performed eight times this week seem true and immediate?

Forgetting doesn't mean losing things from your mind – everything we have ever done is stored in our limitless memories – forgetting means misplacing things in your mind. Everything's there, you just can't or won't find what you're looking for. The playwright David Mamet describes an actor's process un-improvably: plan it, know it, forget it, do it.

*

We know we are present in the world when we see our effect upon other people and things. Our core consciousness – our basic awareness of being present in the world – comes from our awareness that we change and are changed by other people and things. Here you are, reading this book. You are aware of your environment, of the book, and are aware of a 'you' reading this book. Self-awareness comes when you feel yourself turn a page, shift in your seat or feel yourself changed by a sentence in the book. This thread of awareness is only broken by deep dreamless sleep – when you are not present in any relationship, real or imagined.

So presence comes from an awareness of yourself in relationships. Learning to become present, or 'in the moment', means learning to connect with other people and relationships. It means learning to connect not to what you think is happening, nor to what you wish were happening, nor to what happened the last time you played the scene, but to what *is* happening here and now. Receive, follow and respond. Deal with the world.

Being present is an attentive, alert energy. It is not a generalized state; it operates in the here and now, with intimacy and immediacy. It is a state of specified dependence, which requires drawing energy not from within you, but from people and objects around you. Being present demands true listening: not waiting to speak, but rather needing what someone else has to say.

How can we tell when we are present? The experience of being present feels like ease. It is an organic state of flow and connection. Often when we have been present in a scene, afterwards we cannot really remember it or what we did – though there may be clear memories of what others have done. We certainly have no idea of whether it was any good or not; it just was.

*

Presence is selective. We attend to specific people or things, and tune out the rest in order to manage the flood of data available at any one time. Think of your friend's noisy birthday party, at which you select one voice to hear from the babble which surrounds you. Humans have an internal spotlight or zoom lens. Attention spotlights areas which we deem valuable, important. Train your spotlight so it is laser-guided in its precision and can shutter out the world around you. You won't need to ignore the camera or the audience (perversely that puts them in the spotlight): take them for granted and let them drift out of the light.

Find your focus-point within a scene, and spotlight your attention onto it. Connect your presence to its needs; define yourself through its responses.

Out of connected presence, we carve identity. I am whoever others find me to be and I am whatever I am capable of making others around me. I am tall because everyone else is short. I am strong because I find this bag to be light. I am scary because others are scared. I can transform who I am by transforming my relationships to other people and objects. I rely on them to prove my existence; they can also transform my existence. Acting is transforming how you sense the world. I make myself Macbeth not by making myself a murderer, but by seeing a Macduff who needs to be killed.

The work is never about you. Playing Lady Macbeth, the focus is not on making yourself Lady Macbeth, but on seeing a Macbeth who needs you. This liberating idea is the deepest root of the presence we cultivate in our craft. The work will always come through you; it will come to life all around you – but it won't be about you. It will be about ideas, stories, people, but never you.

You need a source of energy which is outside of yourself for every moment in your work: a god, something in nature, an object or most likely, another person, to provide energetic momentum. This is written into the laws of thermodynamics: energy cannot be created or destroyed, only transformed. When we talk about presence in acting, it is with nature's law in mind: *reach out for existing energy and transform it.*

Exploration

These simple exercises can be done in preparation for class or as starter exercises to a session. Develop an understanding and awareness of operating with different levels of focus and attention (what Stanislavski called 'Circles of Attention').

Engage the first principles of receiving and following.

- Be aware of when you are operating in different circles of attention. When in your day are you in circle 1, connected

only to yourself and sinking inwards, drifting back? When do
you enter circle 2, connecting intimately in an exchange with
another person or object with alert presence? When do you
enter circle 3, playing out to multiple people/the environment,
taking and controlling space? Note different moments in your
journal. Note in particular what happens and how your body
behaves when you move between circles (from sitting at the
back of class in circle 1 with your mind wandering, to the
moment of being called into the action of the class in circle 3;
leaving a conversation with a large groups of friends in circle 3
to having a private conversation in circle 2, for example). How
does this introduce/release tension and change your breath
pattern? Draw yourself in each of these three circles. Colour in
your drawing, communicating tension and focus through colour
and shading.

- Watch this incredible TED talk, in which the deaf percussionist
  Evelyn Glennie discusses listening with your whole being:
  www.youtube.com/watch?v=383kxC_NCKw.

- Look at an animal like a frog, a chicken or a pigeon – an animal
  that lives entirely in the present tense, unaware of future or
  past. For these animals there is only immediate impulse and
  response. Write a repeating monologue for the animal – like
  the seagulls in Pixar's *Finding Nemo* who can shout only
  'MINE!' My father-in-law's terrier seems to think only in terms of
  'What?', 'Love me!' or 'Go away!'

- Work in pairs. You will need an image for this – a painting, a
  photograph, an advert or whatever. Keep your image hidden
  from your partner. Sit back to back. Partner A, describe your
  image to Partner B in as much detail as possible – what's in
  the image, its colour, textures, moods. Partner B will draw
  what you describe. Partner A, your objective is to help Partner
  B draw what you see. Compare the drawing and the image
  once you have finished. Try the same the other way round.
  Reflect on the intimacy of this exchange and the experience of
  receiving and following someone else's engaged imagination.

- Work with a partner. Tell the story of your name to your partner:
  include its history, its meanings, how you feel about different

ways people use your name, who named you and what derivatives of your name people choose to use. Now perform the same story to the whole group. Try and talk to them with the same intimacy and ease which you found with your partner.

Exercises

I have divided the exercises in this chapter into two sections. The first section, 'Receive and follow', builds connection and situational awareness. The second section, 'Receive, follow and respond', moves this organic, connected state into an active and potentially transformational one.

Whenever I refer to the objects, ideas and people that transform you and that you seek to transform, I will refer to them as your *target*. Your target is whatever you want to change in any given moment. It is a term I am borrowing from Declan Donnellan.

Receive and follow

Count to three (5 minutes)

Engage with intimate presence and alertness. Train a basic exchange of energy with a scene partner.

- Work in pairs.
- Repeatedly count one, two, three, alternating between you as you go. So:

    A: One.
    B: Two.
    A: Three.
    B: One.
    A: Two.
    B: Three.

    And so on. This requires no forward or backward thinking; hear what is said and say the next thing. It is oddly difficult and a nice quick warm-up for outward facing, present-tense listening.

- Replace the number three with a sound you decide on (i.e. one, two, bing!).

- Now replace the number two with a shape (i.e. one, *jump*, bing!).

Teaching Tip: You can extend this exercise by including more numbers, more people and more physical play. Try it in a full circle, counting in groups. It leads well into the Meisner repetition work I will outline later in this section.

Finger following (10–20 minutes depending on how far you develop it)

Train connected presence, bound to a specific external target (the finger) and clearly defined objective (following it).

I

- Work in silence with a partner.

- Remember, working in silence does not mean holding your breath. Breathe freely.

- Partner A, hold up your index finger about 30 centimetres/12 inches from the bridge of your partner's nose. Partner B, focus on the finger.

- Partner A, your task is to lead your partner carefully through the space, guiding them with your finger and maintaining an even distance between you.

- Partner B, your task is to follow that finger and maintain that even distance.

- Let your focus be absolute. Take care of each other. Move up and down, back and forth, side to side as you travel. Mobilize your spine, pelvis and thighs. You are not exploring objects in the space, since you are focusing on each other; you are exploring yourselves in space and the imagined connection between you that makes you one body.

- As you move, imagine the space is like water: it supports you like water supports a fish.

- Do not test or trick your partner; this is not a competition. Move through space together.

- Be aware of other people in the space. Move in relation to them; explore how the two of you, as one body, can relate to others.

II

- Switch your role from leader to follower or vice versa. Exchange with silent agreement and without breaking your journey.

- Reflect on this exercise. Do so in your journal, in a group discussion or in your pairs, depending on the available time. How broad was your circle of attention? What was your relationship to time – did the exercise seem to last a long time, or no time at all? How did it affect your relationship to your partner? How was your breathing affected? What thoughts or images came to mind as you worked?

Teaching Tip: You might develop this further by leading more than one person at a time – working in threes or fives.

You can also try changing the point of focus – lead your partner from their solar plexus or hips (instead of the nose), for example. This significantly shifts the tone and feel of the exercise.

Triangles (20–25 minutes)

Train active presence amid a busy ensemble, connected to an imagined target (the triangle) and clear objective (make it equilateral).

- Work as a full group. Work in silence and with a rule of no physical contact.

- You will need a clear space for this exercise, with chairs and tables cleared away. Notice any potential physical dangers, as you will use the whole space as this unfolds.

I

- Move through the space, walking point to point. Spot something specific in the space, and move directly to it. Make contact with it, then move off towards something else. Walk freely, with ease and flow.

- As you move through the space, become aware of two other people. Don't choose two people, just let two bodies catch your attention which happen to be near you at this moment.

- Retain an awareness of them as you continue to move through the space. Your circle of attention has broadened to include them. You will not always be able to see these people, but without looking, build an awareness of their journeys. As you move, your peripheral vision will clock them.

II

- Now try and make an equilateral triangle in the space, with yourself and the other two bodies as the three points of that triangle. Make it a perfect equilateral with the same length sides and the same size angles.

- Don't stop to see the problem develop as the two other bodies move away; move yourself to achieve your equilateral triangle. Do not wait for it to happen; make it happen. Move.

- Allow this exercise to ebb and flow as you get close to achieving your triangle and then see it disappear. Go for absolute perfection with your triangle; you may be tempted to compromise in order to complete the exercise. Completion is not the point.

- Pause the exercise. Where are you looking? What is your relationship to the space? What is your relationship to time? How broad was your circle of attention? Which are the moments of drama in this exercise?

- Continue the exercise.

- You are in a state of intense situational awareness as you play this exercise. Your core consciousness is fully engaged (where you are here and now in relation to what you want); your extended, autobiographical consciousness is diminished (who you are in relation to past events). Focus fully on a target outside of yourself, pursuing an objective utterly in the present tense. This is the definition of a state of situational awareness: here, now and reliant on the actions of others.

- Notice the dramaturgy of the exercise as it unfolds: the rhythm of the play and its peaks and troughs; the moments of tension, suspense and release as people move closer to and then further from their goals.

- Bring the exercise to an end and consider how the skills developed in it might relate to acting.

Triangles and threes are strangely important in human history, with great divine significance in the major world religions now and in the past. It takes three legs to make something stable and bear a load: a triangle represents stability (the Hittites even used it as a sign to mean 'healthy' or 'good'). Three is the magic number. How might this relate to drama and acting? How might it impact on our understanding of a scene between two people, or a soliloquy with an audience? I would suggest one person is always in relation to two other targets – at the very least who they wish they could be and fear they might be (more on this in Part Two).

Mirroring (25–30 minutes)

The receive-and-follow principle extends to its natural end.
Train total situational awareness and presence. Train intimacy
through imagined connection.

I

- Work with a partner.
- Stand facing your partner, about 1.5 metres/5 feet apart.
- Find alignment and a centred, calm breath. Make comfortable, easy eye contact with your partner.
- Partner A, begin to perform a simple, flowing physical action. Partner B, exactly mirror that action. Work initially in two dimensions – up/down and side-to-side.
- You are absolutely not trying to catch each other out, but to work in unison and find a point of communion in your work in which it is impossible for the outside observer to see who is leading.
- Ultimately, you may not be sure who is leading, perhaps you can do this exercise without a nominated leader. You are both taking responsibility for your shared movement.
- As you continue into this exercise, you will enter a total situational awareness of the other person. The exercise drives out awareness of anyone other than the person before you and what they are doing here and now. You are engaged in a meditative state of alert connection.

II

- As you continue, allow your imagination to play a trick on you. Imagine you are looking into a mirror. The person in front of you is you looking back. Those are your eyes, that is your skin, that is your hand. You are what you see in the mirror right now. Explore yourself and what you look like. Open your mouth if you want to see inside, widen your eyes and lean forward if you want to see your eyes in more detail. Look in the mirror.

- Continue in this state as long as you care or dare. If you have continued in this exercise for a while – say 10 or 15 minutes – you will need to really shake it off. Jump around, look about you at other targets in the room and, crucially, start to talk about it with your partner.

- Reflect on the quality of attention you found, and the effect it had on your sense of yourself, space and time. Discuss what you noticed. Discuss how you felt. Discuss how this state of awareness and connection might relate to the work of an actor.

Receive, follow and respond

Rounds of applause (anything from 10 to 40 minutes)

Train active and immediate presence, at first in pairs and then among an ensemble with changing targets. Play the same moment many times as if for the first time, always 'in the moment' because what other moment is there than this one?

I

- Find a partner. Stand facing your partner, about 10 feet/3 metres from each other. Stand with your feet hip-width apart and your weight spread evenly over both feet. Have soft knees and be ready to move and be moved.

- Partner A, 'throw' a clap towards Partner B. This should involve a clear clap with a definite gesture towards your partner. Partner B, 'catch' that clap (by clapping of course).

- Partner B then 'throw' the clap back to Partner A. Partner A, 'catch' that clap with another clap. Continue playing this special game of catch, using a clap instead of a ball.

- Catch exactly the clap you are sent. It will have an energy and a direction all of its own. Your partner may offer a looping, soft clap which will arc through the air gently. Your partner may throw a clap like a dart which zips through the air. They might be slightly off-line with their throw, in which case you will need to move to catch it, or they may throw it right at your throat. Receive the clap that is sent.

- Try throwing the clap back and forth for a while, building up an energy like two tennis players in a rally. Try not to drop or miss a clap, but be honest if you have and start the rally again.

- Move your feet to receive or send any clap; let it be a physical act engaging your whole body. Remember there are always two claps at a time from each partner: one to receive, one to send.

- If you are an observer to this exercise, it is striking how obvious it is when someone has not received the clap they were sent. Sometimes a clap is unexpectedly soft or small; does the person receiving it move forwards to catch this gentler energy, or pretend it has made its way over to them, even though our mind's eye saw it drop a metre short? This is an exercise in connection: is your body responding to the action of your partner? Are you receiving the energy that is given, or impersonating connection?

- You might ask pairs to take it in turns to play in front of the group, allowing everyone the chance to see this active exchange. You are basically improvising a scene.

II

- Now stand in a large, open circle.

- Throw a single clap around the circle in a random order. Use clear eye contact and definite gestures as the indicator of its direction. The clap could get thrown to you at any time, so everyone will need to stand alert and ready to receive throughout. Make yourself an available target.

- Remember there are always two claps at a time from each person: one to receive and one to send.

- The goal is not speed here, though that can be enormous fun; the target is free flow. Speed may happen, but that is not what you will try and achieve.

- Pause after a while and observe your own behaviours. Where is your eye-line focused? How are you breathing (or not)? What tensions are introduced into your body? What is your circle of attention?

III

- Now build an agreed order for your game of catch. Slowly throw the clap around the circle. Once you have both sent and received it, sit down so that everyone knows who has had a turn and who has not. Make sure everyone gets it once, before it has made its way back to the person who started it.

- Now start again, throwing the clap around the circle in this fixed order. Do not deviate from this order; let the pattern build and allow everyone to become confident with it. Know from whom you receive the clap, and to whom you send it.

- Pause what you are doing after a while and observe your own behaviours. Where are your eyes? How are you breathing (or not)? How are you holding your weight? What tensions are introduced into your body by this exercise? How is all of this different from the exercise when you were throwing it at random?

- Now begin to throw it around the circle in your fixed order again, but this time try and do so *as if* the order were random. Adopt the behaviour patterns of the unknown, random throwing, even though you really know exactly when you will receive the clap and who will throw it to you.

- You are effectively playing a scripted scene. Remember, it is of no importance how the actor actually feels; it matters how the actor seems to feel to an audience.

Teaching Tip: You can play this exercise with sounds, words of a poem or lines from a speech or scene passed around rather than a physical action (in this case a clap, but it could be any move or sequence of moves). Be inventive and apply the same principle to other forms of communication. The thing to explore here is physically listening: vividly connected exchanges of thought, action and will.

Communion exercise (15–20 minutes)

*Make the state of presence active, as you respond to
a partner, not simply receive and follow. Respond to
unmediated inner impulses in a state of connected situational
awareness. The target is dictated by the exercise (the other
actor), your action is a response to their behaviour. This
is based on work I learned from the acting teacher Katya
Kamotskaia.*

- Work with a partner.
- Stand facing your partner, around 2 metres/6 feet from your partner. Find alignment and a centred, calm breath. Make comfortable, easy eye contact with your partner. Allow yourself to see and be seen.
- Imagine a coiled spring of light is running between your solar plexus and the solar plexus of your partner. It presses back on you, wanting to spring out. It is currently coiled tightly enough that it requires a deliberate choice from you to stand where you stand, facing your partner. It is not coiled so tightly as to cause discomfort or make it hard to breathe. It is a definite choice to be this close to your partner. Do not demonstrate this, or act the coil's presence; allow it to be there in your mind and trust that the thought will condition your body.
- You could move closer to your partner, but if you did it would cost you: it would be harder to breathe as the pressure from the coiled spring would intensify.
- You could move away from your partner; if you did the coiled spring would slowly release its tension.
- Explore simply moving towards and back from your partner down this channel.
- Eye contact is everything in this exercise. Do not break eye contact.

II

- Try working with a simple curiosity. Imagine a simple, non-invasive quality of contact. It might be holding a hand or touching a shoulder. Be curious about how that contact might feel. Move towards or away from your partner, but know that it will cost you to get close enough to achieve that contact.

- The exercise is concluded either when you achieve that contact, or realize you cannot.

- Reflect on the physical impact this imagined tension had on you. Consider how it affected your relationship with your partner and how this imagined bond changed you.

Extended communion (30 minutes or so, depending on how deeply you are able to investigate)

This extends the training of the last exercise, embedding it within psychophysical dependence: it raises the stakes. It is based on an exercise taught by Robert Cohen.

- Follow the instructions for the exercise above, establishing a connection with your partner down a single channel of energy. Again, eye contact is everything.

- This time, rather than allowing yourself to be affected by curiosity about contact, try having a thought.

- Think this: *I can be hurt by you.* Know that this is true. The person opposite you has the capacity to hurt you. They won't because you are working in a safe environment and within a trusted ensemble, but they could hurt you. They could hurt you physically, and more than that they could hurt you emotionally and psychologically. They won't, but they could. Have this thought, and dare to know it is true. Dare to understand what it means. Allow the thought to grow into meaning and to see it, know it, own it. Allow yourself to lean into the thought. Speak it aloud. Repeat it if you need.

- Explore moving towards or away from your partner, as you possess this thought. Respond to your partner's presence and behaviour. You can only move towards or away.

- Release this thought and focus on your partner. See their face and take the time to notice something you have not noticed about them before.

- Think this: *I can hurt you*. Know that it is true. You have the capacity to hurt the person in front of you. Not just physically, but more than that – emotionally and psychologically. You don't, you won't, but you could. Be aware of your potential.

- Don't just repeat the words in your mind; move beyond the words to more profoundly own the thought. See what it means. Think it, mean it, know it, own it. Lean into it. Speak the words aloud. Repeat them if you need.

- Explore moving towards or away from your partner, as you possess this thought. Respond to your partner's presence and behaviour. You can only move towards or away.

- Release this thought and focus on your partner. See their face and take the time to notice something you have not noticed about them before. Find your centre and settle.

- It can be difficult to come to terms with our own power to effect change, and to accept how profoundly other people can affect us. Acknowledging, even accepting, our own power and consequent vulnerability is a crucial part of preparing to act. This exercise challenges the actor to begin this process.

- Which thought did you find harder to understand and possess? How did the two thoughts differently affect your body and breath? How did each make you feel? Discuss the relevance of this for an actor in their work. Remember, one thing acting is profoundly concerned with is playing and receiving actions: changing and being changed.

- This exercise reaches back to the core question of dependence and the artifice of human independence. Reflect on this. What does dependence mean? Upon whom are you dependent? How does dependence feel? What is the opposite of dependence? How does that feel?

Teaching Tip: **This is a very simple exercise, but can provoke strong reactions. It needs to be allowed time and space to develop and you must factor in time for in-class reflection and evaluation.**

Basic Meisner repetition (30 minutes)

Train receiving, following and responding. Train active presence. Bring language into this work in a simple, non-threatening way.

This exercise is very well-known and can be intimidating because it is talked about so much. It is in fact very simple and can be very liberating.

- Find a partner.
- These are the rules: listen, observe and tell the truth.
- Listen, in this exercise, means repeat exactly what is said.
- Observe means say what you see, not what you feel or think or imagine.
- Tell the truth means be specific and say nothing which you cannot directly see to be true.
- Sit in a chair and face your partner, centred and aligned. Make eye contact. Observe your partner.
- Partner A will begin by stating something which both of you would absolutely agree to be true. For instance A might say 'You have green eyes' or 'Your hair is curly'. Partner B will repeat this exactly, though turning it from the second to the first person, so Partner B says 'I have green eyes' or 'My hair is curly'.
- Continue with this simplest truthful exchange, repeating the words while perhaps varying intonation, pitch, intensity and therefore meaning if this naturally occurs. So:

A: Your hair is curly
B: My hair is curly.
A: Your hair is curly.
B: My hair is curly.

- This is a very basic verbal exchange. Although the words do not change, meaning will shift.

- Continue like this until another observation strikes one of you – until a new impulse arises. For example, perhaps Partner A smiles and Partner B says 'You're smiling'. Partner A would then repeat this, 'I'm smiling'. Crucially you are stating something which is incontrovertibly true. And so this two–word, truthful exchange repeats until a new impulse arises.

- Let yourself be affected by what is said, and by your partner's behaviour, observing moment to moment. As your work becomes more detailed you might notice smaller changes: 'You raised your right eyebrow' or 'Your hands are clenched'.

- Initially, do not engage in supposition or suggestion and do not offer your point of view – don't say 'You look tired', for example. Keep it about outward behaviour, action and physicality, without further judgement about what that behaviour means.

- So a typical exchange might run:

    A: Your hair is curly.
    B: My hair is curly.
    A: Your hair is curly.
    B: My hair is curly.
    A: Your hair is very dark and curly.
    B: My hair is very dark and curly.
    A: Your hair is very dark and curly.
    B: You moved your feet.
    A: I moved my feet.
    B: You moved your feet.
    A: I moved my feet.
    B: You tilted your head.

And so on.

- The very fact of being seen in this way – openly, as yourself and with direct honesty – is very exposing and affecting. It provokes strong reactions and, at least at first, should be done with an observer close by to redirect the exchange if it ever becomes inflected with judgement or inference. Keep it simple.

- Reflect on this exercise, and do keep coming back to it: it reaps its rewards through, well, repetition.

Teaching Tip: As you develop confidence with the exercise, move your repetition beyond statements about physical behaviour, to allow reflection of what is perceived to be true. At this point, you become able to say 'You look tired' or 'You look embarrassed', for example. This is clearly more provocative territory. As such, it moves us into the territory where most of the actor's work will take place: it also moves us into territory which needs careful leadership from a teacher who really knows their class.

This exercise extends well into the beginning of scene work. Take an exchange from a scene and submit it to repetition: a line is said and then repeated in turns until it is fully received, followed. Move on to the next line only when a response becomes *necessary*. This exercise helps us move beyond words to discover behaviour within language – see 'Repetition' in *Chapter 8* (page 238).

Declan Donnellan's repetition (30 minutes)

Bring the repetition exercise into dramatic form. Work within the simplest dramatic structure. Train active presence, responding to the behaviour of a scene partner with scripted language.

- Work in pairs.
- Have a conversation. Your text is – 'No, there's you, there's me and there's the space.' These words will be all you can use in your exchange.

- These three vital points of coordination – you, me and the space – are as crucial as they are obvious. Because they are obvious, it is often easy to take them for granted and blur their distinction.

- The 'no' provides the impulse to drama. The 'there' keeps us reaching out (more so than 'here' would). The 'you, me and the space' are the divine triangle of conscious presence.

- This demands behavioural specificity about each element: locate exactly what you mean as you talk to each other.

- A finger touching the heart when you say 'There's you' or 'There's me' is hugely different from two fingers pointing at the eyes or your foot. Be equally specific with 'the space'. Don't waft a hand generally through the air; locate something in the space that you mean: a chair, a window, the sun, a friend … Each will communicate something entirely different.

- Repeat the words, but allow a conversation, an interaction to occur. It will.

- If you feel like you can't think of anything to do, find energy from a target: move.

- Any choice – even no choice – will make something happen in your partner. They will discover meaning in it: human beings are supremely well programmed for finding narrative sense in seemingly random actions. See what happens in your partner and respond to that.

- You might also try this exercise with different text – 'No, it's not you who is in control, it's me who is in control and this is my space', or 'No, it's not me who is in control, it's you who is in control and this is my space'.

- Remember what the movement specialist Lorna Marshall says: 'It's enough to be human.'

Follow-up

Extend and embed understanding of situational awareness and presence away from class, or as reflective exercises to end a session.

- Notice how you make absent targets present – perhaps when you talk about someone who isn't in the room, or negotiate a complex idea while working. Where do you 'put' these imagined targets in space? Does your absent friend come and sit next to you as you gesture? Does that idea get attacked with a pen as it dances on your desk? Note these in your journal as you discover them.

- When do you enter a state of situational awareness in your everyday life? During sporting activity? In an absorbing class? When are you utterly present in your life?

- Teach something simple to a classmate – a game you know or an exercise you particularly like. Notice the level of listening and understanding you have to employ in order to teach and learn.

- Watch this famous experiment and notice how attention operates with a spotlight (www.youtube.com/watch?v=vJG698U2Mvo), or search online for the gorilla experiment by Daniel Simons and Christopher Chabris.

Further reading

Chekhov, Michael (2002), The gorilla experiment – *To the Actor*, Routledge. Chapter 3, 'Improvisation and Ensemble'.

Damasio, Antonio (2000), *The Feeling of What Happens*. Vintage Books. Chapter 1, 'Stepping into the Light'.

Donnellan, Declan (2002), *The Actor and the Target*. Nick Hern Books, pp.139–145.

Marshall, Lorna (2008), *The Body Speaks*. Methuen Drama. Chapter 10, 'Connecting to Others'.

Meisner, Sanford and Longwell, Dennis (1987), *Sanford Meisner on Acting*. Vintage Books. Chapter 2, 'Building a Foundation: The Reality of Doing' and Chapter 3, 'The Pinch and the Ouch'.

Rodenberg, Patsy (2009), '*Presence: How to Use Positive Energy for Success,* Penguin Books. You can also see her speak brilliantly about presence on stage if you search online for 'Patsy Rodenberg second circle' or via www.youtube.com/watch?v=Ub27yeXKUTY

Stansilavski, Konstantin, trans. Jean Benedetti (2008), *An Actor's Work.* Routledge. Chapter 5, 'Concentration and Attention' and Chapter 10, 'Communication'.

4
ADAPT

Train skills for fulfilled psychophysical transformation (changing your form, nature, appearance), adapting yourself to an imagined environment and situation.

Framework

What is an actor's job? You make yourself into somebody else. The only material you have to work with is yourself. Training teaches you to marshal yourself as a radically flexible resource.

Transformation in acting is the process of physically, emotionally, imaginatively adapting to the character's circumstances. You won't dash into a telephone box like Clark Kent transforming into Superman: the process is evolutionary. Preparing a role is a slow emergence into new social behaviour, new psychology, new physicality because of a social survival need.

So transformation begins with adaptation to your character's *given circumstances*.

In acting, by given circumstances we mean: who you are, where you are, when you are, what your relationships are, where you have come from and why you are here. These given circumstances are the source of transformation, since you will adapt yourself around them. They define what you are, who you are and how you are, here and now.

As you adapt and transform, use your unique humanity as a basis for characterization. Rearrange and reform the person you already are. Harness your full expressive potential, as you adapt yourself to the role – not the role to yourself.

Bring your whole self to bear: don't play the part how someone else might play it. The person you are is infinitely more interesting than the actor you hope to be. Stretch yourself to the limits of the role. You never lose yourself in your character; you discover yourself and new potentials within yourself.

So let's train flexibility and availability. The craft of acting demands a body, will and spirit which are ready to evolve and transform with ease and flow. You need a thin skin. Train yourself as an instrument to be tuned by given circumstances and played by the will of your character.

*

We are always engaged in unconscious adaptation. There is no such thing as stillness in life: your eyes flicking faster than we can see to read your surroundings, tiny muscular adjustments to keep you balanced and upright, your hypothalamus adjusting your body temperature, your breathing managing oxygen intake. There is always adaptation in response to your given circumstances.

Adaptation is a response to habitat and situation. An actor's transformation is a truthful response to imagined habitat and situation. Tap into the energies of your environment.

This adaptation and transformation need not deliver consistency. A chameleon has adapted to the needs of its habitat. Your characterization can present contradiction and sudden change, as you react to your changing circumstances.

Adaptation doesn't necessarily mean blending in to your environment – a peacock has adapted to the demands of its habitat. Your characterization can deliver bold, vivid, colourful life. Don't be afraid of being extreme in your transformation.

Nor are we are pursuing beauty. The gloriously odd-looking duckbilled platypus is the ultimate in adaptive pragmatism. Adaptation serves exactly and only the environmental need. Your transformation can be as ugly as your role requires, or your situation demands.

Take the risk of fulfilling each transformative gesture. Life can be extreme, so don't be afraid of being extremely truthful.

*

The first tool for transformation is our imagination. But the subject of all our work will be our body. This will be where the transformation will be seen and heard – with breath as the vital connective tissue between one and the other.

Train your breath and your body to become responsive, and more than that, adaptive to imagined given circumstances and needs. Train yourself to act on your feelings, insights and impulses.

Crucial to the adaptation of the actor into their role, therefore, is an understanding of movement (both conscious and unconscious) in relation to the elements of space and time, weight and flow. Particularly, actors will work with time through tempo-rhythm.

By tempo we mean the speed at which movement occurs: how many beats (like heartbeats) there are per minute. Intuitively, tempo is associated with mood in music: something to be played slowly is marked by the Italian word for mournful (*mesto*); something to be played quickly is marked as triumphant (*trionfante*). Tempo is governed by pulse and mood.

By rhythm we mean patterns within time: repeating sequences of strong beats which operate upon time and shape time into units (the number of beats in every bar). Rhythm is pattern, repetition, ritual in time. Rhythm is governed by impulse and repetition.

In a character then, tempo is the height of your mood and rate of your heartbeat. Rhythm exists in the regularity of your changing desires and your repeated habits of action and impulse.

Often our inner tempo-rhythm contrasts with the tempo-rhythm we want the world to perceive. Think of yourself as you walk in for a job interview: inside you are racing, with a sustained and strong force – wringing yourself out; yet you are working very hard to show the world a state of steady calm and ease, gliding into the room. Only shadows of the inner condition are visible or audible: everything about you seems steady, light and graceful, except for that hand throttling your pencil. This fault line offers rich material for the actor to mine: the disjunct between how we feel inside and how we want to seem to the world is a source of tension and therefore performable action.

*

A language for describing expressive movement potential was defined by the dancer Rudolf Laban (1879–1958), a pioneer of modern movement studies. His system gives us the vocabulary of four key elements of motion: *space*, *time*, *weight*, *flow*. Each element of motion exists on a continuum.

The element of space runs on a continuum between *direct* movement and *flexible* movement. Moving like either an arrow in flight, or a ball rolling.

The element of time travels between *sudden* movement and *sustained* movement. Moving like either a lion pouncing or a lion prowling.

The element of weight occurs between *strong* movement and *light* movement. Moving like either Daddy Bear climbing out of bed, or Baby Bear chasing a playmate.

The element of flow moves between *bound* movement and *free* movement: either stop-and-start jerks like an old bike up a steep hill, or uninterrupted free-wheeling down a gentle slope.

Laban combines the first three elements (space, time and weight) to define different *effort actions*. Effort action defines the type of energy we bring to movement, relating to our inner life and impulses.

Below is a table of the eight effort actions:

Effort Action	Space	Time	Weight
Float	Flexible	Sustained	Light
Flick	Flexible	Sudden	Light
Wring	Flexible	Sustained	Strong
Slash	Flexible	Sudden	Strong
Glide	Direct	Sustained	Light
Dab	Direct	Sudden	Light
Press	Direct	Sustained	Strong
Punch	Direct	Sudden	Strong

Actors must learn to adapt their mind, body, will and spirit to time, space, weight and flow. A simple understanding of Laban's effort actions will be a vital tool as we work our way through this and subsequent chapters. It provides a clear vocabulary through which to discuss specific movement choices.

Exploration

These exploratory exercises can be done as pre-class work, or as starter exercises. Consider adaptation, adapting to an ensemble and the basics of tempo-rhythm and Laban movement analysis.

- Research how humans adapt their homes around their environments. Quickly and crudely draw your childhood home. Now research traditional housing in: Bangladesh, Ethiopia, the Arctic, the Gobi Desert. Extend this to research how these environments have conditioned other human survival choices. Stick images in your journal, do drawings, make notes on human adaptation and imagination in response to need.

- Make some notes in your journal considering teamwork and how you adapt to work in a team. Pick a team you are a part of, to consider closely. This might be a sports team, a dance company, a class, a family. What is the shared objective of that team? What is your role within that team? What individual responsibilities do you take? What is the greatest realistic risk you undertake in pursuing that objective? What is the greatest possible reward? How is your behaviour different when you are part of this team? How do you adapt your physicality and psychology?

- Choose a favourite piece of music and imagine you are conducting it. Fill your body with the interpretation of that music.

- With your foot, as you read this, tap out the tempo-rhythm for: someone who is late for class; someone lying on a holiday beach reading; someone cooking a dinner for ten friends.

- Tap the outer tempo-rhythm (which we can see) for: someone in a job interview for their dream job; someone waiting in a cafe for a blind date; someone picking up their child from their first day at school. Now beat their inner tempo-rhythm: what they feel inside. How are these different?

- Look at the table of Laban effort actions on page 80. Use the language of Laban's effort actions to describe the movement of: a prowling cat, a squirrel running up a tree, an eagle soaring, a hyena eating its prey, a hummingbird feeding at a flower. In each case consider weight (light or strong), space (flexible or direct) and time (sudden or sustained), then correlate these to an effort action. So, for example, a prowling cat is: strong, direct, sustained – this movement's effort action is a press. Separately consider this effort action's flow: is it free or bound? Try moving your arm with a bound press: is your arm prowling forward?

- Work with a partner to consider and discuss your own Laban states and habitual tempo-rhythm. Do you have states to which you habitually return? Consider yourself as you are in your classroom. Are you habitually sudden or sustained in your movements? Direct or indirect? Light or strong? What is the correlating effort action to these states? Is there an effort action with which you very rarely move – e.g. you only rarely float or glide; maybe you hardly ever jab and punch? Is your outer state different to your inner state? Discuss this with your partner, particularly talking about any discrepancy between your inner and outer states. Perhaps you often feel an inner wring, though you rarely show it.

- Reflecting on the last exercise, find a piece of music in the tempo-rhythm in which you think you mostly operate. Are you more thrash metal, funk or lounge jazz? This is not about your taste in music, but rather your habitual tempo and rhythm of movement. Really think beyond your fashion choices and tastes, to the tempo and rhythm of your movement. Share this with the group or a partner. Work with a partner to reflect on your habitual movement patterns using Laban's vocabulary.

Exercises

I have broken this chapter into two sections: 'Transforming yourself' and 'Adapting to the world'. The first section trains you to transform psychophysically. The second section trains you to use these transformational skills to adapt around shifting given circumstances.

Transforming yourself

Shared count (10 minutes)

Train acute listening and connection among the ensemble. Adapt tempo, rhythm and inner state around a shared ensemble objective.

- Stand in a circle. Centre and align yourself, facing into the circle with your eyes closed.

- Once everyone is centred and focused, open your eyes and focus on the centre of the circle.

- Allow your circle of attention to be large enough to include the presence of everyone in the circle – not who they are nor what they make you feel; simply build an awareness of bodies related in space.

- As a group – one person speaking at a time – try and count to twenty. If two or more people say a number at the same time, start counting again from zero.

- No one is in charge: no one will dictate who speaks when. One by one, without following any system, count up to twenty. Don't forget to breathe.

- The exercise concludes either when you get to twenty, or when you have had enough until the next time …

- Reflect on this exercise. What is the quality of listening? How are your body, breath and inner/outer rhythms changed by this task?

- Return to this exercise more than once, and work to release tension as you play again. Allow a connection to build between

the group as you share responsibility for this simple but
challenging task. The one guarantee is that if someone drives
or pushes the exercise towards its end, the connection will
break and people will be denied the opportunity to take joyous
responsibility for the successful outcome whenever it does
come. Enjoy the shared failures in the journey, which make any
ultimate success joyous.

- There is a simple equation here, which carries on into lots of
  our work: the more you fail, the more joy you'll discover.

Shared speech (15 minutes)

*Bring shared intention and meaning to the shared breath,
tempo, rhythm and inner state of the previous exercise.*

- As an excellent and natural extension of the last exercise, do
  the same thing with a speech or poem.
- Work as a full group, in a circle. As preparation, everyone learn
  the same piece of text.
- Speak this speech or poem aloud taking a word, sentence or
  verse line each without a preordained order. If more than one
  person speaks at once, start again. No-one should speak more
  than one sentence at a time. If you get good at this, make it
  one word at a time.
- The quality of listening is remarkable and the value given to the
  words by the exercise can be exhilarating.

Teaching Tip: Extend this by removing the rule that you cannot
continue the speech if two people speak at once. Anyone can speak
at any time, but work with the same intensity of listening.

Shared shape making (15 minutes)

Deepen and extend your adaptation to the ensemble into physical action. Explore unified action within the ensemble.

- Work in silence and as a full group. Centre and align.

- Spread yourselves evenly throughout the space, balancing and filling the room with where you stand. Everyone must be involved and there must be no one taking charge. Use only your bodies as the resources with which to make:

  A circle

  A triangle

  A square

  A cathedral

  A working car.

- Take absolute responsibility for yourself and your shared physical objective as brilliantly as possible. This is not a race, so allow everyone to find their place; achieve the tasks through the spirit of cooperative play, not the spirit of competition.

- You can, of course, extend this as far as you care or dare:

  Make a new-born baby.

  Make the sinking Titanic.

  Make a melting ice lolly.

  Make a god.

- The rules are: work in silence, work with complicity (everyone must want to make it) and work without managers.

- Use your journal or work as a group to reflect on this exercise. How easy was it to work in silence? How easy was it to work without someone in charge? Notice that we can kill the ensemble by telling each other what to do. How did you communicate collectively?

Listen, follow, respond (15–20 minutes)

Train physical transformation of tempo-rhythm and inner life in response to an external stimulus, and take this into honest action.

- Work as a full group. You will need a sound system for this exercise. Stretch and mobilize your body before you begin.

- Choose a piece of music which can stimulate strong but shifting emotional responses. I like Franz Schubert's *Serenade*, for example.

- Play the music. It may help to do this with your eyes closed initially, though as you grow in confidence with it, do work with your eyes open. Responding to other people's movement as well as your own sensations will really enhance this work and your potential learning.

- Listen to the music. Follow it, breathe with it and then begin to respond to it physically.

- Let the music stimulate an inner reality and inhabit this: activate your body to make alive whatever the music triggers in you. Don't feel that you have to follow the rhythm, though you may.

- As you get into this, listen to your own body more than you listen to the music, and respond to its pulses and impulses. Tune into the shifting pulse and impulse of your body, as it responds to the music. Listen to the music, follow it and respond physically to what it makes you feel.

- Allow yourself time to develop within this work. Settle into it, grow within the music.

- Continue this until the music comes to its end.

- Once the task is done, reflect on the work. How were you transformed? What happened to your weight, tempo, force: did your responses to the music make you feel or seem heavier or lighter; your energy more sustained or more sudden; your force more direct or indirect? What happened to your breathing and body temperature?

> *Teaching Tip:* You can very easily take this into scene work: respond to a piece of music which connects to the rhythm and mood of a scene and work with this playing underneath a rehearsal.
>
> See 'Suggested material' for further suggestions. It certainly helps if this is music the students are unlikely to have heard much before. Don't choose dance music, since this will prompt social performance.

Effort action (45 minutes)

Practically introduce Laban's movement vocabulary and guide transformation based on the stimulus of his language and imagery. Explore and expand your expressive movement potential.

I

- Work individually. You might do this with music playing underneath, perhaps something from 'Suggested material'.

- Explore the qualities and effects of inhabiting the Laban effort actions.

- Try pressing (sustained, direct, strong). Feel it first with palms of hands. Press against a real wall. Imagine the walls are closing in on you and you have to hold them back – like Chewbacca in the Death Star's trash-compactor in *Star Wars*. Now extend your pressing activity in all directions. Let your other body parts lead in pressing, for example, the back, the knees, top of head and elbows or feet. Try walking. Press down with your feet as you walk, taking the body in different directions.

- Try flicking (sudden, flexible, light). Imagine a fly landing on your shoulder. Flick it away with your hands by quickly twisting the wrists and fingers. The fly keeps coming back from all directions: flick it away from every part of your personal space.

Flick the fly away with your shoulders, head and feet. Involve the elbows, hips and knees. Try jumping, flicking the feet in the air. Include your whole body and enjoy a sense of intense lightness and buoyancy.

- Try wringing (sustained, flexible, strong). First, wring out imaginary wet clothes. Now imagine you are a wet blanket and wring yourself out. Move to both sides – right and left. Wring your wet-blanket-body out part by part. Feel the counter-tensions that your body enlists to make the individual body part wring.

- Try dabbing (sudden, direct, light). Dab at a canvas you are painting. Type a letter in a hurry. Dab with the feet. Try with the knees, hips, shoulders, head, elbows, chin, back and chest. Take plenty of time to experience dabbing in all these parts of the body. Take dabbing steps forward. Notice the counter tension your body produces to dab into the air (unlike typing or dabbing a canvas, where we receive object resistance). Feel how that tension runs through your whole body.

- Try slashing (sudden, flexible, strong). Slash that canvas you just painted in two with a razor-sharp knife. Slash it in many directions, so you shred it. Slash it with each leg. Use large jumps to slash with your legs and arms and even your trunk.

- Try gliding (sustained, direct, light). Smooth the icing on the surface of a delicious birthday cake. Waft away cobwebs from in front of the door to your attic: remove them with your palm (don't worry, there aren't any spiders). Move forward, gliding over the floor. Go ice skating. Feel the tension through your body as you do this.

- Try punching (sudden, direct, strong). Practise thrusting your sword at a mortal foe; punch your sword forwards. Thrust with your whole body in this action: let your feet stamp into the ground as you make the thrust forwards; your trunk should punch too. Notice what happens to your body as you create counter-tension to stop yourself falling forwards and make use of the resistance of the floor with that noisy stamp. Avoid using your head in this action (head-butting); without resistance, the counter-tension you create can give you whiplash.

- Try floating (sustained, flexible, light). Without moving, imagine you are flying. Put your arms out and soar on the warm air, looking down on the world below. See how high you are, feel the great open space around and above you: think upward, outward and forward. You may recognize this sensation from the moment after you wake up and before your day truly begins. Now wander around the space smelling sweet flowers – just for its own sake. Indulge your lightness.

II

- Choose a state to explore further. Move through the space, travelling from point to point in the room. As you reach a point, make contact with a specific object in the room, turn and move to another. Use the Laban state you have selected to guide the quality of your movement.

- Allow the state to exist within your mind and breath as well as your body. This is an inner as well as an outer state.

- Continue to move the space, interacting with objects and other people as you pass them. Perhaps explore a simple physical activity through this state (stacking chairs or packing a bag).

- Now gradually internalize the state more and more, so that you are in fact trying to hide this state from the world. You don't want anyone to know that inside you are floating, wringing or punching. The outer life will now merely reveal the shadows of your inner state.

- Give yourself time enough to really inhabit and be possessed by this state, so that your every gesture is conditioned by your negotiation of it.

- Release. Shake out and return to a free breath.

- Reflect on this exercise. How did negotiating this inner life affect your interactions and behaviour? How did it inhibit you? What shadow tensions of your inner life were there in your body?

Effort actions in action (15 minutes)

Apply Laban's effort actions, exploring them as inner and outer states.

I

- Work in pairs, with one observing and providing feedback.

- Decide upon a simple physical task. You might stack all the chairs in the room, place the chairs in a careful circle, arrange all the shoes in the room in a line or simply tidy up and pack your bag to go. Any simple, non-intensive task will do.

- Choose a Laban effort action. Perform your task exploring that effort action, allowing it to condition both your inner and outer state.

- Feedback. What story does this tell the observer? What did the observer infer had happened or was happening? What might the unwritten motive for this task have been? How did you feel and how did working with this effort action condition your inner state and thought patterns?

II

- Perform the task again, but first decide on an inner effort action and a contrasting outer effort action. Conceal your inner effort action with this outer. You might have an inner wring but an outer glide – much as I experienced when waiting to pick my son up from his first day at school.

- What story does this tell to the observer? What did the observer infer had happened or was happening? What might the unwritten motive for this task have been? What shadow play (subconscious activity) revealed the inner effort action? Was there a dabbing finger, or a wringing foot, despite the broader outer glide? As Freud taught us, your fingers never lie.

Animal exercise

Transform your habitual physicality and psychological patterns in extreme and unexpected ways. Reveal new potential behaviour and transformation.

- Work individually.

This can begin as a pre-class exercise (Part I) and become a 60-minute class exercise (Parts II and III).

I

- Choose an animal to use as the basis of a transformation. Reflect on what you considered about your habitual tempo, rhythm and movement in the last two Exploration exercises on pp. 81–2. Choose an animal whose physicality and behaviour patterns are in specific ways very different to your own.

- Will you choose predator, prey or scavenger? From land, sea or air? Quick moving or sedentary?

- Your choice should be based on an animal which is different to how you habitually see and experience the world. If you are nervous and anxious, look for a high-ranking predator who sees not threats, but opportunities. If you are a loner, look for a pack animal. If you are a calm, generous soul, perhaps choose a scavenger. Are you a social butterfly? Perhaps choose a gliding bird of prey.

- Be specific about your choice: not just a cat, but an alley cat or a Siamese cat; not just a snake but a cobra or a constrictor; not just a lion, but an old ragged alpha male or a young adolescent female.

Once you've chosen your animal, research their physical behaviour and interactions. You might go to the zoo and watch them, as well as watching footage of them in their natural environment. Use your understanding of Laban and tempo-rhythm to help. Look at how they move their limbs – the lion's padding, swaying, heavy-pawed shoulder roll. Observe their eyes and gaze. Study especially the alignment of the spine and its full extension – how the head might move as the animal moves (the bobbing head of the horse as it moves).

- Look at the rhythm of their breath and how that breath reaches into the body. Watch them in motion and in stillness. Watch them asleep and feeding, or seeking their prey. See the rhythm of their body in states of desire and satisfaction – of having and not-having. See how they clean themselves. Watch them playing.

- Try inhabiting some of their behaviours. Move your arms like their legs; try making your hand a paw; move with their rolling shoulders; crane your neck as they might and so on.

II

- You will need a clear space, ideally with mats and even some basic gym equipment if you can get it. Otherwise, a clear and safe space with some load-bearing objects in it (chairs, tables) will help.

- If you are carrying any injuries, either sit out or, if you safely can, incorporate these as an injury your animal is also protecting.

- In class, prepare with a proper physical stretch: mobilize and tune up your body. Make sure you flex key joints, roll through the spine, loosen the neck and stretch leg and arm muscles.

- At any point in this exercise, do stop to release tension before it becomes uncomfortable.

- Begin walking through the space at a natural and easy rhythm.

- First adopt the basic breath pattern of your animal as you move. Allow this to naturally affect the weight, rhythm and tempo of your movement (from your spine) and thought patterns.

- Now allow your gaze to become the animal's. Look for what they look for, see what they see – threats, opportunities, meals, safe places, dangerous places. This will further affect the weight, tempo and rhythm of your movement and thought. Extend into it. Lean into transformation.

- See a safe place and move to it – or if necessary, gather a few things together to create a safe place, continuing to use breath and sight as your key in. Allow your imagination to transform objects in the room to other things if necessary: a chair might become a tree stump, for example.

- As you are moving objects about, begin to relate to them as if you were the animal. You won't have thumbs now, and probably not hands. Perhaps you're pushing with a powerful paw or nudging with your head; perhaps you gather things with your beak or clutch with a claw.

- Once you've made your safe place, come to rest in it and fully adopt the physicality of the animal. As you settle, check through your pelvis, spine and out into your neck and limbs.

- Remember most animal faces are not as expressive as a human's. Release unnecessary tension in your brows and around your mouth and lips.

- Your tail, or long neck, or wings grow out from your spine. Allow your imagination to feel the sensation of this extension of your spine. Be aware of the sensual connection from the top to the very base of the spine.

- Have a stretch. Groom yourself.

- Take a nap.

- Perhaps move out from your safe corner to look for food, or investigate your environment.

- Have a play, exploring an object you find, to discover its potential and explore your own.

- Explore vocalizing breath as your animal, though beware of straining your voice: no roaring, for example. Keep open and supported.

- Explore the different senses: how acute is the sense of smell; what smells good? How far into the distance do you see; what

are you alert for? How does your tongue behave? How acute
is your hearing and what are you listening for?

- You don't have to carry your weight on four legs if it is
  uncomfortable; simply carry your weight on your legs and move
  your arms as if load-bearing.

- If you're flying, you might stand still and lean forward from the
  waist, arms open wide as wings to give you the sensation of a
  glide. Your imagination will make you travel.

- Give yourself plenty of time to explore these different situations
  and sensations, though beware of physical strain.

- If you end this exercise here, be sure to stretch and do a
  proper physical release after this. Reflect on your experience
  and especially on what happened to your inner life through this
  physical exercise: the rhythm of thoughts, your experience of
  desire, fear, having and not-having.

III

- Begin to humanize your animal.

- Become aware that you are among humans. Be aware that
  if anyone discovers that you are an animal, they will probably
  cage or kill you.

- Allow your pelvis to free up, so you can stand upright,
  and slowly begin to disguise yourself as a human so
  no-one can tell what you really are. You are that animal in
  disguise.

- You will need to learn to walk upright, but how much of your
  animal can you keep alive and still convincingly pass for a
  human?

- Explore a few words as you start to move through the space,
  exploring your human environment. You might start with simply
  'yes' and 'no', or naming things you see in the space. What
  rhythm, pitch and tone naturally and easily come through this
  animal? This may be extreme, but it should never be forced or
  a strain on your vocal instrument.

- You might even head out of class and make a short journey around 'the real world'. If you are doing this, you will have to be really confident of your disguise, and clearly this should only be done if you're happy it's safe to do so.

- More simply, explore a basic physical activity. Work in role as your animal, and write a letter, tidy a room, dress to go out or whatever you choose.

- Release and stretch after this exercise. Reflect on it with a partner or in your journal and especially on what new potentials you discovered in yourself. What kind of animal are you most days? When in your life might it be useful to be more like the animal you have explored here?

Adapting to the world

Shifting given circumstances (30 minutes)

Consider how subtle shifts in given circumstance can deliver radical transformations. Locate the necessity for specificity. Adapt around shifting given circumstances.

I

- Work as a full group or in small groups of around five.

- Stand in a circle. The first person name any two specific objects – for example, a cocktail glass and a beach towel. Where and when does everyone imagine we are because of those imagined objects in the middle of the circle?

- Now the next person go in and remove one of those objects and replace it with another imagined object. For example, remove the beach towel, keep the cocktail glass and add a regency table. Where and when does everyone imagine we are now?

- Now the next person do the same. For example, remove the cocktail glass, keep the regency period table and add a bone-china teacup. Where and when are we now?

- Continue round the circle, each person replacing one imagined object in the pair as you go. How extreme and sudden a transformation can one object deliver?

II

- Call new objects out at random. If two or more people speak at once, then all the objects they have said go into the space. Where and when are you now?

III

- Now put an actor in the middle of the circle. The actor must relate to the objects and discovered given circumstances. As the objects change, adapt your behaviour around them and the worlds they propose; find activity from them and explore it.

- Keep the new objects coming, so the actor in the middle has to keep imaginatively adapting. It can be fun to do this fast, but it is more worthwhile to let the actor find and fully inhabit each world before transforming it again.

- Reflect on how the actor's behaviour was conditioned by each new object and implied circumstance.

Given circumstances (45 minutes)

Extend the learning of the last exercise. Explore how subtly changing given circumstances condition transformation. Train yourself to be physically available and responsive to subtle shifts in imagined given circumstances.

- You will need lots of colouring pens/pencils and blank paper for this exercise.

- Work in pairs. Take it in turns to be actor and observer, providing summative feedback on what you experience and witness.

I

- Actor, perform a short (1 minute at most), simple physical task (arranging chairs, polishing shoes, packing a bag, putting on make-up). This could involve elements of mime.

- Observer, notice the initial effort and rhythm. What Laban effort action would describe it? What rhythm would you beat out to conduct it? Quickly, and without any artistic pretension, draw their dynamic movement in your journal. Don't draw them or their body: draw their movement. Focus on colour and line, not form. Put your eyes on the person more than the page: communicate their dynamic movement through the marks you make.

II

- Actor, repeat the task but add a specific 'when are you'. Keep this a secret from the observer. Perhaps it is very early in the morning, or late at night. Perhaps it is just before lunchtime and you are very hungry, or maybe it's 1879 and all this is being done with a corset and bustle.

- Adapt yourself to these new circumstances. Do not demonstrate them, simply let them subtly condition your behaviour. Allow it to be a point of concentration in your mind and trust your body will follow.

- Observer, draw their movement. Make a note of any Laban effort actions you observe or shifts in tempo-rhythm. Sketch, write, colour and shade the page to communicate the quality of the movement you see.

III

- Actor, repeat the task but now introduce a simple point of environmental concentration: the heat, the rain, the cold; a point of concentration for your mind and body. Keep this a secret from the observer.

- Allow this to affect the rhythm and effort of your physical actions. Do not demonstrate the condition; simply allow it to be a point of concentration for your mind and trust your body will follow. Try chewing over an inner monologue relating to it: 'Why is it so hot?' … 'This rain is miserable …'. Let a thought like this roll around your head as you perform your task.

- Observer, draw their movement. Again focus on colour and line, not form – draw the space around their body and how it is changed. Is the space colder? Have they become smaller in it? Does it seem more threatening? Note down any effort actions you see in your journal.

IV

- Actor, repeat the task but now add a clear previous circumstance. Keep this secret from the observer. Where have you come from prior to performing this task? Perhaps you've been having an argument with your mother, or been searching for a lost precious object. Perhaps you've just heard you got a part in the play, or have heard a close friend is coming to visit. This will simply provide another point of concentration for your mind.

- Explore how this conditions your physical action.

- Observer, again note the changing Laban effort action and tempo-rhythm and draw what you see. What story begins to form around their action for you? Who might this person be? Perhaps note down a few characteristics to describe them (e.g. ambitious, passionate, weary, lonely).

- Reflect together on this exercise and how your subtly developing circumstances conducted rhythms and efforts, thoughts and feelings. Look at the drawings together.

- Now switch over and repeat the exercise.

Teaching Tip: Some students find the drawing element of this task inhibiting. You can always just leave out this element of the exercise, but I do encourage the actor to make any marks on the page of your journal that communicate the movement quality they perceive.

Endowment exercise (30 minutes)

Extend the learning of the last exercise. Train yourself to receive identity and transformation from given circumstances and especially the behaviour of your scene partner. Develop openness.

- Work in pairs.

- As preparation for the exercise, Partner A plan a scene between two people which you can improvise with Partner B. Plan your given circumstances and both characters' basic wants in the scene. The scene should have two characters who cannot both get what they want. The stakes must be significantly lower than life or death.

- For example, Partner A might plan a situation of a relationship ending (with all the specifics of who, where, when, why, what your relationships are, where you've come from). Partner A wants to stay together and Partner B wants to end the relationship. These are your wants. Neither character will die if they don't get what they want (the stakes are therefore not life and death).

- Partner A, do not tell Partner B any of the circumstances of the scene. Partner B should only know their want or objective: in this case that they are coming in to end a relationship.

- Partner A, set up the basic scene. Partner B enters. Play the scene. Partner B, you will need to discover exactly who you are, where you are, when you are, why you are here, what your relationship is to Partner A, as you work. None of this is known before you enter: it will all be discovered by listening, receiving, reading your surroundings and scene partner.

- Don't play the game, play the scene. Partner A, your aim is neither to communicate nor to hide your given circumstances: it is your job to serve your character's need. Partner B, your aim is not to find out your given circumstances as fast as possible and 'win': your job is to serve your character's need – get what you want.

- When you begin, this will probably be lots of fun. Let it grow beyond this into serious play of the scene.

- Now swap around so Partner B plans a scene for Partner A to enter, blind to everything except their objective.

Teaching Tip: As an extension to this, you can take given circumstances from a play you are working on: Partner A could prepare the unwritten scene in which Rosaline breaks up with Romeo, or the scene in which Lady Macduff finds out Macduff has fled to England. This can also be an excellent basis for devising original drama.

Adapt to text (30 minutes)

Explore how you might adapt your physicality to text and inhabit its tempo and rhythms. Treat the text as a physical score. Words are behaviour.

- Actors work with limited time and space, like poets work with a white page. Both the whiteness of the page and the time on stage/screen are ineluctably limited and will run out. Poets and actors shape journeys through them deliberately and precisely in order to express meaning.

- The word 'verse' comes from the Latin word *versus*, which refers to the turn of the plough at the end of a field. Treat reading verse as a physical act, with a heavy turn of your ox and plough every time you reach the end of the field – the end of the line. Reading a poem is like ploughing a field ready to be sown.

- Read Edward Thomas's poem 'As the Team's Head-Brass', a poem about a man sitting on a fallen tree watching a ploughman work. If you can, learn it.

- Notice the white space as well as the black marks: the
  negotiation of the emptiness, by those words. The black
  mark on a white page is like an actor walking onto an empty
  stage.

- Perhaps think of the white space as the end of the field, or as
  empty space, perhaps think of it as silent time passing, or if
  you're feeling especially bold, as steps towards mortality.

> As the team's head-brass flashed out on the turn
> The lovers disappeared into the wood.
> I sat among the boughs of the fallen elm
> That strewed the angle of the fallow, and
> Watched the plough narrowing a yellow square
> Of charlock. Every time the horses turned
> Instead of treading me down, the ploughman leaned
> Upon the handles to say or ask a word,
> About the weather, next about the war.
> Scraping the share he faced towards the wood,
> And screwed along the furrow till the brass flashed
> Once more.
>   The blizzard felled the elm whose crest
> I sat in, by a woodpecker's round hole,
> The ploughman said. 'When will they take it away?'
> 'When the war's over.' So the talk began –
> One minute and an interval of ten,
> A minute more and the same interval.
> 'Have you been out?' 'No.' 'And don't want to, perhaps?'
> 'If I could only come back again, I should.
> I could spare an arm. I shouldn't want to lose
> A leg. If I should lose my head, why, so,
> I should want nothing more. … Have many gone
> From here?' 'Yes.' 'Many lost?' 'Yes, a good few.
> Only two teams work on the farm this year.
> One of my mates is dead. The second day
> In France they killed him. It was back in March,
> The very night of the blizzard, too. Now if
> He had stayed here we should have moved the tree.'
> 'And I should not have sat here. Everything

Would have been different. For it would have been
Another world.' 'Ay, and a better, though
If we could see all all might seem good.' Then
The lovers came out of the wood again:
The horses started and for the last time
I watched the clods crumble and topple over
After the ploughshare and the stumbling team.

- Read it aloud.

- Feel how the plough team turns as it reaches the end of every line.

- As you read, move through the space, driving an imaginary ox and plough along with the line, and at every line ending turn round to plough a new furrow. Press forward. Every line is a new journey across the space, every line ending a turnabout.

- Feel how the punctuation operates on time and movement; how it tries to hold it up or move it along; how it provides resistance to time passing, or eases its passing. Feel how it changes the weight of your ox and plough. What is the effort action of a full stop – a punch? A comma as a glide? What about an ellipsis (…)? Does this float through time? What would a dash be; a slash? And so on.

- Decide how you think each punctuation mark behaves. Physicalize the effort action with your arm, leg, trunk, as you meet each of these marks on time and move through the field you are ploughing with the poem.

- What happens when you reach the space hanging beyond the line 'Once more.'?

- You could split the poem up between the entire group and plough it out in the space together; break it into units according to full stops which coincide with a line ending. Take a chunk each and physicalize it. Pass the plough onto the next person when you reach the end of your unit. Try and plough deep furrows through the entire room.

- Reflect on this exercise and the physical experience of a poem moving through your body. How does the language on the page conduct rhythm, tempo and effort in your breath and body?

Teaching Tip: Give students time to look over this poem in advance of class, so those with dyslexia or who struggle with literacy have time to prepare. Ask everyone to look up any words they do not know and come with a basic comprehension of the poem.

To get into this exercise, try the 'Shared speech' exercise on page 84, using this poem as your material. Pass the poem on at the end of each verse line.

Follow-up

Embed and extend the consideration of tempo-rhythm, Laban movement analysis and an adaptive process.

- Go online and watch a great conductor at work. Try Daniel Barenboim for starters. Go to www.danielbarenboim.com/video and watch him conduct the Prelude to Act 1 of *Die Walküre*, a piece of music written by an anti-Semite that this Jewish conductor makes vital, necessary and profoundly moving. How would you describe his physicality using the language of this chapter? Watch an interview with him (try How to listen to music https://www.youtube.com/watch?v=LCKZDSIHV80). How is he transformed by the music as he conducts?

- Look at this TED talk by Benjamin Zander: http://www.ted.com/talks/benjamin_zander_on_music_and_passion. Consider what this musician says about impulses and what implications it may have for our work as theatre makers and actors. Two actors in space can create harmony or discord like two notes on a piano. Each dramatic event in a play is like a strong impulse within a piece of music. Consider also the tempo, rhythm and Laban state of the speaker himself as he presents: he has a very distinctive movement pattern. How would you describe it?

- Watch pianist Ivo Pogorelich play *Für Elise*: www.youtube. com/watch?v=e4BysqPWgfc. Consider his relationship to the piano through his arms and fingers. Watch his spine and its flow, its tension. Observe the new impulses. Notice how our relationship to time is altered as we listen. How can this take only three and a half minutes to listen to?

- Choose a famous person and create a movement profile of them, using the vocabulary of this chapter. You might choose, for example, from: Woody Allen, Hillary Clinton, the Dalai Lama, Michael Jackson, Mick Jagger, Meryl Streep. Include your own drawings or pictures of the person in your movement profile, as well as the following information: direct/indirect; sudden/ sustained; heavy/light; bound/free; their animal; their tempo-rhythm. Below is a list of the Italian words for different tempi for you to choose from when describing the person's tempo:

  Larghissimo – very, very slow
  Grave – very slow
  Largo – broadly
  Lento – slowly
  Larghetto – fairly broadly
  Adagio – slow and stately (literally 'at ease')
  Adagietto – slower than walking pace
  Andante – walking pace
  Andantino – faster than walking pace
  Marcia moderato – the speed of a march
  Andante moderato – quicker than a march
  Moderato – moderately
  Allegretto – moderately fast
  Allegro moderato – faster
  Allegro – fast and bright
  Vivace – lively and fast
  Vivacissimo – very fast and lively
  Allegrissimo – very fast
  Presto – extremely fast
  Prestissimo – fastest.

Suggested material

Other music you might use in 'Listen, follow, respond', 'Laban action
    sequences' and 'Effort action':
Frederic Chopin, *Tristesse.*
Franz Liszt, *Un Sospiro.*
Modest Mussorgsky, *Prelude to Khovanshchina, Dawn over the Moscow
    River.*
Sergei Rachmaninov, *The Isle of the Dead.*
Camille Saint-Saens, *Danse Macabre.*
Franz Schubert, *Piano Trio Number 2, II.*

Other poems and speeches you might use in 'Adapt to text':
Robert Frost, 'Birches'.
John Keats, 'To Autumn'.
Sylvia Plath, 'Blackberrying'.
William Shakespeare, *Macbeth*: Act 1, Scene 7 – Macbeth, 'If it were done'.
William Shakespeare, *Othello*: Act 4, Scene 3 – Emilia, 'Yes, a dozen'.
W. B. Yeats, 'The Song of Wandering Aengus'.

Further reading

Adrian, Barbara (2008), *Actor Training the Laban Way,* Allworth Press.
Benedetti, Jean (1998), *Stanislavski and the Actor.* Routledge. Tempo-
    Rhythm, pp. 87–95.
Donnellan, Declan (2002), *The Actor and the Target.* Nick Hern Books.
    Chapter 20, 'Time'.
Newlove, Jean (1993), *Laban for Actors and Dancers.* Nick Hern Books.
Stanislavski, Konstantin, trans. Jean Benedetti (2008), *An Actor's Work.*
    Routledge. Chapter 21, 'Tempo-Rhythm'.

5
PLAY

Train skills of truthful, imaginative, free action playing: trying to get something you want through vivid, organic, free role-play.

Framework

As an actor, you break free from the here and now in which you find yourself. Play makes all imaginable action possible. The key language of the actor's play is that of want and need:

A *super-objective* is the main want which drives you through the drama.

A *target* is whatever or whoever you want to change (and are changed by) in any given moment.

An *objective* is whatever you want to do to that target.

An *obstacle* is anything that blocks you from getting what you want.

An *action* is whatever you do to overcome those obstacles, in order to get what you want.

Romeo's *super-objective* is (perhaps) to experience perfect love. In the balcony scene, Romeo's *target* is Juliet: through her he can experience love. His *objective* is to make love with her. His *obstacles* include a wall, a balcony, her family's hatred of him, and her loyalty to her family. His *actions* include trying to climb that wall, keeping hidden and discreet, and all the words he speaks to conjure desire in her.

*

An action, then, is the pursuit of a specific objective or goal. Below are twelve rules of action.

1   *There is always action.*
Something is always happening; deal with whatever that is. Don't feel you are not exciting or interesting enough in your action. Don't feel that someone else is not exciting or interesting enough in their action (the actor can never accurately say 'I'm just not getting anything back'). Deal with the world.

2   *Action is play.*
Be curious, be interested, explore desire. Look to your target and ask, 'What could I do to get what I want?' Don't ask, 'What should I do?' or 'What would I do?' – actions are not limited by the social 'should', nor the ego's 'would'; liberate action with the boundless 'could'.

3   *Action is physically possible.*
What you want to do can be done. You may not get what you want for years, you may not get it all or you may get it and discover it doesn't deliver satisfaction (a tragedy), but you are visibly chasing something you believe to be possible.

4   *Action serves desire.*
If you truthfully invest in your character's desires, you will be moved, and the audience will be moved by the image of that desire. Pursue your character's desire with Cain's will (he sacrificed his own brother Abel, and with it his soul, to get what he wanted). If action has no equal motivating desire to balance it, we are left with melodrama.

5   *Action is selfish.*
Acting is problem-solving. Give your acting colleagues a problem to deal with, give the audience something to respond to, by selfishly pursuing your objective. The more Tybalt wants to hurt Romeo, the more the actor playing Romeo is offered. *Be selfish to be generous.*

6   *Action is specific.*
Action is focused on a specific, necessary and changing target. Focus your spotlight on a specific target.

7 *Action is immediate.*
What you are doing happens here and now. Make imagined targets present: that lost love is in the empty chair beside you; that absent father is standing in his empty boots by the door.

8 *Action transforms.*
Whatever you are doing changes your target. Whatever your target is doing changes you. Make yourself available to change. Empower yourself as an actor of change.

9 *Action reaches out.*
The target must be external. Need something outside of yourself, or externalize something which is inside you: your fear is in those shaking hands – manage them.

10 *Action serves the text.*
Action has no interest in life beyond the needs of the text. Play only what drives you towards your character's desire, as defined by the text. Great drama is efficient. Drama is life without the boring bits.

11 *Action is active.*
Before you step on stage, remind yourself, 'I am here to get something and I'm not leaving until I've got it.' Don't train yourself to be more perceptive; train yourself to act on your perceptions. Get on with it.

12 *Words are the last resort.*
As a species we take the path of least resistance to our desires. If we can, we get what we want through simple physical action (to grab, push, lift). If we need to, we make that physical action psychological (to soothe, reassure, cajole). If we are forced to and as a last resort, we make physical and psychological actions also verbal (by talking). A script is a collection of every character's last resorts. If there were an easier way for your character to get what they want, they would take it. Language is the most extreme action.

*

One thing action is not: emotion.

Emotions are non-conscious, physiological reactions: increased heart rate, accelerated breath, sweat, tears, muscular tensions. There are seven universal emotions: *joy, fear, anger, sadness, arousal, surprise, disgust*.

Culturally, you may attach secondary feelings to these emotions. You might learn to feel shame or guilt about anger, sadness, arousal or fear. Perhaps you were told little boys don't cry, or little girls shouldn't be angry; perhaps you developed feelings of confusion or shame about experiencing arousal and sought to resist it.

Emotions are a natural and universal part of being human; accept them while interrogating feelings as a social, cultural act.

Emotions are also, often, an obstacle. Juliet's shame, arousal and fear are very real obstacles she has to overcome in order to achieve her objective. The action of overcoming or controlling those emotions and feelings is what the actor will play – never the emotions or feelings themselves. Strong emotions are the currency of our work. But do not work for them – trust they will come naturally.

Think of emotions as being like a dynamo light on a bike. Emotions are not a light you turn on with the flick of a switch. In order to turn on the light, you will have to get on the bike and ride. Pedal harder and the light will shine more brightly.

Want to get where you're going, and do something about getting there: emotions will follow; that's just how you're built. Romeo will smile, and therefore so will Juliet.

Ultimately, we are not concerned with how the actor feels. *We are not trying to make our feelings and emotions real and truthful. We are trying to make our actions real and truthful. Action makes meaning.*

Exploration

These exploratory exercises are good as pre-class preparation or starters to a session. Introduce working with actions and build awareness of them in your everyday life.

- When discussing character actions, use a vocabulary of transitive verbs (direct doing words, e.g. to shove, to tickle, to tease), not nouns (naming words, e.g. beauty, beast) or adjectives (describing words, e.g. beautiful, happy). The verb helps us name how we want to change someone or something else. Take a state and transform it to action with verbs:

  I am furious with him = I want to scold him
  I am frustrated = I want to find an escape
  I am madly in love = I want to hold him/her
  I am irritable = I want to silence you
  I am confused = I want to find an answer.

  Take a noun and transform it into action with verbs:

  I want my dinner = I want to find a cafe
  I want a lover = I want to seduce him/her
  I want a moment of peace = I want to eliminate distractions.

- Make your own list. Try transforming these states into action with active verbs:

  I am tired
  I am angry
  I am passionate
  I am hungry.

- Try transforming these nouns into action with active verbs:

  I want a new house
  I want a coffee
  I want her attention
  I want to be cool.

- Observe and label your own actions in life: what are you doing, using the vocabulary of juicy, active verbs? Be as specific as possible: I scoff my sandwich, I applaud my son's drawing, I charm the waiter, I challenge my teacher, and so on. When you find yourself in a queue at the shops, observe and label the actions of those around you.

- When you find yourself talking to yourself, ask: To whom or what am I specifically talking (my clumsy hands, my laziness, my late friend, this stupid kettle)?; What is the action (e.g. to organize my clumsy hands)?; What is the objective (i.e. what is this action for?, e.g. to get to school on time)?

- Consider your own current super-objective (main driving want). Is everything you are doing coherently working towards a singular goal? Perhaps not, since this is life and more complicated and less coherent than a play, but there may be a dominant goal: e.g. to train as a professional actor; to support and nurture your family. Consider the objectives you pursue which move you towards this super-objective, and what visions of your future (who you wish you could be and fear you might be) motivate you as you work towards those objectives.

- Romeo's super-objective is to experience perfect love. Juliet's might be to achieve freedom. Define the super-objectives (main wants that carry a character right through a story) for:

  Simba from *The Lion King*
  Woody from *Toy Story*
  Frodo Baggins from *The Lord of the Rings*
  Little Red Riding Hood.

- Work with a partner. Without speaking, play these actions on your partner. Play them psychophysically, not just physically (so don't just warm their body, warm their whole person):

  To warm
  To cool
  To reassure
  To charm.

- Work in pairs. One of you can only say: 'Please'. The other of you can only say: 'No'. You can repeat these words as much as you like. Improvise a 1-minute scene between you, exploring a wonderful range of tactics to achieve whatever objective you discover. Share your scenes with the rest of the group.

Exercises

Teaching Tip: Many exercises involve students sharing work in front of the class. When you're asking students for feedback from such an exercise, encourage them to say what they see – not what they infer or imagine is happening, but what they can see is happening. Observing behaviour keeps student feedback away from qualitative judgement (good/bad, better/worse).

The brilliant British comedian Eric Morecambe used to call the round of applause at the end of a performance the 'who's-the-best'. I discourage students from clapping each other's work in the classroom. I realize this sounds somewhat miserly, but it discourages short-term focus: it's distracting when you finish a piece of work and hear a less-enthusiastic applause than the last student was offered. This can provoke chasing the applause. Often the exercises which 'fail' provide the most valuable learning, and are in our terms the true successes.

The bowl of water (5 minutes per student)

This exercise was devised by Peter Brook. Reveal the value of an objective in providing focus and release for an actor.

- Work one at a time in front of the group (your audience).
- Carry a bowl full of water from one side of the room to the other.
- How does it feel to perform this simple physical task in front of an audience? How does the presence of the audience affect your physical behaviour (tension, circle of attention, rhythm, effort)?
- Try defining an imagined need (an objective) for carrying that water across the room and an imagined set of circumstances for the environment, and perform the task again.

- Perhaps it's hot water for your sister giving birth at home; perhaps it's to clean your boyfriend's bleeding nose; perhaps it's to wash the carpet before your mum gets back and finds out what you've done …

- How is the journey changed?

Get the pen (20 minutes)

Introduce the vocabulary of motives, targets, objectives, obstacles and actions and reveal how they can serve you.

- Work as a full group.

I

- One or two nominated observers stand aside to provide feedback at the end. Everyone else line up along one side of the room.

- The exercise leader will put a pen on the other side of the room. This is your target, i.e. the focus of your objective.

- Your objective is given to you by the exercise: you want to get the pen.

- The rules are absolute and must not be broken at any cost: you cannot begin to pursue that objective until the exercise leader says 'Go!'

- Before you begin, discuss the following:

   What are the obstacles to achieving your objective (getting that pen)? Primarily, the distance between you and it, and the other people who want the same thing. The rules are also an obstacle, but you will not break these in this exercise or you break the fair play of the ensemble.
   Name some actions you could play to overcome those obstacles and get what you want.
   The target is the thing you want: the pen.
   The objective is what you want to do to that thing: get it.
   The obstacles are what stand in the way: space and people.

The actions are how you could overcome those obstacles in order to get what you want: snatch, shove, beg, bribe …

- Now get ready. Exercise leader, count them in: 'One, two – relax'.

- The exercise leader will never get to three, let alone 'Go!'

- Analyse your action. What were your behaviours as you prepared to go?

II

- Repeat this exercise from the very beginning (including all the explanation, since repetition of the terms won't hurt), knowing the exercise leader will never get to three. A few different people stand aside as observers. There will be no race to the pen. See if you can make it believable none the less.

- Analyse your action in this little piece of rehearsed theatre. Did you believe it? Did your audience of observers believe it?

III

- Think a little more closely about your objectives and introduce the question of motive here. What was the motive for getting the pen? What were you doing this for?

- Perhaps you really wanted the pen. Perhaps, though, your motive was to show you were a committed ensemble member. If so, your objective may not really have been to get the pen. Perhaps it was simply to play the exercise – or be seen to play the exercise. Getting the pen may have been exactly what you *didn't* want – you didn't want to be *seen* to be the most aggressive, competitive one in the ensemble, maybe you thought you'd get hurt if you did. Or perhaps it was something completely different. But analyse, discuss and then define your motive and objective with specificity and thoughtful honesty.

- Now define the obstacles to that specific objective and the actions that can get past those obstacles.

- Play the exercise once more (safe in the knowledge that there will be no race).

- Don't underestimate the importance of the leader never getting to the number three. This is what generates complicity between us; this is what makes it theatre: when people really get hurt, well that's just life, and life can be rubbish. The privilege of acting is that we can be as ferocious and filthy as we please and no-one will get hurt because it's a game we've all agreed to play, underwritten by trust.

- Reflect on this exercise, on the nature of complicity and on the importance of fully considered and specific motives and objectives.

Psychophysical actions (15 minutes)

Introduce the physical action with a psychological function. Apply psychological intent to simple physical action.

- Work with a partner. Take it in turns to observe/act.

- Define a simple physical action, for example:

    To dress myself
    To polish my shoes
    To clear the room
    To pack my bag.

- Define three simple psychological actions, with yourself as the target, for example:

    To reassure myself
    To calm my nerves
    To energize myself
    To steel myself.

- Try performing your physical action partnered by each psychological action, i.e. to pack my bag in order to reassure myself; to pack my bag in order to calm my nerves; to pack my bag in order to energize myself; to pack my bag in order to steel myself.

- Observer, describe what you saw. Describe physical behaviour, and what story you inferred from it.

Point to point (25 minutes)

Draw energy and actions from the world around you. If in doubt, reach out. Introduce the principle that objectives are planned, while actions are improvised responses.

- Work as a full group.

- This exercise works best in a room with plenty of things in it – chairs, tables, props, costumes, and so on.

- Centre and align yourself. Work in silence.

- See something across the space and move towards it. Make contact with that thing, turn, spot something else and move towards that. Simply move through the space, walking from point to point. Walk with purpose but nothing more than purpose: do not add artificial intensity to your walk, but don't wander either. Enjoy the pleasure of walking towards a target with ease and flow.

- Continue this for a short while, allowing yourself to settle into the rhythm of your walk, making contact with objects and points in the space.

- Now make a choice to change each object when you arrive at it. Move to your target and physically change it when you get there: you might turn it, polish it or even just warm it up, but you will change it.

- Continue this for a short while.

- Try moving to the object without knowing how you will change it until you have reached it. Change it because of what you find it to be on arrival.

- Continue this for a short while, in a spirit of play: with exploration and curiosity.

- Try adding an objective for these actions; you might want to make the room more beautiful, more ordered, to explore balance or to arrange things according to colours, for example. Continue to walk and change objects in the space, pursuing this objective.

- Now allow yourself either to say 'Yes' or 'No' to each object as you change it, as a verbal response to the change you effect or part of how you effect that change.

- If you find yourself aware of and interacting with others, do so non-verbally and through objects.

- At a certain point, when you feel you have explored this dynamic, or when your room is at the peak of mess you'll safely allow, let everyone discover a shared objective: to tidy the room.

- Achieve this in silence, then come together and reflect on what you did. How did your simple actions and objectives change you – your body tensions and breath patterns? How did these tensions and patterns in turn change how you felt? How is this rhythm of seeing a target, seeing the need to change that target, changing it and discovering a new target useful to an actor? How does it feel to discover objectives through physical action? How might this be useful to an actor?

Teaching Tip: This exercise will make your room into a creative mess and objects in the space will be moved around. Agree on a corner of the space as a no-go zone. Gather all precious or personal objects you don't want moved around into this corner.

   I use this as a way in to lots of different exercises: it quickly gets you outward-facing, curious and responsive.

Status improvisation (25–35 minutes)

Pursue an objective without digression or qualification. Test and train your readiness to play completely with and without power. It demands you relinquish, imagine, arrive, adapt and play.

- Work as a full group. Work without words, though not necessarily in silence.

- One of you will leave the room. That person – the 'leader' – will privately conceive a clear set of imagined circumstances, with a clear and powerful objective. They might, for example, need to hide themselves from people hunting them, comfort themselves after a great shock, celebrate a triumph or prepare themselves for a great speech.

- For everyone else, there is a single shared objective: to serve that person in the pursuit of their objective. Endow them with great power over you: they can have you whipped and imprisoned, or they can free you from servitude, depending on your service.

- Accord them the appropriate status:

    Do not come within touching distance unless invited.
    Do not make eye contact unless invited.
    Do not turn your back unless invited.
    Follow their every order or suggestion.

- You will not know what your leader's objective is, so you will need to read their every move closely to correctly assess and serve their needs.

- Do not 'act' serving them. Serve them. Do not show your servitude, serve. The best referees, umpires and butlers largely make themselves invisible, as they facilitate the actions of others. This exercise is absolutely not about you: it is about the leader.

- Allow the exercise to unfold over time. This exercise particularly benefits from being allowed to move beyond its initial burst

of busy energy. As the opening objective is achieved, a new
one will emerge and the temperature of the room will change.
The leader will have to settle into their position of power.
The servants will have to settle into submission to the will of
another. The quality of listening will intensify.

- If the empowered leader indicates they wish you to leave, you
  should step out of the exercise and join the teacher as an
  observer.

- Allow this to be serious play. Move this beyond a game that
  you play; let it be an exercise that you play.

- It may become desirable to allow the leader language. If so,
  only they can speak.

- Reflect on this exercise. How does it feel to lead? Are you
  at ease with holding this status? How does it feel to serve?
  How at ease are you with submitting to or leading the will
  of another? Comment on the dramaturgy of the exercise –
  its peaks and troughs, moments of reversal and dynamic
  shift. Discuss as a group and reflect in your private journal.
  You probably found yourself playing out your role in key
  power-relationships in your own life, i.e. being the child or
  pupil to parents, guardians and formative teachers. Were
  you: eager to please; desperate to rebel; silently resentful of
  their authority; content and safe; or something else entirely?
  Reflect.

Play script (35 minutes)

*Bring the work of objectives and actions to scripted text for the
first time. Prepare to work on scripts, introducing basic textual
analysis.*

I

- Work with a partner. Learn the following script, or write one of
  your own which is equally open to interpretation:

    A is standing. B enters.
    A: What do you want?

B: Don't you know?
A: I told you last time.
B: What do you mean?
A: You know what I mean.
B: Why do you say that?
A: I can't stay here.
A exits.

- You could simply improvise a basic scenario in 5 minutes using this text.

II

- In your pairs, write three possible objectives, e.g. to steal a kiss, to arrest A, to punish B.

- Write three possible answers to the questions 'Where are you?' and 'When are you?', e.g. I'm in a corner shop in Bognor Regis at 8 a.m., I'm in a Paris bistro at lunchtime or I'm in a sheep field on the side of the Wyoming mountains at 1 a.m.

- Write three possible answers to the question 'What are you?', e.g. a politician, a mother, a teacher.

- Allow your imagination free reign and don't edit your first impulses – even if they seem mundane. It doesn't really matter for the purposes of this exercise what you choose, it only matters that you choose and are specific.

III

- Everyone swap objectives with another pair in the room. Everyone swap given circumstances with a different pair in the room. Everyone swap 'What are you?' answers with a third pair in the room.

- Given these objectives, circumstances and identities, rehearse and then present the scene.

- Reflect on this exercise. How did these given circumstances and objectives change the way you saw the world? Did the world seem bigger or smaller, more daunting or more surmountable? Did the other person seem stronger or weaker,

more open or more closed? How did this way of seeing
transform your body and behaviour?

IV

- What if we go so far as to plan our actions before we play the
  scene?

- Write seven active verbs into the script and swap with another
  pair. Define an action for each line, e.g.:

      A: *I challenge you*. What do you want?
      B: *I mock you.* Don't you know?
      A: *I implore you.* I told you last time.
      B: *I press you.* What do you mean?
      A: *I jab you.* You know what I mean.

  and so on.

- Rehearse and play the scene, being specific about playing
  exactly the actions scripted. Inhabit the action physically: put it
  in your breath, body and mind. Change your scene partner.

- How did it feel to plan the scene so fully and fix its shape? Was
  it liberating or restricting to have defined actions for each line?
  What story emerged from this?

Basic object exercise: Public solitude (20 minutes per student)

*Train to play private actions in public. Devise your own scene
and begin to understand basic dramatic form.*

- Work one at a time, with the rest of the group as an
  audience.

- This exercise explores one of the most basic challenges for an
  actor, which Stanislavski called 'public solitude'.

- In this exercise you will use the room you are in, and treat it as
  if it were empty. The rest of your class will sit at one end of the
  room, and you throw an imaginary wall up between you and
  them (called the 'fourth wall').

- In advance of the class prepare an imagined set of given circumstances (you will play yourself in your classroom, but you will need to choose when you are, where you have come from, where you think you are going to, any relationships and why you are here). Also prepare a single objective you can pursue, and three physical actions which will move you towards achieving that objective. For example, it is the end of the school day today; the weather is as it is now. You have hurried directly from your least enjoyable class and are coming into your favourite classroom. Your objective is to prepare the room for a research presentation on Stanislavski, which you must give to the class tomorrow. You are pleased with what you've prepared and hope it will impress your class. Your simple physical actions are:

  1 To pin up the posters about Stanislavski that you have made.

  2 To lay out chairs for your class in a semicircle, with a chair for you at the front, on which you will put your notes for the presentation having double-checked they are in the right order.

  3 To put the music of Gilbert and Sullivan's *Mikado*, in which Stanislavski acted, onto your sound system and check the technology works.

  Once you have completed each of these actions to your satisfaction, your objective will be achieved and you will begin to pursue a new objective, e.g. to go and catch your bus home.

- Come up with your own scenario and play it in front of the class.

- Reflect on what you did. How did the presence of your audience condition your action and behaviour, if at all? Did your audience believe you were in private and doing what you prepared? How did clear actions, related to specific targets, free you into playing the scene?

Basic object exercise: The obstacle of time (20 minutes per student)

Extend the previous exercise's learning, now also training to play against the obstacle of time, answering the question 'Why must this be done now?'

- As with the previous exercise, work individually in front of the class, to present a prepared improvisation.

- Add something to your scenario which will give your action greater urgency. Perhaps your bus goes in 10 minutes, and the bus stop is a couple of minutes run from here. Perhaps it is the following morning and you are setting everything up before the class starts in 10 minutes' time. Make up circumstances of your own.

- You are introducing time as an obstacle, and your actions will be conditioned in order to combat this obstacle. Probably, they will simply become accelerated and intensified.

- Play this exercise. How does the new urgency condition your behaviour? How does it change the focus of your attention? How was your physical tension altered? What happened to your circle of attention? What happened to your tempo-rhythm and effort actions?

Basic object exercise: The inner obstacle (20 minutes per student)

Extend the previous exercise's learning, now also training to play against an inner obstacle of emotion.

- As with the previous exercise, work individually in front of the class, to present a prepared improvisation.

- Now add an inner obstacle of fear to your scenario, which will raise the stakes for you. Perhaps this presentation is being marked towards your final grade. Perhaps you are on a final warning for missed work-deadlines, and this presentation can save or lose your place on the course.

Keep the condition of urgency (running late for the bus) from your last exercise too.

- Play this exercise. What new targets (imagined or otherwise) come to the fore because of the new stakes? Did the new problem help you focus your energy on the scene and away from the audience? How were the physical actions altered by your psychological state? How was the psychological state altered by the physical actions?

- Consider how strong motives, clear objectives, defined obstacles and specific actions can help an actor.

Basic relationship exercise: Opposing objectives (30 minutes per pair)

Extend the previous exercise's learning. Collaborate with another actor in the devising process and play a scene together.

- Work with a partner.

- In advance of your class, prepare a shared set of given circumstances. You will play yourself in your classroom, but you will need to choose when you are, where you have come from and where you think you are going to. You are playing yourselves in this classroom; the rest is up to you.

- Prepare an objective each (something you want) – these objectives should be mutually exclusive. In other words, define a scenario in which you both want different things and cannot both get what you want.

- Each prepare three physical actions which could help you achieve your objective. In other words, come up with three things you could do to get what you want. For example, Partner A wants to prepare the classroom for their presentation tomorrow. Partner B wants to prepare the classroom in a different way for their presentation tomorrow. You both need the whole space if you are to do this satisfactorily. You both have buses to catch.

- Your obstacles are time, the space and each other.

- Your planned physical actions are identical to those in the previous exercise.

- Devise your own scenario. Play this exercise.

- Words are the last resort. It is easy to make this exercise all about two people talking. Use language only when it is necessary: see how much of your objective can be achieved without the need for words. See if you can get what you want physically and without speaking.

- Do not anticipate or play for conflict; perhaps it will not be necessary, perhaps you can just get what you want.

- Do not play to entertain, interest, or otherwise engage your audience. Play to get what you want, and trust that your interest in your objective will interest the audience.

- Remember, your main interest is in achieving your objective, not affecting your partner unless that becomes necessary. Only do what is necessary to get what you want.

- Do not prevaricate, do not delay, do not digress. Get what you want.

- Your objective may be changed during the course of the action; respond honestly to the events that occur within the action.

- Reflect on this exercise with the observers. What transformed behaviours did they see? Did you pursue your objective at all times? Did the audience believe it? Were you pursuing your objective because of a clearly defined need, or did it just look like an acting exercise?

Basic relationship exercise: Shared objectives (30 minutes per pair)

Extend the previous exercise's learning. Collaborate with another actor in devising a scene, and play actions together in the face of strong inner obstacles.

- In advance of your class, prepare a shared set of given circumstances. You will play yourself in your classroom, but you will need to choose when you are, where you have come from and where you think you are going to. Prepare a shared objective you can pursue together, and for each of you, three physical actions which could take you towards achieving your objective. In other words, you both want the same thing and will work together to get it. You will each have planned three things you could do to help you get it.

- In this instance, also plan a definite inner obstacle which makes it hard for you to get what you want. Perhaps you are having an affair with your scene partner's boyfriend: your inner obstacles are guilt and fear of being found out. Perhaps you know your partner is having an affair with your girlfriend, but you don't want to get into the argument until you have completed this crucial piece of coursework: your inner obstacles are anger and shame.

- Perhaps you have not told your partner, but really you are acting as a decoy because outside everyone is setting up a surprise birthday celebration for them: your inner obstacles are excitement and anxiety about failing. Perhaps it is your birthday and you have not told your partner that you know perfectly well there is a surprise party being prepared for you outside, as you don't want to disappoint them: your primary inner obstacles are anxiety (you hate parties) and minor shame (at the lie).

- Use the defined physical actions to overcome these obstacles, as well as to overcome the already discussed outer obstacles.

- Play the exercise.

- Do not demonstrate or play your obstacles: we do not want to see your fear, anxiety or guilt; we want to see the counter-tension in your body which you are using to suppress those forces. So provide psychophysical resistance to fear, anxiety or guilt. Apply this resistance in order to play your physical actions and get what you want: to get the room ready for tomorrow's presentation.

- Reflect on this exercise with your audience. Where did we see the counter-tensions of resistance to the force of the feelings? How were the bodies and behaviours changed? Again, look for tension, rhythm, tempo, effort. Use the language of actions (i.e. verbs) to describe what you were seeing happen (try to avoid 'I saw fear'; and say instead 'I saw her press down her fear' or 'wring out her guilt': be specific).

- You can continue these object and relationship exercises to your imagination's content, and as far as you wish to stretch your skills. You might introduce richer imagined given circumstances – transforming the space and time more dynamically. You might project yourselves into the future and imagine a fantasy scene of your life in five years' time. You might raise the stakes, making the problems you have to solve more costly to confront. You might work with more than one other actor in the scene.

- At every stage, the core principle remains: play three physical actions to overcome defined inner and outer obstacles and achieve an objective. Which is to say: do specific things, to solve particular problems and get what you want.

- Do not play character, do not play problems, do not play the scene, do not play conflict, do not play states or conditions: play actions. Above all though, play.

Follow-up

Extend and embed the training of the exercises away from class with these simple tasks.

- Take a five-line exchange from any play you know well. Define the character objectives. What verbs, what actions could you use on the lines to effect the change the character seeks?

- Look out for moments in real life, when we see people fighting against the obstacle of emotion – in interviews, police news conferences or in your own home.

- Look out for rare moments in your own life when expressing emotion is an action or your objective – for example, expressing grief in many cultures.

- Behavioural economist Dan Ariely discusses how decisions (actions) are made because of given circumstances and the behaviour of others. Context massively alters our perceptions and choices. Watch his TED talk at: http://www.ted.com/talks/dan_ariely_asks_are_we_in_control_of_our_own_decisions?

- Amy Cuddy is a persuasive scientist who has done extensive research on how human body language shapes who you are: our minds change our bodies, and she shows that our bodies also change our minds. Watch her TED talk at: www.ted.com/talks/amy_cuddy_your_body_language_shapes_who_you_are

Further reading

Alfreds, Mike (2007), *Different Every Night*. Nick Hern Books.

Brook, Peter (1988), *The Shifting Point*. Methuen.

Caldarone, Marina and Lloyd Williams, Maggie (2004), *Actions: The Actor's Thesaurus*. Nick Hern Books. Introduction.

Stanislavski, Konstantin, trans. Jean Benedetti (2008), *An Actor's Work*. Routledge. Chapter 3, Action, 'if', 'Given Circumstances'.

PART TWO

THE ROLE

Learn processes for rehearsing a play. Learn to analyse, interpret, inhabit and play an authored role.

Mostly actors work as interpretive artists, inhabiting words and worlds predefined by authors. A writer pens a plot which the actor enlivens through rehearsal. Such rehearsals are a steady process, working to uncover and truthfully inhabit the role you will play and the story you will tell. In this part of the book we will look at exercises that can form part of a script-based rehearsal process.

In our craft there is a common lie that what we do in rehearsals is based primarily on talent. It is not. Talent is necessary; but talent is just as necessary to become a civil engineer or an accountant. The things that will bring a script to life are your skill, craft and hard work.

However, you are not only a technician. You bring your own soul and psyche to the writer's material. If you play Medea, Lady Macbeth or Blanche Dubois you are involved in an interpretive, but also a creative act. Your unique body, breath, voice and imagination will deliver a unique chemistry when you inhabit an authored role: something new will naturally be made.

I find it most useful to think of the actor's creative process as one defined by inevitable discovery: you discover something new when you bring yourself, your soul, to a script. You take yourself on a voyage of discovery. I favour doffing the burden of achieving originality and creativity (since these are inevitable), and using language of exploration and adventure. It seems simpler and more fun. Rehearsals analyse and refine the unique products of the natural chemistry which occurs when a company of actors meet a script for the first time.

*

In 1492 Christopher Columbus set sail from Spain with three ships. He sought a path west, which would provide a quicker route to the riches of India, China and the Spice Islands. After sailing for ten weeks, Columbus reached what he thought to be islands lying just west of India: the West Indies. He sailed on, and found only a vast, barren land. This was not India.

He returned to Spain frustrated, oblivious to the fact that he had revealed to Europe the gateway to a whole new world.

Columbus went on three further missions to find his new passage to India. Although he found Cuba – which he took to be Japan – reached the South American mainland and unlocked the door to North America, he never did reach the west coast of India. Columbus, blind to what he had done, died in poverty a lonely, disappointed and bitter man.

In our work, like Christopher Columbus, let us set off looking for something – anything – specific. A clear target and a hunger for its rewards will draw us into adventures. Maybe we will eventually find exactly what are looking for; maybe like Christopher Columbus we won't. But unlike Columbus, let us care to look closely at the specific value of who or what we do find and dare to realize when we have stumbled upon something special.

6
THE MAP

Learn to analyse and interpret a script.

Framework

This chapter involves work you can do before you begin to rehearse and early in rehearsal. The exercises guide you towards a deep understanding of your only resource other than yourselves: the script.

The text has primacy, precisely because it comes first in this kind of process. It is the map which guides you.

The journey you take through the landscape of the play will become truly thrilling only once you have dropped the script and can adventure freely. But in order to get to that point, we must do more than learn a script, we must discover a role.

At first, you will work on the script as if it were an ancient map: inaccurate, without scale, but heavily decorated with images of beauty and meaning for the map's author (have a look at the Hereford Mappa Mundi). Mark on the script your own beliefs, ideologies and reference points. Describe your personal fascinations with the world of the play, and locate your reason to make the journey. You need a personal relationship with the story you will tell.

Next move beyond personal intuition to root your insight in the script's structural foundations. The modern Ptolemic map (plotted from above with grids and to scale) plots structure with reliable coordinates. Your next step treats the script as if it were a Ptolemic map and marks its internal narrative structures. These coordinates plot your course.

Analyse the script to reveal the precise setting, values, politics and culture of the story world through which you will travel. Look at the acts, scenes and events built into it, which are the boundaries you will cross. These mark your changes of direction along the way: they are the moments of choice, which reveal character and plot as you discover them.

The script will mark the literal and emotional space between people. The language of the script will guide all your physical choices and suggest all necessary behaviour. It will reveal where you are here and now, suggest possible futures and imply significant pasts.

As you reveal the story world and each character's journey through it (character through-lines), name the different bits of the story – act by act, scene by scene, unit by unit. These will help you remember where you have been and locate where you have yet to travel. These names will make return journeys simpler – whether in your imagination or in action – and ease your process as you plunder the story world in ever greater depth. Early maps of the Antarctic show Gale Ridge, Stench Point, Despair Rocks, even Exasperation Inlet and Inexpressible Island. Crucially, these names evocatively describe the traveller's sensory experience of that landscape.

Most importantly, of course, the script will reveal a story. We move ourselves towards that. You are a conduit for the big ideas – social, political ideas – which run through the story. Work in search of these big ideas and ways to animate them.

*

A warning: in 1798, the map-maker James Rennell did something mind boggling in its audacity; he invented a mountain range. Not a small one he thought others might miss, but one as large as any in the known world: it stretched right across West Africa for thousands of miles, all the way from modern Nigeria to Sierra Leone. He called this range *The Mountains of Kong* (no, honestly). Because others took his word for it, The Mountains of Kong became a standard feature of European maps of Africa. For more than a century, this mountain range stood as an impassable barrier to European explorers and travellers. Finally, 100 years later, a curious Frenchman went to have a look at the mountains – and found that they weren't there. We must not be overwhelmed, like Rennell, by the desire to make a radical discovery of our own. In this kind of process, we are discoverers, plotting what we find, not originators building a new world.

The script is our starting point for everything. It defines our action and is the source of all creative discovery and interpretation. The script is more than a curiosity helping us locate our place in the world; it makes the world. The actor's textual analysis is an artistic, active process of discovery, which is more than preparation for adventure: it is the first step on that adventure.

Exploration

These exercises are necessary preparations before rehearsals begin, which ready you for the work that follows.

- The first time you read a play is vital: give yourself uninterrupted time and space, make yourself comfortable and read it in one sitting with a pencil, a good biscuit and a cup of tea. Your first responses to the script will stay with you and, as they are intuitive, they are often very valuable. You will only meet the script with truly fresh eyes once, so give it a fair chance. Note your reactions down in your journal: how it made you feel as you read it, when it was particularly clear or dense, what strong ideas it prompted. Note the obvious and be specific about when the text aroused specific feelings within you. Be honest, not clever.

- Immediately after you have read it for the first time, make a drawing of the play. Draw the major events and all the key moments or images that you remember from the play. The most important moments will be at the centre and be bigger than the rest. Include the play's mythology (absent characters or mysterious unseen events) as they appear in your imagination. You will necessarily be inaccurate, but you will map an honest representation of the play's first impression on you.

- Make a rehearsal script. Your script should have a blank page facing every page of text. I photocopy or print out a script and stick it into a large A4 notebook, with one clean page facing one page of text. This workbook becomes a place for all my notes, drawings, pictures etc.: a book of maps.

- Sit with a dictionary and access to the internet or a library and read through the script, ensuring you understand the exact meaning of every word in the play. This is not primarily about etymology, it is about giving yourself clear images to fulfil language and give it substance. If you refer to a 'tree', search for an image of the kind of tree your character will be referring to where they live (when I say 'tree', I unavoidably picture the old pear trees in the garden of my childhood home. How about you?). If you mention a city, search for images of that city and the landscape your character would know. Find pictures to fill your imagination and root the language of the script. Do sketches or stick pictures into your working script; note specific meanings on your facing pages.

Exercises

These exercises are necessary preparation projects before you begin to play scenes in role. They are relevant to all styles of dramatic text – whether Restoration, Greek, Shakespeare or realism.

I have broken this chapter into three sections. 'Beginning rehearsals' includes exercises which establish focuses for your later work. 'Research' includes exercises to prepare factual and imaginative reference points for your work. 'Narrative events' focuses on detailed analysis of the plot and story. All the exercises are entirely focused on text.

If there is not time to do this work during a rehearsal process, I will do this work independently before I begin rehearsals. Almost all the exercises are easily adapted for an individual working at home (though that is less rewarding).

Beginning rehearsals

What makes a play? (20 minutes)

Open up the different elements which form the focus of rehearsal's active analysis. Define your rehearsal's terms of engagement.

- Work as a full group in a discussion chaired by a teacher, or in groups of four or five.

- Nominate one person to be the group scribe.

- Below is a list of the ingredients which are a necessary part of a traditional play or film script (not a production, simply the map for a production). Write it out and pin it to the wall:

  Writer(s)
  Reader(s)
  Words and punctuation
  Plot
  Story
  Character(s)
  Objectives (character wants)
  Obstacles (the problems those characters face)
  Actions (whatever characters do to resolve that conflict)
  Events (the things that happen to characters)
  Genre (thriller, horror, tragedy, farce and so on)
  Style (surrealism, naturalism, absurdism, symbolism and so on)
  Tempo (the speed of time passing)
  Rhythm (pattern within time)
  Theme (whatever the play is about – honour, love, power and so on)
  Setting (location, period, duration, level of conflict)
  Structure (five act, three act, one act and so on)

- Add to or edit this list as you interrogate it.

- Choose a film or play of this script you all share as a reference point. Go through this list and discuss each of these elements in relation to that script, to help clarify your understanding both of these terms and of the script. In each case, ask what the element is (e.g. what is an event or what is genre), what it is not and then what it might be in your script.

- Reference one other script as a tool for comparison as you go (e.g. discuss *Toy Story* as well as whatever script you are working on).

- These ingredients will be the terms of analysis: each of these elements will ultimately need to be interrogated and analysed as you work on a script.

- Each element can be analysed as you work through the following exercises. Leave your list on the wall for reference later and to help support subsequent work.

The first read-through (allow an hour more than you think the play will take to read)

Explore instinctive responses to the play and its initial impact.

I

- Sit together in an open circle. Have scripts and pencils in hands as well as access to the internet or a dictionary available for reference.

- Read as the first rehearsal, do not read to give a performance. Uncover the events of the play in your reading – meaning read with generosity, allowing the language to move you, but with no pretension to performance.

- Do not read the parts you will play in performance. Read someone else's part, if possible reading a role you are unlikely ever to be cast in (the wrong gender or age, for example). Change roles at the end of each act or after a few scenes. Everyone will *hear* the role they will play. Soon you will have to commit to it with driven subjectivity; this is one moment to hear it objectively and follow, rather than drive, its arc.

- Because this is a rehearsal, allow yourself to stop and repeat lines or words for clarity: there is no rush and this is not performance.

- As you listen to the play unfolding, note down:

  What your character is (doctor, butler, father, sister)
  Where your character is
  When your character is (scene by scene)
  Facts about major unseen events (e.g. Juliet's funeral or Macbeth's coronation)

Facts about major unseen characters (e.g. Rosaline in *Romeo and Juliet* or the father in *The Glass Menagerie*).

- Take a definite break at what might be a natural interval.

- Because this is the first time the script has been heard aloud, you will hear things you have not noticed in the script before: story beats, relationship dynamics, desires or secrets you had not seen when reading the black marks on your own. Now you are hearing the story. Share these discoveries and allow a free discussion to flow from them.

- Do not feel that you need to drive this discussion too much – allow it to flow. Use the ingredients you have agreed make a play (from the previous exercise) to focus the discussion. What genre is it written in? What possible styles are present? How does its structure affect the reading? What words repeatedly spring out at you?

- Do not feel you need to answer every question, simply open the dialogue.

II

- Break into pairs. You will need colouring pens and a large piece of paper, ideally A3 or bigger.

- Together draw a map of the play you have just read. Draw a definite journey across the page – like a snakes and ladders board – with key events, characters, ideas or themes drawn on too. This will not be as accurate as the classical Ptolemic map (with grids and precise scale), but it will truthfully reflect your relationship to what you just heard. Use colour, scale and location on the page to indicate the importance of events or relationships.

- Share these with the rest of the group, discussing differences between what you have drawn, then pin them to your wall.

Research

Research projects (allow a week or more for research to take place and 10–15 minutes per presentation)

Locate the script's cultural, social, political and biographical reference points. Free the actor's imagination into the world of the story. Fill language and action with image and meaning.

- All research is imaginative. It is there to trigger imagination and help an actor inhabit the world of the script.

- All research relies on memory: look into your own experiences for corollaries to the events of the play.

- Research involves gathering images, music and stories. These help you to: understand the situation of the play; imagine yourself in those situations; and visualize/improvise those scenarios.

- Give each member of the group a different area to research. Research can be into any and all of the ingredients of a script (as outlined in the first exercise). It could therefore be:

  Biographical about the author or their historic readers/ audience
  Etymological about the meanings of words in the play
  Psychological, spiritual or physical about characters and actions
  Social, political or historical about conflicts, events and themes
  Artistic about genre, style or structure
  Musical or dance-based about tempo and rhythm
  Cultural, geographical or social about setting.

- Our work is primarily concerned with given circumstances. Research will build imaginative bridges to link us to: who, where and when we are; character relationships, histories and motives.

- Research whatever you find necessary in order to richly inhabit the world and words of the play.

- To research, for example:

    Learn new skills or rituals (for events, actions, e.g. learn to march for a contemporary staging of *Othello* or learn the Italian Catholic marriage ceremony for *Romeo and Juliet*)

    Listen to/play music and learn dances (e.g. learn the Tarantella if you are in a production of *A Doll's House*)

    Visit art galleries and museums (for style, genre, setting, theme)

    Go on trips (for setting or events)

    Interview people (who have experienced relevant desires, events or conflicts)

    Read relevant literature (for setting, conflict, events, theme, author)

    Watch films or documentaries (for style, genre, setting, events, conflict, character, theme)

    Cook and eat food (for setting and character).

- Research to stimulate your imagination and senses; don't let research become desk-bound or it will quickly become academic.

||

- Prepare presentations. These share relevant learning. You might share images, maps, music or art work. You might prepare a full-class improvisation in which you will act out a marriage ceremony. You might invite a trained friend in to teach the class to march like a soldier. You might do a sock-puppet show about the rise of Lutheranism in northern Europe.

- These presentations are by and for actors. They should stimulate imaginations and senses.

- Research is an ongoing process and is not concluded in a single session: as you work with the script you will discover new questions to answer. Fill rehearsals with active learning, prompted by the demands of playing the text.

Thematic wallpaper (30 minutes)

Find the relevance of the script to your own lives and society. Link the where and when of the script to the here and now of your world. Engage with the immediate meaning of the story for your audience.

- Work as a full group. You will need a large pile of recent newspapers and magazines, with lots of pictures in them.

I

- Discuss the key themes in the script. By themes, let's agree we mean big ideas which recur in the writing and pervade its action. Crucially, themes affect the lives of every character in the script, for example: honour, death, love, power, freedom, glory.
- It can be useful to identify binary opposites which the play is exploring thematically, for example: honour/dishonour (in *Othello*); spiritual love/sexual love (in *Twelfth Night*); imagination/reality (in *A Midsummer Night's Dream*); innocence/guilt (in *Macbeth*).
- Agree on between three and five dominant themes in the script. Identify clear moments when *every* character is related to these themes in the script.

II

- Share a pile of current magazines and newspapers around among the group.
- Search through the newspapers and magazines and find images or articles which relate to the themes you have identified. You are looking for the political relevance of the script: examples of how its themes viscerally run through our contemporary lives.
- Plot these images into your script at the moment when you think the theme is most viscerally manifest for your character

– so for honour/dishonour in *Othello* that is clearly when Othello murders Desdemona.

- Alternatively, you can pin these images and articles to your wall, creating a gallery of contemporary images.

- Discuss the relevance of each image among the group, showing how this story continues to be necessary. Actors make meaning.

Research from memory (45 minutes)

Connect the events of the script to your life, generously sharing those connections among the group. Make the relevance of the story immediate and personal.

- Work in pairs.

- The most relevant research about the script will be into our own lives.

- In this exercise you will find a corollary for the events of the story: find an analogy from your experience to help understand the script. It is through analogy that humans learn the world. By the age of three children use metaphor and simile to help describe their experiences ('I'm a monkey!', 'My broccoli's like a tree!'). We often work out what something is by working out what it is like.

- Take one of the key themes from the script, which you feel particularly reaches into your character's experiences in the story.

- Close your eyes.

- Think of an experience in your own life – something that happened to you, or something that you witnessed – which reflects that theme: a moment when you felt in conflict with guilt and innocence, for example.

- The memory you choose must be one you are happy to share with your partner and hear shared with everyone else in the room, so choose carefully. Take time to choose.

- Revisit that moment now. Where were you? Who else was there? When were you? What key event happened? How did the people around you react? What sounds could you hear? How were you changed?

- Open your eyes and, in your pairs, take it in turns to tell your stories. Remember, we are always training ourselves as active, empathetic listeners.

II

- Once you have both told your stories, move on to a new partner.

- Tell the story you have just heard (not your own story which you have just told), to your new partner. Tell the story in the first person, as if it had happened to you. Alter as little of the story as you can in order to make it your own: allow your imagination to own these events as if they had happened to you. Make the story live.

- Once you have both told these stories, move on to a new partner.

- Tell the story you have just heard (not the story you have just told), as if it had happened to you. Stretch yourself, but enliven the story with detail from your own imagination if you need: make the story live.

- You can continue sharing stories around the room in this way as many times as you will. You might even find you hear the story you first told, told back to you.

- After you have done this, reflect on the experience. What was it like to own a story that was not your own? What responsibility did you feel towards the story's original 'author'? Did you need to free yourself from this in order to let the story live? If so, how did you do that? What big ideas, themes, were explored and what new lights did these stories shine on the script?

- Write notes or make drawings in your script about the stories you have heard or told, at the points when you think these are most thematically relevant and alive for your character. Plot them onto the map of your journey through the play.

Where are you? (30 minutes)

Bring specific, detailed understanding to the given circumstances of the space, ensuring your later work is not taking place within generalized or abstracted space. Ground your work and relationships somewhere particular and provocative.

You will need plenty of paper, some of it large (ideally A3) and lots of coloured pens.

I

- Split into small groups, sharing the locations of the play among these groups (in *Macbeth* that would mean: the heath, Macbeth's castle in Inverness, the Scottish royal palace, Macduff's castle in Fife, Macbeth's castle at Dunsinane, the lands around Dunsinane and Birnam Forest). If the play has only a single location (as in *A Doll's House*), each group takes a different time we meet that location – the beginning of each act, for example.

- Read through the relevant scene or act for each location.

- Note down all the factual information given about the location in the text: what is in it, who is in it, its thresholds, light sources, climate, relative size, neighbouring spaces.

- Note down all the character responses to the space: its atmosphere, its effect over the people in it and differentiated character relationships to it.

II

- In your groups, draw a big map of the space. Mark out all its features, but also note (in the manner of an ancient map) atmospheres and moods on it; draw the space's atmosphere and mythology into the map. Use colour and allow your map to be as much social commentary as geographical analysis (though it must also be this).

III

- Come back to the full group and share your maps. Pin these to the wall for ongoing reference. As follow-up work, bring images in and stick these onto the maps, e.g. period furniture, views from the windows, flora and fauna.

> **Teaching Tip:** If you want to accelerate this process or integrate it earlier, you could build it into a read-through of the play, asking scribes to make these notes and share them at the end. You can even set the map drawing as a research project outside of class.

Story world (30 minutes, assuming you split into groups)

Extend the work of the previous exercise, locating the specific setting, values and politics which define the mapped space. Locate the cultural context of the world you will bring to life.

- Work as a full group or in three groups, each taking one of the three tasks listed below.
- Nominate a scribe.
- Know the world in which the story of your script operates. By story world, I mean a script's setting, values and politics.
- Consider the following issues in your groups, or as a group:
    1 What is the setting of your story? First, in what period or periods is it set? Second, in what location or locations does is it take place? Third, what duration of time does it encompass? So, for example, *A Doll's House* is set at Christmas 1879 – the year in which it was written. The action takes place in a middle-class, well-furnished home (described in great detail by Ibsen) in Trondheim, Norway.

The action encompasses three days (the morning of Christmas Eve until late at night on Boxing Day), across the three acts.

Be as specific as you can (much more than I have been in this example) and consider the implications of each of these for your work. What difference does it make that it is 1879? That it is in Norway? That it is during the Christmas holidays? How would the play change if it were set in 1979? In a working-class district of Boston, Massachusetts? During a busy working summer? Over two months? Why must it be this here, this now, this duration?

2   What are the values in your story-world? At my sons' school, the words 'friendship', 'perseverance', 'safety', 'honesty' and 'kindness' are set over the main entrance. These values are enshrined into the code of conduct and rules of the school; all the children know these words by heart and these values condition their behaviour. What values are central to the aspirations of the culture in this story?

Usually there is one dominant value, which the events of the script move us alternately towards and away from. In *Othello* that value might be honour. In the TV show *Columbo* that value is justice. In the film *The Godfather* that value might be loyalty. In *A Doll's House* that value might be freedom. What is the central value dominating the lives of the characters in your story? Each scene will move the characters and the action a little closer to or further from that value. Each act will move the action a lot closer to or further from it. The final act of the drama probably involves a shocking and fabulous surge towards or away from that value: in *Othello*, Othello realizes he has committed the most dishonourable act possible in the name of honour. In *A Doll's House,* Nora discovers that what she thought was freedom is actually bondage.

3   What are the politics of your story-world? By which I mean: how is power distributed? In British society today, power is distributed through – among other things – nationalism, racism, patriarchy, capitalism. It is easier to get power if you

are rich, white, male and British than if you are poor, black, female and have emigrated from Uganda. Is the world of your story matriarchal, feudal, autocratic, egalitarian, theocratic? Where does this put your character in relation to power and their sense of having a respected voice? Create a status line for the characters of the play – on your feet ideally – defining the arrangement of power at the beginning of the play, and then do the same for the end of the play. How has it changed?

- If you have worked in small groups, share your reflections with the group.
- You can extend and deepen this work, if you have time, with exercises outlined in Chapter 9, pages 267–71.

Narrative events

Units of action

Reveal the script specific coordinates – points of departure and arrival, which will locate and focus your character throughline. Reveal moments of choice for your characters and from this, the story – beat by beat – which you will tell together. Create a physical score for the script, marking moments of physical shift and transformation (which is what each new event/unit represents).

There are many different systems for exactly how to do this. The important thing is to do it. It requires gentle reinventing and rediscovery with each new play.

Stanislavski asks us to think of a play as a great big meal. A meal is not eaten whole and in one go. We break a meal into more digestible parts: perhaps a starter, a main course and a dessert – the three-act drama. But we don't eat our main course in one go; there are distinct units within that too: perhaps meat, vegetables, potatoes – three scenes within the act. But we don't try and eat all that in one go either: we cut it up into small mouthfuls. These mouthfuls are what we eat.

Most plays and screenplays in Western drama are broken into acts for you, either by author or editor. Most break these acts into scenes (though not all). I can think of none (though I am sure many exist) that present the scenes broken into smaller, bite-size units of action. The actor needs to break the scene into smaller units, just as the dinner guest will cut up the plate of food you present to them. You won't be able to swallow and digest it properly otherwise.

Acts

- Let us start with acts. The end of an act marks a major change in the play: a significant transformation takes place, which brings the act to a close. Usually this throws the central character (protagonist) significantly closer to or farther from the state they long to achieve (their super-objective). Sometimes a new act also marks a significant shift in location or time. A five-act drama has five major shifts to and fro; a one-act drama has only one major shift.

- Work as a full group, or in small groups taking an act each to analyse. Identify the events which conclude each act.

- Let us observe this in Macbeth, considering the protagonist's swings towards or away from his super-objective (to secure the crown of Scotland for himself and his heirs). Below are the events which conclude each act in *Macbeth*:

  Act 1 ends as Macbeth resolves to kill King Duncan.
  Act 2 ends when Macbeth is named king.
  Act 3 ends with the news that the English are planning to attack Macbeth's Scotland.
  Act 4 ends as Macduff resolves to kill Macbeth.
  Act 5 ends as Macduff kills Macbeth and Malcolm is crowned king.

- Notice how clearly the basic plot is told through these events.

- Now title the acts. For example:

  1 The prophecies

  2 The murder of Duncan

3　The murder of Banquo

4　The murder of Lady Macduff and her sons

5　The murder of Macbeth.

- The titles should be simple, clear and ideally define the narrative thrust of the act.

- Write out your titles and stick them on the wall.

Scenes

- Scenes may be given for you. If they are, go through the same process, noting the major events which mark the climax of each scene.

- Either do this as a full group, or split into smaller groups and work on an act of scenes each.

- Let us observe the concluding events in the seven scenes of Act I in *Macbeth*:

    1.1 The three witches prepare to meet Macbeth.

    1.2 King Duncan pronounces the execution of the Thane of Cawdor and the passing of that title to Macbeth.

    1.3 Macbeth fantasises about becoming king.

    1.4 Macbeth plots to remove King Duncan's son from his path to the crown.

    1.5 Lady Macbeth urges Macbeth to kill Duncan.

    1.6 Duncan is welcomed into Macbeth's castle.

    1.7 Macbeth resolves to kill the king.

- The major concluding events of each scene give us the bare plot of each act.

- Now title each scene in the act. For example:

    1　When shall we three meet again?

    2　What Cawdor hath lost, noble Macbeth hath won

    3　All hail Macbeth and Banquo

    4　The Prince of Cumberland

    5　The king comes here tonight

6 Fair and noble hostess, we are your guest tonight

7 Screw your courage to the sticking place and we'll not fail.

- In this case, I have chosen lines from the scenes to title them. This is often liberating. These titles will help us remember each scene more easily than referring to them by number, and focus our attention on narrative function and action. Titling is an interpretive act, so be ready to change your titles as you work and learn.

- Write out the titles and stick them up on the wall, under each act.

French scenes

- Either work on this as a full group, or for speed split into groups and take an act of scenes each.

- Break the scenes (or if you are working with a script without scene divisions, go straight to this stage) into classical French scenes. In eighteenth and nineteenth-century French drama, new scenes were marked on each entrance or exit of a character. This acknowledges the significant impact of one person leaving or entering a shared space. It helps reveal the rhythm and pacing of the action, as we see the regularity with which definite dynamic changes occur.

- Simply draw a straight line across your page where the exit or entrance is marked.

- Act 1 Scene 3 of *Macbeth* has five entrances/exits which mark new French scenes:

    1.3.1 Enter the three witches
    1.3.2 Enter Macbeth and Banquo
    1.3.3 Witches vanish
    1.3.4 Enter Ross and Angus
    1.3.5 Exeunt.

- Title these French scenes, if you do not have scenes marked already. For example:

    1 The weyard sisters hand in hand, thus do go about

2 All hail Macbeth and Banquo

3 Were such things here as we do speak about

4 He bade me call thee Thane of Cawdor

5 Let us toward the king.

- Share your divisions and titles among the group. Write them out and stick them up on the wall under each relevant scene.

Units

- This should be done by the whole group working together.

- Break these French scenes into units. A new unit will begin when something happens – an event – which affects every character on stage. An event creates a new objective for everyone on stage. These events mark the forward motion of the narrative action. Often there is a change in topic at the same time.

- Let's look at the second French scene in I.3 of *Macbeth* ('All hail Macbeth and Banquo') and pinpoint the events which mark the beginning of new units. I'll mark the events where I think they are with **//** and a number.

Enter Macbeth and Banquo **//1**

Macbeth
So foul and fair a day I have not seen.

Banquo
How far is't call'd* to Forres*? **//2** – What are these *is it said to be
So wither'd and so wild in their attire, *Scottish town
That look not like the inhabitants o' the earth,
And yet are on't? Live you? Or are you aught* *anything
That man may question? You seem to understand me,
By each at once her choppy* finger laying *chapped
Upon her skinny lips: you should be* women, *would appear to be
And yet your beards forbid me to interpret
That you are so.

Macbeth

Speak, if you can: what are you?

First Witch

//3 All hail, Macbeth: hail to thee, Thane* of Glamis*!   *a military
                                                           nobleman
                                                           *Scottish town

Second Witch

All hail, Macbeth: hail to thee, Thane of Cawdor*!   *Scottish town

Third Witch

All hail, Macbeth, that shalt be king hereafter! //4

Banquo

Good sir, why do you start*; and seem to fear   *flinch
Things that do sound so fair? – I' the name of truth,
Are ye fantastical*, or that indeed   *imaginary
Which outwardly ye show*? My noble partner   *appear to be
You greet with present grace* and great prediction   *immediate honour
Of noble having* and of royal hope,   *gain
That he seems rapt withal*: to me you speak not.   *entranced
If you can look into the seeds of time,
And say which grain will grow and which will not,
Speak then to me, who neither beg nor fear
Your favours nor your hate*.   *neither begs your favour nor fears your hate

First Witch

//5 Hail!

Second Witch

Hail!

Third Witch

Hail!

First Witch

Lesser than Macbeth, and greater.

Second Witch

Not so happy, yet much happier.

Third Witch

Thou shalt get* kings, though thou be none: **//6**   *beget, conceive*

So all hail, Macbeth and Banquo!

First Witch

Banquo and Macbeth, all hail! **//7**

Macbeth

Stay, you imperfect speakers, tell me more:

By Sinel's* death I know I am Thane of Glamis;   *Macbeth's father*

But how of Cawdor? The Thane of Cawdor lives,

A prosperous gentleman; and to be king

Stands not within the prospect* of belief,   *field of view*

No more than to be Cawdor. Say from whence

You owe* this strange intelligence, or why   *own, got*

Upon this blasted heath you stop our way

With such prophetic greeting? Speak, I charge* you.   *command*

Witches vanish **//8**

At each of these points I have marked, I think a new unit can be said to begin. The characters on stage are all affected by what occurs. The events are as follows:

Event 1 – Banquo and Macbeth enter

Event 2 – Banquo sees the witches

Event 3 – the witches hail Macbeth

Event 4 – the witches hail Macbeth as king

Event 5 – the witches hail Banquo

Event 6 – the witches hail Banquo as the father of kings

Event 7 – the witches begin to depart

Event 8 – the witches vanish.

I mark a straight line out from the event. Everything between one line and another is a unit. Let's title these units:

1   How far is't call'd to Forres?

2   What are these?

3   Hail Macbeth

4   King hereafter

5 All hail Banquo

6 Thou shalt get kings

7 Stay you imperfect speakers

8 The witches vanish.

Again I'm using lines from the play to title the units. You may feel the bald descriptions of the events serve as well or better.

- The unit of action is all the stuff that happens as a consequence of the event. A unit continues until another event occurs. There is a cycle flowing through the drama: Event – Reaction – Action. We mark the events to locate the new action in the script.

- These units are our bite-size mouthfuls, which we can digest. They give us the most specific delineation of the changing action of the drama. They also provide us with a structure for our analysis of the text. They provide a physical score, showing where psychological and therefore physical changes take place. They allow us to plan or recall our journey through the story world – or check our route as we travel. Each event marks, in every sense, a move in the play.

Story vs plot (30–45 minutes)

Bring vivid connection to the story, and develop ownership and understanding of that story. Discover the vibrant unseen activity in the story, and begin to bring this to life.

- Work as a full group.

- The story of a play is different to its plot. The plot is everything we see happen. The story is more than that.

- If I were to tell you the story of *A Doll's House* I might begin by telling you about the day Nora fraudulently took a loan out to save her husband's life. This is a crucial part of the story of the play, but it is not an event in the plot. We do not see this moment on stage, we only see its repercussions.

- Your unit by unit breakdown and analysis will have given you the plot in great detail. Now return to the story.

I

- Sit in a large circle.

- One of you get up and start to tell the story of the play to the rest of the group. Tell it with passion, but playfully. Tell it in the third person and past tense ('Macbeth was riding over a Scottish hillside when suddenly …'). Explore and uncover the story.

- When another of you feels like adding more detail, more colour, or wants to help out a struggling colleague, get up and tap hands with the person in the middle, taking over the task.

- Allow yourselves to go backwards and add detail if an event has been forgotten, or a secondary story (subplot) needs attention. Tell the whole story – not the plot. Tell it together and for each other.

- Notice especially which events in the plot were diminished in the whole story, and which events not in the plot were particularly dominant. Reflect on why this might have occurred and what it teaches you about the play.

II

- Repeat the exercise, but try telling the story from different characters' points of view. As a group, choose one character and tell the story entirely as that character experiences it. Tell it in the first person and dramatic present tense ('I am riding along the shoreline towards Forres when suddenly …').

- You might find yourself acting sections out as you do this – don't inhibit that instinct. Others in the group might jump up to join in at these points.

- If you have time, you will benefit from telling the stories of every character in the play.

Summaries (40–45 minutes)

Extend the learning from the previous exercise. Focus on the core of the story and plot, and take ownership of the script to become its authors. Learn and plot the mapped landscape.

- Work as a full group. Sit in a circle.

I

- Go round the circle. Tell the story of the play, with each person speaking one key narrative sequence at a time, ending with the phrase 'and then'. For example, it might begin:

  Macbeth single-handedly defeats the Norwegian rebels, and then …
  Macbeth rides home with Banquo, and then …
  King Duncan hears the news of Scottish victory over the rebels, and then …
  King Duncan finds out the Thane of Cawdor is responsible for the rebellion and then …

- And so on round the circle until the story has been told.

II

- Now go round the circle again, but this time tell the plot scene by scene, not the story bit by bit. For example:

  1.1 The witches meet and get ready for Macbeth's return from battle, and then …
  1.2 Victory is announced and King Duncan declares Macbeth Thane of Cawdor and then …
  1.3 The witches prophesy Macbeth will be king and Banquo will father kings and then …

- And so on until the plot is summarized.

III

- Now break the circle into as many groups as there are acts in the play (in the case of *Macbeth*, five). Allow a short amount of time to prepare. Go round the circle again, this time telling the story act by act. So, for example:

> Macbeth decides he should be king, and then …
> Macbeth kills King Duncan, and then …

IV

- Now work as one group. Allow a couple of minutes to prepare one sentence to describe the entire action of the play. For example:

  > Macbeth murders his way to the throne of Scotland and is overthrown by a grieving father's revenge and England's forces.

V

- Work individually. Do the same from each character's point of view. What is their story within the script? Summarize each character's journey in one sentence. For example:

  > Macduff supports the rightful heir to the throne, has his entire family murdered for it and enacts revenge.

- Discuss your summaries among the group.
- Reflect on what insights you may have brought to the play.

Teaching Tip: It can be useful to return to this exercise at the end of a rehearsal process as well, to reconnect the company to the story they are telling together. It is easy to forget what we are here to serve.

Mountains of plot (20 minutes)

Consider levels of tension and conflict within the script – a crucial element of setting. Map the rising and falling tension as an independent through line, which will help guide your later choices in rehearsals.

- Work as a full group.
- Write the major events of the play, scene by scene, onto pieces of paper. Use a separate piece of paper for each event.
- Starting at the beginning of the play, stick the events onto the wall of your rehearsal or classroom. Put them up in a long line horizontally across the wall, so they come in order. The higher you put them up on the wall, the higher the level of conflict within that moment. The most intense moment – the climax – will be highest on the wall.
- Feel free to move events up or down as you work and make discoveries about the relative tension and conflict in the events.
- You will end with a mountain range of events, which shows the relative peaks of the drama. Sometimes there will be sudden cliffs; sometimes action will gradually rise or fall.
- Observe the rhythm and growth of the drama. Discuss what you see. Draw it in your working scripts, marking the points of highest tension for your character.

Timeline (35 minutes)

Bring linear specificity to the story work, analysing the script to draw out the necessary events which precede it. Provide a foundational platform for further character research, role-play and rehearsal exercises.

- Work as a full group, or in smaller groups on different sections of the story.

- You will need lots of pieces of paper stuck together horizontally – about 1.5–2 metres/5–6 feet depending on the length of the script.

- Draw a long, straight, horizontal line, running the full length of your roll of paper. This is the arrow of time flying.

- Engage the spirit of a detective for this exercise and enjoy delving into the detail of the script.

- When is the opening of the play? Mark a vertical line at the extreme right-hand end of the timeline to mark the moment the play begins. Write on the date and the opening event.

- Who is the oldest character in the play? Establish their age. Mark a vertical line on the timeline at its extreme left-hand end, which will be the birth of that character. Write on the date, and label it as their birth.

- Now mark on the births of all the other characters in the play, at the relevant points along the timeline.

- Now mark on the trigger events for the play. These are the events, which directly trigger the action of the play. In *Macbeth*, these might include: the beginning of the war with the Norwegians; the loss of Macbeth's and Lady Macbeth's baby; the Thane of Cawdor's treason; Macbeth's triumph in battle. These are the events that could form the direct prequel, if you were ever to write it.

- Now mark any other events which have a definite moment attached to them on the timeline: the death of Macbeth's father, when Duncan took to the throne, the marriages of the Macbeths or the Macduffs, the birth of Lady Macduff's son and so on. If you can, write a date on each event. Use a different colour for factual events given by the script and conjecture. If the order of events is uncertain, also indicate this with colour choice.

- Finally, put this timeline up on your wall.

- Reflect on what you have learned about the play and your role from this: what surprises were there? How has your sense of your character's personal history changed? Are there events you might want to further research and improvise?

Unseen events (30 minutes)

Locate key off-stage events within the course of the action, ensuring your work on the text is filled by a rich, sensory understanding of all the events which trigger and propel it.

I

- Start working as a full group.
- Look through the script and locate the major events, which occur during the action of the play but which we do not see – either because they happen between scenes or happen off-stage. For example, we never see the great feast welcoming Duncan to Macbeth's castle, the murder of King Duncan, the coronation of Macbeth or the death of Lady Macbeth.

II

- Work in small groups, each group taking one unseen event.
- Note down all the available factual information about that event given in the text.
- Now each member of the group complete a different task around the event, in under 5 minutes:

    Write a description of the environment in which the event took place, from one character's point of view – the location, atmosphere, smells, sights and sounds. Focus on the five senses.
    Write a diary entry from another character's point of view describing the event with the advantage of hindsight.
    Write a monologue for another character involved, telling the story of the event immediately after it has occurred.
    Write an inner monologue for another character, observing the event occurring in real time.

- If there are more than four in the group, deliver the same tasks from other characters' perspectives.
- Stage these into a short scene of monologues and share them with your group.

III

- As a natural extension of this work, define the exact given
  circumstances and objectives for this event, and prepare and
  perform an improvisation of it.

Shared storytelling (30–40 minutes)

*Bring the whole story to celebratory life, and build the
ensemble around that story.*

I

- Break into pairs. You might begin with a basic mirror exercise
  (page 64). Partner A begin to tell Partner B the story. Tell it
  slowly, and use *lots* of physical actions to help tell it. Move
  around, become different characters in the story, act out
  scenes, depict all the scenery in immense detail … Really go to
  town on telling this story with all the enthusiasm you can muster.

- As Partner A is telling the story, it is Partner B's job to physically
  mirror the storyteller as closely as possible. As Partner A
  moves, Partner B moves, mirroring exactly what is done. Eye
  contact will help you a lot here.

- Partner A, this is not a competition. Do not test or trick your
  partner; work with them, inviting them along on the journey.
  You couldn't have it better: you truly and completely get to take
  your audience along with you. Allow your partner to keep up;
  see if you can tell the story in physical unison.

- As you get into the story and achieve a unified, focused rhythm
  for the physical mirroring, extend it. As Partner A speaks,
  Partner B speaks too. You will move and also speak in unison.
  Your speech may for a while become rather deliberate and
  over-articulated, but take your partner with you.

- Now try ceding control of the story to your partner. So without
  explicit agreement, Partner B can take control of the story and
  Partner A will be the one mirroring. See if you can truly tell the
  story together.

II

- The group leader can now join pairs together, so four of you are working together telling the story, organically exchanging leadership. All move and speak in unison.

- Now do it in eights. Move and speak as one to tell the story.

- Now do it as a full group. Take over the whole room as you tell the story.

- All of you together, tell the story of the script in vivid detail, sharing out the responsibility of moving and speaking in unison. Try and be sure everyone gets a moment leading the group storytelling.

- Bring your story to its glorious resolution.

Follow-up

- Find more images from the press and other sources that you can cut out or print out, which capture the key themes of the script. Bring these into class and post them on your wall. Write a single-word caption to explain the connection.

- Find images of people who capture something of your role in these cuttings. They may be the wrong gender or age, but you see something of your character in them. For Macbeth, images of Nikolai Ceausescu, Idi Amin or Stalin might be appropriate, for example. Bring these images into class and stick them up on your walls. Annotate them with key words that explain the connection – in this case perhaps tyrant, narcissist, murderer.

- Come up with an alternate title for the play. What if *A Doll's House* had been called *Nora Helmer*? How would it change the play? What if *Macbeth* had been called *Throne of Blood* (as in Akira Kurosawa's 1957 film adaptation of the play) or *The Lost Son*? Think of your own title for the script and see how it changes the piece. Consider why the play has the title that it does.

Further reading

Alfreds, Mike (2007), *Different Every Night*. Nick Hern Books. Part 3, 'Preparation – Preparing the Text'.

Merlin, Bella (2007), *The Complete Stanislavsky Toolkit*. Nick Hern Books. 'Mining the Text', pp. 56–112.

Mitchell, Katie (2009), *The Director's Craft*. Routledge. Chapter 10, 'Building the World of the Play'.

Stanislavski, Konstantin, trans. Jean Benedetti (2008), *An Actor's Work*. Routledge. Chapter 7, 'Bits and Tasks'.

www.themappamundi.co.uk is a remarkable site with wonderful ways to explore this beautiful map.

7
A ROUTE

Learn to interpret and truthfully inhabit a character in a script.

Framework

This chapter involves work you can do before and during a rehearsal, to bring your role to life in a vivid and transformational way. The exercises enrich and brighten your role-play.

Nowadays we have a remarkable kind of map, which plots itself around every one of us. Pocket-sized technology places each of us at the very centre of the world. Wherever I go in the world, I can access an online map which spins the world around me and guides me turn by turn towards my chosen destination.

This is the map you ultimately need the script to become. You will plot the world of the play from one point of view, utterly subjectively – lost beyond the next turn you need to take towards your character's destination. To read the script as a GPS map, you need to define a point of view: given circumstances, objectives, actions. These plot the world with your character at its centre.

This kind of detailed navigational positioning relies on triangulation. The GPS map works out where you are, by working out your relationship to two or more fixed, known points. It is the same for you in acting. You will work out who, what, where, when you are, by measuring your relationships to at least two other points outside yourself.

Because characters are always on a journey of transformation, you will need to plot coordinates regularly in order to discover the direction of travel. Every narrative event (a moment of change in the story) marks a change of direction on your journey. As part of rehearsal, for every new unit (a chunk of action running between two narrative events) you need to plot your new position and direction of travel in order to achieve the specificity the craft demands.

*

Below are ten questions which provide a framework for all the work from here forward, and a focus for much of the work you have already done. Through active analysis of them, you can plot your position and locate your next course of action, unit by unit. Ultimately, working with them will empower free play. All this planning ensures we have a clear direction of travel – not a fixed journey or destination.

1 Who are you?
2 Where are you?
3 Where have you come from and where are you going to?
4 When are you?
5 What are your relationships?
6 What do you want?
7 What for?
8 What is at stake?
9 What are your obstacles?
10 What can you do to overcome those obstacles?

Answer each of these questions for yourself as we go through them in more detail. Subject yourself to the same analysis you will later impose on a role in a play.

1. Who are you?

- Let's rephrase this question, to give us two external points for triangulation:

  Who do you wish you could be?
  Who are you afraid you might be?

- The specific answers change moment by moment (unit by unit).

- Who you are is a series of movements in opposite directions: you want to be this; you don't want to be that. You are held in a dynamic tension between flight and pursuit.

- Within this question, ask: What are you? Mother, sister, daughter, teacher, gardener and so on.

- Now triangulate this question:

   What are you *not* that you wish you were? Macbeth, crucially, longs to be a father.
   What are you that you wish you were *not*? Juliet, crucially, wishes she were not a daughter to Capulet.

- These are social roles which you pursue or resist, and by which your imagination and behaviour are bound. Plant these identities into your body: the bad eyesight of the seventeenth-century British author who writes by candlelight; the wide stance and tight jaw, habitually shut against the dust, of the cowboy horse-rider.

- You never act or play who you are: this will arise out of the cumulative sum of your actions. As Aristotle put it, you are the sum of your actions.

2. Where are you?

- Five senses locate you. What do you see, smell, hear, feel and taste? What objects, climate, colours, familiarity surround you? Environment conditions behaviour both consciously and unconsciously (consider how rooms painted different colours prompt different behaviours).

- Place has status, which conditions behaviour. Cathedrals are designed to make us feel small: the human experience is diminished, given godly perspective, as we walk into these cavernous spaces. Space conditions behaviour.

- I am a different person sat in my front room than I am sat in my boss's office. The relative statuses of the two rooms condition my behaviour, bind my imagination.

- Be clear and specific about your surroundings; they are part of who you are and what you are capable of imagining for your future.

3. Where have you just come from and where are you going to?

- Where you have come from (your immediate previous circumstances) defines the tempo-rhythm of your body, its flow, texture, tension and energy as you enter. Arriving in a scene after a long, hot horse-ride creates a different body to that which enters after a short dash across a snowy courtyard.

- Where you are going to means what do you expect to happen next? This is almost always disappointed or surpassed in drama. Be clear about what situation you expect to discover on your entrance; know what you are anticipating will happen. Entering a scene expecting to find your long-lost friend with her arms open wide creates a different body to that which enters expecting to meet a scornful, resentful ex-lover.

- Your immediate past, the anticipation of your immediate future, conditions your body, breath and action.

4. When are you?

- What time is it? What day is it? What month is it? What season is it? What year is it? What era are you living through?

- I have a different body at 6 a.m. than I do at 9 p.m., capable of different behaviours at each point.

- How does your body feel on a Monday morning compared to a Friday morning?

- How would your life be different had you been born in exactly the same place, but in the year 1600?

- How is your body different getting up on a summer morning from a winter morning?

5. What are your relationships?

- This includes your relationships to objects. Flip flops make me a more easy-going man than leather brogues. How do the shoes you are wearing now make you feel? How is your behaviour conditioned by the seat you are in? Is there a precious object you are currently wearing? What would it mean to lose that object?

- Then there are people. To understand these relationships, let's ask two questions of each person to whom you are connected, which will triangulate your position:

  How do they make you feel?
  How do you *think* you make them feel?

- Your behaviour towards someone else is significantly conditioned by the pull of these two poles. It is irrelevant how you actually make someone feel: you cannot truly know this. Your body and behaviour are partly created by your expectations and (mis)perceptions of others.

- Also consider the same issue through these questions:

  What do you think they want you to be? e.g. a daughter, a wife, a lawyer
  What do you want them to be? e.g. a mother, a lover, gone

- Either resist or attempt to serve the role you think they want you to play. Try to make them the person you want them to be.

6. What do you want?

- 'Want' is derived from the Anglo-Saxon meaning 'lack' or 'need'. I've discussed this at length in the 'Framework' of Chapter 5.

- What is your *objective* and who or what is your *target*? Juliet wants to make Romeo kiss her. Romeo is the target. Getting him to kiss her is the objective.

- Implicit within this question is understanding suffering: suffering when you do not have what you want; suffering when you get what you want and find it is not what you wanted; suffering when you have what you want and fear you will lose it. Macbeth suffers because he wants to be king and is not. Macbeth suffers because he is king and finds it does not deliver the fulfilment he expected. Macbeth suffers because he is terrified someone will take his kingship.

- What kind of suffering is your character experiencing? Who do they blame for it?

7. What for?

- What is your motive? This is not psychoanalytic: don't look back into your previous life for the answer. This is cognitive and behavioural: look forward into your future life for the answer. What future are you trying to secure for yourself by achieving this immediate objective? Triangulate:

  Why do you need it here?
  Why do you need it now?

- Your motive must have urgency to have dramatic currency. Like Odysseus trying to get home, it may take ten years to get what you want, like Sisyphus cursed forever to push his rock up a hill it may be never-ending – but like both of them you must be bound to it, long for its fulfilment, this moment. That urgent need is the currency of your action.

8. What is at stake?

- Every moment is about to get either better or worse. How bad or good it could get is what is at stake.

- Split the stakes, triangulating your position in order to locate the force of your need:

  What can you gain if you get what you want?
  What can you lose if you don't get what you want?

- Build a specific image of what can be lost and gained. In each moment, what can be lost will be as terrible as what can be gained is wonderful: the stakes balance. Gaining Romeo's love can save Juliet's life; losing his love can kill her.

- You never play or act the stakes: they arise through the urgent strength of your actions.

9. What are your obstacles?

- An obstacle is anything that is blocking you from getting what you want.

- It is useful to think that there are two types of obstacle: inner and outer.

- Outer obstacles are things like walls, physical distance, the cold, other people and their contrary wants. These are tangible problems which need solving.

- Inner obstacles are things like fear, hatred, love, loyalty, guilt. These are unseen but fiercely felt, and make it hard or even seemingly impossible for you to get what you want.

- Romeo wants to kiss Juliet. In order to do so, he must overcome outer obstacles like the balcony and inner obstacles like his fear of her family.

- Obstacles are measured by the counter-tension in your action. I know the traveller's bag is heavy in his right hand because I see his left arm sticking out to counter-balance its weight. I know his journey ahead scares him by the shallow breath, tight jaw, furrowed brow and tense shoulders that bind that fear. I don't see fear. I see its resistance.

- You never play or act an obstacle: it is the problem. Play the solution.

10. What can you do to overcome those obstacles?

- What physical, psychological and verbal tactics can you employ to get around, over, under or through your obstacles?

You might have to push, charm or cajole something out of the
way to get what you want. These are your actions.

- This is the only bit you act: play the solution, not the problem.
  Play your actions: because they are a consequence of all the
  other questions, they reveal (even if that is because they are
  trying to hide) all that life.

- Acting is problem-solving.

*

It only takes one tiny shift in an element of these given circumstances
to transform you.

Most days, I see the same man. We pass each other every morning
when I leave the house. He is the street-sweeper who works on our
road. He wears a bright yellow high-visibility jacket and pushes a
dust-cart. Each morning he greets me exactly the same way: 'Hey
boss'.

Last week, I met him as I was walking back from work. It was late,
and he was walking home, carrying his high-visibility jacket and without
his dust-cart. Same two faces, same street, different time, one of us
in a different coat. He greeted me in a totally new way: 'Alright mate'. I
was a different man (no longer his boss, now his mate) because he was
not wearing a jacket or pushing a cart. A subtle shift in given circumstances delivers a major transformation of two characters and their
roles – all captured in a single verbal action. Take care to be specific.

Exploration

*The following exploratory exercises can be done outside of
class to build initial comprehension and connection with your
role, opening an initial dialogue between actor and character,
as preparation for later, more detailed work.*

- Tell (or note down in your journal) a story from your own life,
  which demonstrates how you are like your character. Do not

look for ways you like your character, look for ways you *are* like your character. Ask yourself, how am I similar? What do they see like I do? When in the script do they do something that I know I would do too in those circumstances? These likenesses are an excellent starting point for your research into your connection to the character. Your transformation will stretch out from this connection.

- Locate a decision your character takes which makes you think 'Who would do that?!' Whether it is Polyxena leaving her mother and walking willingly to her own death, Medea killing her own children or Nora walking out on hers, you have found a crucial decision which you will need to own and inhabit. Your project is to answer your own reactive question: 'Who *would* do that?' You don't need to answer it yet, but locate the question. And know this: you could do that.

- Select your character's *Desert Island Discs*: the eight pieces of music they would take with them if they were stranded on a desert island (don't be bound by the period of your play). What single luxury would they take with them? What work of literature might they take (you have the Bible and the complete works of Shakespeare already)?

- Write your character's name in the centre of a blank page. Fill the page with the roles they play in society: mother, daughter, writer, teacher and so on. Once you have filled the page with as many roles as you can think of, write next to each role what the character *does* that makes them this. So if you have put Christian, don't write down 'she believes in God', since this is not something she actually *does*. Write actions, e.g. she goes to church, reads the Bible, prays. Now look particularly at any social roles which lack action. How does your character relate to these identities? This opens up the crucial 'What am I?' part of question 1 (Who are you?).

- We rarely think of ourselves as animals. We feel we are different – we have windows, dishwashers, golf, garden hoses … all sorts of odd things. Below is a list of things that we have or do which make us think we are different from cows or pigs.

As I write this, I'm not thinking of other animals which seem to have higher-level functioning (dolphins, chimps, your pet dog):

Opposing thumbs
A free pelvis
Abstract language
Knowledge of death
Emotion memory
Self-consciousness
Recreational sex
Moral conscience
Abstract imagination
Sense of humour
Control over environment
Collective faith systems.

- This list is not scientific: it is about human culture and the story we *tell* of our superiority to other animals. This list describes what makes us *feel* distinct in our humanity. Edit or add to it as part of your process. Interrogate your character's relationship to each of these areas. What is their unique relationship to death, language, humour, recreational sex, faith and so on? You do not need to know the answers yet; simply open a dialogue about your character's unique humanity.

Exercises

These exercises all either prepare text for rehearsals or are exercises which you can do 'off-text' to help explore your character and their journey through the script. They are designed to deepen and extend your relationship to the role, but only ever in the ultimate service of the text. This is crucial: these only have value if they enrich your relationship to the text.

These exercises are not all necessary. I will indicate those which I think particularly important. Again, many of these exercises can be done by an individual preparing at home.

I have broken the exercises into three sections. The first section, 'Find your role', includes exercises which analyse the text for information about your character, in order to answer the ten questions. The second section, 'Build a character', includes exercises which bring your answers to these questions to life. The third section is 'Improvise in role', and this asks you to devise and play scenarios in role (but off-text).

Find your role

All of the exercises included in this section are useful for any role you play, in any script. They ensure that detailed, text-based transformation occurs.

Role lists (timing for this depends on the size of the role and length of play, but putting together one list may take around 30 minutes. It is worth the investment of time)

Open up question 1 and question 5 (Who are you? and What are your relationships?), looking in close detail at your character's social identity and ego, both as projected onto them by others and as they project it out to the world. I think this is crucial to any process.

- Work individually, probably outside of class.
- Make six lists about your character, working carefully through the script to gather all the information you can about the role.

I

- *Make a list of facts about the character.* Go through the script and write out any information which is non-negotiable. This might include age, family relationships, information (not opinions) about appearance, education, work. Note the page or line number when it is said and by whom ('We've been married now for eight years', says Nora to Torvald at the end of *A Doll's House,* for example).
- *Make a list of everything your character says about themselves.* Note the page or line number on which it is said, observing

your character's progressing relationship with themself ('I am so thoughtless!', says Nora at the beginning of the play, for example).

- *Make a list of everything your character says about other people*. Note the page or line number on which it is said, and about whom, arranging the list so you can see the progression of character relationships through the play. You might even separate these lists for each character relationship. Include anything in which your character expresses a clear opinion about another character ('You do look paler, Kristine, and perhaps a little thinner … Poor Kristine', says Nora).

- *Make a list of everything other people say about your character*. Note the page or line number and who says it, observing shifting perceptions of your character through the play. Include anything in which your character is clearly described by another person ('My little bird that fritters', says Torvald of Nora, for example).

- *Make a list of everything your character says about the world*. Note the page or line number, revealing their shifting moral or social attitudes. Include anything in which your character presents a specific world-view or philosophy ('It is gorgeous to have pots and pots of money and never have to worry', says Nora, for example).

- *Make a list of everything the author says about your character*. Note the page or line number. Include any stage direction which describes your character and include adjectives describing behaviour ('cheerfully … playfully … briskly … busily …', describing Nora, for example).

- You could write these lists out in columns which line up next to each other, so you can look at any particular moment in the play and see all six sources at once.

- What do you discover about your character and the journey of your role? What information is newly apparent to you from this close analysis? Reflect on this in your journal.

Unit analysis

Prepare specific and playable offers for a rehearsal, which are drawn from detailed textual analysis. Deal in detail, unit by unit, with questions 6–10. I think this is crucial to any process.

- This is preparation that can be done outside rehearsal. Question your discoveries and offers through rehearsal.

- For every scene, establish the basic given circumstances: where and when you are. Find images which help you connect to the setting and stick them into the facing blank pages of your working script.

- In every unit, establish:

  1 Your previous circumstances (where you have just come from and what you expect for your immediate future)

  2 Your objective (the thing you want to achieve in that unit)

  3 The obstacles in the way of fulfilling that objective (both inner and outer)

  4 Your motive for pursuing it (what this is all for)

  5 Actions (or tactics) you could play to try and get what you want.

- Mark any changes between verse and prose and between distinct modes of address (thou/you; cousin/my worthy Cawdor; Nora/my skylark). Notice punctuation (as definite a psychological gesture by the author as any word, since it suggests rhythm of breath), and all like sounds (e.g. alliteration or rhyme). Notice unexpected vocabulary and 'clever' words (metaphor or simile included). No change in the verbal habit of your character is chance; it reflects a psychological shift. Any imagery marks conscious or unconscious desire. Do not worry if you don't understand what it means yet; simply plot it, so you can return to it more easily later. Notice the shift and it will begin to occur.

- None of what you write (or draw) is going onto a tablet of stone. This is a notebook, in which you scribble ideas and thoughts for yourself about your role. These are offers you can bring into rehearsal. This is not you writing down how you will play the role; you are noting starting points for yourself and opening a specific dialogue between yourself and the script. To remind myself of this, I write in pencil.

Through line (timing depends on the size of the role; I would allow an hour if I were playing Juliet)

Pare the script back to its barest action for your character. Follow your character's line of action and how each step is a reaction to the last event. Bring further clarity and detail to your analysis. Deal with questions 9 and 10 (your obstacles and actions). I think this is crucial to any process.

- Work in pairs.

- Tell the story of your character's journey through the play, event by event. If necessary, do this with the units of the script in front of you.

- The language of this will be 'and because of that'. So you will say what happens to you/what you do in one unit, and then say 'and because of that' before describing the next unit.

- Give as little interpretation as possible: communicate the action as baldly as you can.

- You are aiming to expose the architecture and engineering of the role: how it is put together. Be open to discoveries from this simple reading. For example, Juliet's through line in her first scene (1.3) might be:

  > I am called in by the nurse and because of that
  > I meet my mother and because of that
  > I try to keep the nurse in the room and because of that
  > I have to silence the nurse and because of that
  > My mother tells me she wants me to marry Paris and because of that
  > I say I will obey her will as much as I can and because of that

> The servingman is brought in and announces the guests have
> arrived for the party and because of that
> I leave to meet Paris at the party.

- Reflect on how your character's actions are sequential and reactive, and particularly notice the places where you have found an action which was not 'because of that'. What was it because of, if not the thing that just happened?

Teaching Tip: If you are working with limited time and a very large role, you can do this scene by scene rather than unit by unit. In this version, Juliet's first two acts would read:

> My mother tells me to marry Paris and because of that
> I go to the party and fall in love with Romeo and because of that
> I propose marriage to Romeo and because of that
> I arrange to meet Romeo at Friar Laurence's cell to be married
> and because of that
> I meet Romeo at Friar Laurence's cell to marry him and because
> of that ...

The sense of the journey will be less specific, but the structure of the through line will still be exposed.

If you have more time, start by doing the through line scene by scene, then go unit by unit.

Backstory

Colour your imagination with the memories of your character.
Forge imaginative frames of reference for the events which
precede and predicate the script. Enrich characterization and
substantiate your character's language. Deal with question 3:
Where have you come from and where are you going to? I
think this is crucial to any process.

- This can be done as pre-class work, or done individually in class. It can form the basis for later improvisations and relationship exercises (page 205).

- Writing the basic timeline will take around 20 minutes. Developing it into more detailed descriptions will take longer. It could run over the course of the whole rehearsal process, developing as the work progresses. Doing this in one go usually ends in blocked actors making things up; carrying it through the whole process allows the backstory to grow out of active analysis.

- Using your list of facts about your character (developed in 'Find your role' in this chapter on page 175), build a backstory for your character. The backstory is all the events which precede the play and make your character's action necessary. A backstory is not a biography. A biography will include much that is not directly relevant to the action of the drama – a backstory will not.

- For Nora, a backstory would include experiences from her childhood which made her into her father's doll-child, your answer to the question of where her mother was in her childhood, her father's financial difficulties, meeting Torvald and how he helped her father and so on. For Macbeth, it would include when he met Lady Macbeth, became Thane of Glamis, when the Norwegian wars began, how Duncan became king, when he became friends with Banquo and so on.

I

- As you have done for the whole play already, create a timeline. Draw a long line across a page: at one end is your character's birth; at the other end is your character's first entrance. Mark the events of the backstory onto that timeline in chronological order. Mark down any specific dates, and if the order of events is conjecture, indicate this with colour choice.

- Work with a partner and describe one of these events with your active imagination – tell the story of that moment as if you experienced it. Use the first person and past tense (e.g. 'I walked into the room. The air was cold and dry.'). Detail the sense memories: what you could see, smell, hear, feel, taste.

- Turn the other crucial events into memories, by writing diary entries, letters, or drawing them from your point of view.

- This is not a biography for publication; this is a way for you to explore your character's inner life and landscape of memories.

Build a character

Pick and choose exercises from this section according to the text and role you are working on, and the time available. These exercises will offer value throughout your process – not exclusively before you begin scene work. Some can be wisely employed to deepen or revive your work once you have already begun to work on scenes.

Domains of self-esteem (20 minutes)

Consider your character's self-esteem. This is a simple and playful first step for you to move around a rehearsal room in role. Deal particularly with question 1 (Who are you?), and its triangulating forces: Who do you wish you could be/fear you might be?

- Work as a full group.

- Psychologist Susan Harter asserts that there are five separate areas in which children and teenagers measure themselves, which define their self-esteem:

  1 Scholastic competence: how able the child feels herself to be at school work

  2 Athletic competence: how able the child considers herself to be at sport

  3 Social acceptance: whether the child feels popular with her peers

  4 Physical appearance: how good-looking the child believes herself to be

  5 Behavioural conduct: to what extent the child considers her general behaviour to be acceptable to others

  This is useful as it feels a largely accurate description of how we judge ourselves. For many adults, these domains of self-esteem remain current.

- Line up along one wall.

- Treat the far end of the room as 'Absolutely yes!', the other end as 'No way, not at all!', and every point in between as on a sliding scale between those points.

- Move yourself in space, answering the following five questions by where you put yourself in the space. At the start of the play:

  1 Are you academically competent? (I.e. Do you feel clever?)

  2 Are you a good athlete, are you physically able?

  3 Are you socially popular?

  4 Are you physically attractive?

  5 Is your behaviour generally acceptable to others?

- You can do this same thing answering other questions, or making the five questions above more specific to the world of the play. So in *Macbeth*, question 2 might be adapted to become 'Are you a good warrior?', since this is the physical ability which is most valued in the action of the play.

- Answer these same questions at different points in the play and see how it has changed.

- Answer them about your character as a supposed child, if this doesn't seem impossible in your play.

- Reflect on your choices and discoveries in your working script. Where in the play is this sense of self most relevant?

Greatest victories (15–20 minutes per person)

Visualize your character's main goal (super-objective) and find a strong image of desire which you can propel yourself towards, and an image of defeat from which you can flee. Approach your character's super-objective and open up the stakes in the drama (question 8).

- Work in pairs. If you are working alone, you can do this as a written or drawn exercise.

I

- What is the greatest possible victory your character can conceive at the start of the script? Tell the story of this victory to your partner: in that moment, where are you; what do you see; who else is there; how do you feel; what emotions do you see in others; what will you do next? This is a flashbulb memory, imagined and owned. Detail will trigger sensation.

- Tell the story on your feet, and animate it as much as you dare.

- Your partner can ask questions to help stimulate your imagination, but they must be open questions which do not imply an answer. The story must feed off the actor's imagination, not the listener's.

II

- What is the greatest *impossible* victory your character can conceive at the start of the role? Tell the story to your partner in the same way, in the same detail. Dare to glow with the thrill of this victory as you describe it.

III

- What is the greatest *possible* defeat your character can conceive at the start of the script?

IV

- What is the greatest *impossible* defeat your character can conceive at the start of the script?

- Reflect on this in your working script. Locate the closest you get to that victory and defeat in the course of the play. How is your character's action affected by their proximity to triumph/ disaster?

Super-objectives

Extend the work of the last exercise. Analyse and inhabit your character's central desire or need. It deals with question 6: What do you want? I think this is crucial to any process.

- Work individually. Part I can be done as pre-class work, Part II in a single session over about 20 minutes.

- A super-objective is the main, overarching want which drives your character through the play. Everything your character does is in service of this need. Romeo's whole journey is focused on his need to experience perfect love. This is his super-objective.

- What is the single conscious want (there may well be unconscious wants too, but don't deal with those here) which drives your character through the course of the play? For Macbeth it might be to secure the throne of Scotland. For Lady Macbeth it might be to make her children kings. This is an act of interpretation and will push the play in a particular direction.

- The super-objective should make you want to take definite action. It doesn't need to explain your actions, just focus them. It should inspire you to action. Don't let it begin with a passive verb like 'to be'. 'To be king' is not a possible super-objective since it is passive and will not drive you to action. 'To make myself king' would get you started. Let it begin with a verb that drives you into action towards your target. Keep it as simple as you can.

I

- Write a first draft of your character's super-objective

II

- Physicalize that super-objective. You are looking to find a single, expansive physical gesture which manifests your desire. This will be abstract and is about the private sensation – not a demonstration – of the super-objective.

- Start by creating a space to work in. Your imagination will do most of the work. You might want to use objects to represent your goal – a chair becomes a throne, for example. You might block yourself into a corner behind chairs to isolate yourself, or balance on a chair for a sensation of being on the edge.

- Define an action for yourself. Is the language of the super-objective:

  Grasping and seizing
  Searching and reaching
  Imploring and beseeching
  Possessing and overpowering
  Protecting and nurturing?

- Choose one of the above. Perform the action first in your hand and arm. So, for example, playing Lady Macbeth you might try possessing and overpowering with your hand and arm.

- Now allow your shoulders, head and neck to be part of the action.

- Now engage your whole torso. Don't forget to breathe.

- Now use your pelvis, legs and feet.

- Throughout, allow your imagination, breath and will to be stimulated by the action in your body.

- Explore the tempo of your action: how sustained or sudden it is, how quick or slow.

- Explore the weight of your action: how heavy or light it is.

- You might speak your super-objective aloud as you perform the action, softly at first. If your action is effortful (particularly if you are stretching your neck), be careful not to strain your voice.

- Extend your body fully into this action, until you are radiating with it. This does not necessarily imply great physical effort or strength; you might simply be lightly curled in a ball protecting something precious. I mean to direct you towards great psychological effort and strength of will.

- There is no right or wrong to this, since it is about your sensation. If it gives you energy which propels you towards the will of your character as you currently understand them, then it is valid. The challenge is not to get it right, but to fulfil the action.

- You can adapt this action at any point, and use it to help ignite your will in later scene work. Even the thought of the action can trigger your desire.

Hot seating (10 minutes per person)

Start to speak in role, exploring key character questions. Start taking ownership of the role and access new areas of research (as you discover you don't have answers to pertinent questions).

- You can either work in pairs, questioning each other, or as a full group questioning one actor at a time.

- The format is simple: an actor sits on a chair and answers questions about their character.

- The actor can answer in the first person in role ('I love my husband very much!') or in the third person talking objectively about their character ('I think she hates her husband but is terrified to admit it'). It is important to use the third person sometimes – working in the first person you can get stuck saying things you immediately know aren't true simply out of obligation to the terms of the exercise. Both have value; use both.

- The questions must be focused. Decide on a particular area you want to explore while hot seating: a trigger event, a relationship, a set of beliefs or a key objective. Focus your questions on unwrapping this. Ask questions about the sensations the character felt, what they saw or heard, during a particular event. Ask how other characters make them feel or what they wish they could say to them. Ask about their dreams and fantasies.

- It is easy to get off-piste answering questions about what your character's favourite pizza topping would be. Fun, and perhaps worth it for fun alone, but it's unlikely to unlock the words and world of *Macbeth* for you.

- Remember our direction of travel is deeper; use the questions to mine down. Do not ask questions with implied answers: 'Are you angry with your husband?' (these types of closed question are covert direction and notes from other actors on how to play the role). Ask open questions: 'How does your husband make you feel?'

- At the end of a fixed period (even five focused minutes will offer benefits), take the time to note down reflections on any discoveries you make.

Hans Eysenck's personality traits

Consider the behavioural norm of your character, and explore their potential behaviour patterns. Work with different psychological 'personality types' through which to understand

and access your role. Play with different possibilities within text,
examining question 1: Who are you?

- Work as a full group.

Hans Eysenck was a psychologist working during the twentieth century
in Europe. He defined a model of personality based on two key personality dimensions: extravert/introvert and stable/unstable.

I

- For this exercise you will need lots of paper (A4 size is ideal).
  First write down the four points of Eysenck's personality
  compass in one bold colour, each on a separate piece of
  paper: Unstable, Stable, Extravert, Introvert.

- Place the four points of Eysenck's compass out on the floor,
  with unstable as north, extraverted as east, stable as south
  and introverted as west.

- Now write the following personality traits, in another bold
  colour, each on a separate piece of paper:

touchy	sociable	calm	quiet
restless	outgoing	even-tempered	unsociable
aggressive	talkative	reliable	reserved
excitable	responsive	controlled	pessimistic
changeable	easygoing	peaceful	sober
impulsive	lively	thoughtful	rigid
optimistic	carefree	careful	anxious
active	leadership	passive	moody

- Make a pile of these personality traits on the floor in the middle
  of the room.

- One by one, take a trait and place it where you think it belongs
  on the compass wheel. Is 'carefree' a stable or unstable state?
  Is it extraverted or introverted?

- Remember, this is a provocation that opens a useful dialogue
  around personality. Eysenck's proposal is a useful tool. Treat it
  as such, and adapt it for your own purposes as you work.

- Notice that unstable introverts we call neurotic, and unstable extraverts we call psychotic.

- Notice that the four corners of the compass reflect the four Greek humours, or personality types. North-east on the compass would have been called 'choleric' (angry, irascible) by the Greeks (and Shakespeare); south-east 'sanguine' (easy-going, relaxed); south-west 'phlegmatic' (unpredictable, changing); north-west 'melancholic' (mournful, depressive).

- Compare what you have built with the wheel as Eysenck himself drew it.

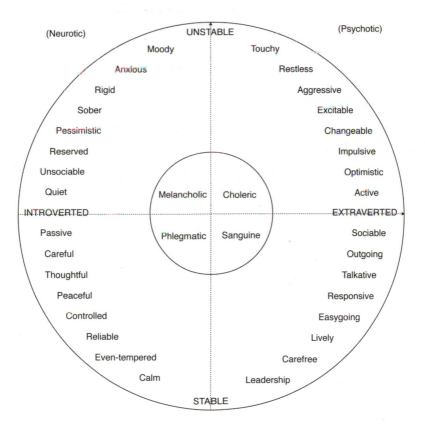

II

- Where would you place your character in their first scene, on this wheel? Eysenck suggests we have dominant traits and temperaments to which we habitually return and which dictate our responses. Do you agree with him?

- Notice that often, when under pressure, people 'flip' across the wheel. So someone who is habitually stable and extraverted (outgoing and sociable), when under pressure may become pessimistic and anxious (retreating into neurosis). Sometimes the quiet, withdrawn person is the one who, under pressure, suddenly becomes aggressive and impulsive; under pressure, the rigid, anxious person may become talkative and lively, and so on.

- Where would you place your character in their final scene?

- Where would you place your character in their moment of greatest crisis?

- What would it be like to play that scene from the opposite point on the wheel?

III

- Try playing a speech or short exchange while moving around this wheel on the floor. Use your physical placement on the compass to condition your reactions (and therefore the specific quality of your actions). Don't move to where you think you should be; find yourself wherever you are and respond accordingly. Keep mobile and allow discoveries to arise.

Characteristics (60 minutes)

Plant your characterization in the world around you. Discover your character's behaviour and choices in their immediate given circumstances, ensuring your work is connected and responsive to the character's environment. Deal with question 1 (Who are you?) and bind it in with your answer to question 2 (Where are you?) and question 5 (What are your relationships?).

- Work individually, as pre-class work, or work on one character in groups of four or five. This is a natural extension of the last 'Personality traits' exercise.

I

- Write a list of characteristics to describe your character in a scene, as they appear to the world (perhaps use Hans Eysenck's list as a starting point).

  In *A Doll's House,* the central character, Nora, has committed fraud in order to borrow money to save her husband's life. Her husband does not know this. At the beginning of the play, she has nearly paid off the debt and thinks she will soon be free of her secret. It is Christmas Eve. For Nora at the beginning of Act 1, among many other things, we might say she seems:

  Outer characteristics
  Cheerful
  Feminine
  Light
  Proud
  Coquettish
  Talkative
  Impulsive.

- See how many characteristics you can write for your character within the scene you are working on; can you write twenty?

II

- Now write the opposite characteristic alongside; so, for example, you might put:

  Outers – Opposites
  cheerful – depressed
  feminine – masculine
  light – heavy

> proud – ashamed
> coquettish – solemn
> talkative – reserved
> impulsive – controlled

- Notice that these opposite characteristics represent the person Nora can or will not be in this scene.

III

- Now write down what inner condition or concealed characteristic you think might be creating this behaviour (the first list of outer characteristics). What inner life prompts the outer life? What private feeling triggers your character's public behaviour? Sometimes the inner life will match the outer life (Nora's husband Torvald is proud simply because he is proud of things he has done). Sometimes the inner life will not match the outer behaviour (you might imagine Torvald is sociable because he is ambitious). So, for example, for Nora you might put:

> **Outer – Opposite – Inner**
> cheerful – depressed – excited
> feminine – masculine – feminine
> light – heavy – nervous
> proud – ashamed – proud
> coquettish – solemn – insecure
> talkative – reserved – lonely
> impulsive – controlled – anxious

Nora, in this interpretation, is cheerful because she is excited about her future; she is impulsive because she is anxious about her past; she is talkative because she is lonely; she is coquettish to conceal her insecurity, and so on.

These are inner states (changeable, not fixed), which can help us discover the specific inner tempo-rhythm and inner life of the scene.

IV

- Now write down what your character sees (imagined or actual targets) in the world around them that makes them behave in the way they do in the scene or act.

  Outer – Opposite – Inner – Target
  cheerful – depressed – excited – her beautiful Christmas tree and all the things she will buy to decorate her house
  feminine – masculine – childlike – a dominating father figure (her husband Torvald)
  light – heavy – nervous – her husband's ignorance of her secret
  proud – ashamed – proud – her husband's good health (which Nora secured)
  coquettish – solemn – insecure – her husband's power and control
  talkative – reserved – lonely – empty chairs
  impulsive – controlled – anxious – her husband's arousal

  So Nora sees her husband's arousal: this makes her anxious and behave in a sudden and impulsive fashion. Nora sees the empty chairs in her beautiful room and feels the loneliness which she manages by chattering away to herself.

  These suppositions may turn out to be misguided, but they mean I will enter rehearsals with offers to share about my character, and offers which have specific and psychologically relevant targets. This connects my work on the character's inner life to the world: it will help me listen and resist the temptation to 'act my character', rather than play my role.

- Your aim is to plant your characterization in other people and the space: see the threat to you, the safe places, the pride and shames of others, the weakness and strengths which transform your behaviour and generate the energy for your behaviour.

Animals

Animal work unlocks compelling psychology and physicality. It can ignite vivid, visceral transformation based on truthful

*insights. Successfully embodied, your audience may never
realize you have done this work. Famously, Marlon Brando's
Vito Corleone in* The Godfather *was based on a bulldog
shot in the throat; Dustin Hoffman's Ratso Rizzo in* Midnight
Cowboy *was a rat; Robert de Niro's Jake La Motta in* Raging
Bull *was a bull, his Max Cady in* Cape Fear *was a cobra; Tom
Cruise's Frank T. J. Mackay in* Magnolia *was a fox. This list
alone speaks for the potential value of this work. It deals with
question 1 and question 10: Who are you? and What can you
do to overcome those obstacles?*

- Work individually.
- This can begin as a pre-class exercise (Part 1) and become
  a 60-minute class exercise. The timing of the final part is
  dependent on the scene.

I

- Look at your character's first scenes.
- What animal would your character be in this scene? Are
  they predator, prey or scavenger? Do they belong on land,
  in the sea or in the air? Are they quick moving or sedentary?
  Make sure your choice is based on suggestions drawn from
  the text.
- Your choice should be based on how your character sees the
  world around them. If they see threats all around them, look
  for prey animals. If they seek company, look for a pack animal.
  If they are an opportunist, always trying to get what they want
  by manipulating other people, perhaps they are a scavenger.
  Do they maintain superior social distance? Perhaps they're a
  gliding bird of prey.
- Be specific about your choice: is Nora a little sparrow or
  starling as Torvald repeatedly suggests, or is she more of a
  horse waiting to be freed into the fields, who has spent her
  life being told she is a bird? Is Lady Macbeth a hooded cobra,
  who winds towards her prey, rears up and widens to spit

and strike down? She would writhe and twist in on herself in madness. If so, does she have eggs in a nest which she is protecting? Or is she a wounded dog, looking for other people's kills to feed off, seeking a pack to protect her and howling to the moon in her final madness?

II

- Work through the basic animal exercise outlined in *Chapter 4* on page 91, using your chosen animal.

- Once you have inhabited the animal and then brought it to human life, begin work with a scene.

III

- With an observer ready to provide feedback, play the opening scene or a speech with this animalization. Dare to be extreme at first and then draw it back to a level where you think an audience might never consciously realize you have done this work.

  If you want to draw this right back, simply imagine your animal is always next to you – like one of Phillip Pullman's daemons in *His Dark Materials* (the talking animals that all the characters have beside them, as a manifestation of their inner lives). Deal with the animal's desire to intervene throughout your scene and the threats they perceive.

- Reflect on what discoveries you made and where else in the script you might take this work. Perhaps it will inform your entire characterization.

Personation

Find sophisticated human transformation, delivering believable and bold characterization. Like the animal work, it deals with questions 1 and 10 – Who are you? and What can you do to overcome those obstacles?

The most famous personations are those of Johnny Depp. Playing Captain Jack Sparrow in *The Pirates of the Caribbean*, he based his characterization on the Rolling Stones guitarist Keith Richards. As Willy Wonka in *Charlie and the Chocolate Factory*, he based his characterization on Michael Jackson. Mike Leigh's work all begins with his actors choosing someone they know to base their character on.

- For this exercise, follow the same process as in the 'Animals' exercise, and allow similar timings. Part I can be a pre-class exercise, Parts II and III can spread across two sessions, or follow each other, each taking around 30–40 minutes.

- Crucially, these are not impersonations. The actor finds the rhythms, vocal habits and physical tensions of someone real, which facilitate a truthful connection with the character's experiences and actions. This should be embedded deeply enough in your transformation that the audience never consciously sees the personation.

I

- Start from your family and work out. Do you know anyone whose behaviour and outer characteristics could serve your transformation here?

- Think first of people you know best – perhaps guardians, parents, brothers, aunts and uncles, cousins. Then think of friends – excluding anyone in the rehearsal room.

- If there's no-one obvious in this circle, then look to people you know less intimately. Are there teachers, colleagues or neighbours you could reference?

- If there's no-one in this wider circle, then turn to famous people, whom you could easily research and study online. Might the characteristic public behaviour patterns of Woody Allen, Princess Diana, Barack Obama or Simon Cowell enrich your work in the scene?

- Are they a political visionary, artist and evangelist – a Bob Dylan or Joni Mitchell figure? Are they an ambitious, passionate absolutist and authoritarian – a Margaret Thatcher or

Mother Theresa? A laid-back, easy-going charmer – like the archetypes played by Owen Wilson and Will Smith, or the Fonz in the TV show *Happy Days*? And so on.

- Once you've chosen someone, observe them and study their physicality, as with the animal. Study their spine, their habitual tensions, their vocal habits and placement. What is their habitual gaze? Princess Diana had that famous 'from behind the fringe' upward gaze; Simon Cowell often looks down over his nose in a 'looking down on you' pose. How do they use their fingers? How much tension is there in their shoulders? How wide is their stance? What is the rhythm of thought, and the tempo and rhythm of speech? And so on.

II

- In class, and after a physical stretch and warm-up, go through a similar process to that with the 'Animals' exercise, adopting the physicality and behaviour of the person in question. You might choose a simple physical task to perform in order to focus the physicality. Perhaps stacking chairs, moving bags into a corner, arranging shoes by colour … anything that can provide you with a focus for your action. It need not have an appropriate psychological context at the moment – it is simply something for you to be doing as you explore this transformation.
- Do explore simple text – a line from the scene, or perhaps a few words (yes/no/naming objects) – as you work.

III

- Explore this transformation by playing the first scene or a particular speech and bring it to the particular challenge of these units.
- Allow yourself a true rehearsal: do fail. Go too far at first in your search for extreme truth, then draw back as necessary. Always ask: How does this transformation serve the text? How does it affect the way I see the world and interact with other people and objects? How does it serve the relationships within the

scene? If it reveals more than it disguises, then it is probably worth pursuing.

- Reflect on this as you work forward, writing up or sketching your learning into your journal.

Teaching Tip: This can be particularly helpful to do if you are playing a historical or mythological character – a Cassandra, Antigone or Queen Anne, for example. It is easy to lose their immediate humanity beneath their mythological or social status.

Improvise in role

These exercises ask you to improvise scenarios in role, in order to expand and deepen your work on text. They can be of use at any point in the process – both before and during your work rehearsing scenes. They are often most useful when employed to add depth as you tackle a scene.

Shared memories (20 minutes)

Bring rich imaginative detail to the landscape of a character relationship. It quickly and simply brings two actors together in an imagined relationship. Add depth to your work on the text.

- Work in pairs, with an actor playing a role with whom your character has a rich history. For example, the actors playing Romeo and Mercutio might do this together.

- If time is short, you can do Part I in class, and let Part II be completed as homework in which you write letters (or emails) to each other describing the moments and sensations you've explored. It can be fun to really post these – a letter landing on your doorstep from Mercutio is obviously a delight.

I

- Sit back to back, with your spines touching. Close your eyes if you want to. Feel the warmth of contact with your partner's spine and ease into that contact. Be aware of the breath moving into your partner's body. Release with your partner.

- Imagine (or rather, remember) a moment from your shared character history when you were together and felt safe with each other.

- Find the sensory detail of that moment, and allow the sensation of it into your breath and your spine, through your mind's eye.

- Where were you? What could you see? What could you smell and hear? What did you feel? What emotions could you see on the other person's face? What words did you speak or did you want to say in that moment?

- Breathe with the memory of this sensation and share the breath with your partner through contact between your spines.

- Now – with the same sensory detail, and focusing on finding the shared breath of that moment – remember a moment when you were together and felt fear.

- Now, still in silence and working with rich imagination, remember a moment when you were together and felt anger.

- Now remember a moment of joy.

- Now remember a moment of surprise or shock.

- Breathe with each of these memories.

II

- Once you have completed this, open your eyes and turn to your partner. Share the memories you found. Tell each other what you now remember of your relationship – describe moments and sensations that your partner has 'forgotten'. Whatever your partner describes, imagine it with them and make it another shared memory.

- Reflect on this in your working script. How and specifically where might these memories enrich the text?

Object exercise (20 minutes each)

Build on the work you have already done on traits, characteristics and relationships, taking these into action. It is an initial rehearsal exercise to help explore your transformation. Make a simple first sketch of your character. Bring your work on all the ten questions together.

- Work with a partner. Each student will need to prepare (as detailed in Part I of this exercise) before class.

I

- Choose a particular couple of characteristics you want to explore in your character, which will stretch you. For example, you might want to explore 'controlled' and 'ambitious' for Torvald.

- Define a specific and simple physical objective. This will give you a set of physical actions which work towards a defined and psychologically necessary objective for your character, through which you can explore these characteristics. So, for example, if you are playing Torvald Helmer you might be writing the letter to dismiss Krogstad from his position in the bank, or dressing to go to work the morning after your promotion. Both these scenarios will allow you to explore his controlled and ambitious persona.

- Make sure you have answered the ten questions in detail.

- Plant the outer characteristics in external targets: ambition is found in Torvald's picture of his father on his desk; control comes from his expensive, neatly worn cuffs and tie.

- To deepen and enhance this work, do the following:

    1   Give yourself an imagined environment to work in that stimulates your senses (heat, chill, humidity, noise, silence …).

    2   Define the Laban effort action of your character's inner and outer states. What are your inner and outer tempo-rhythms? What is your breath pattern?

3 Plan a conscious means to stimulate this energy state in yourself. Perhaps plan an exercise from Chapter 1 to centre yourself, and Laban or tempo work described in Chapter 4 to enliven an inner rhythm. Perhaps trigger your will with an endowment or sense memory exercise from Chapter 2, or perform a simple physical exercise – running up some stairs to make breathing more necessary and urgent, spinning yourself dizzy if you want to feel off-centre and a little lost – or drunk. Be imaginative and find modes of play which can transform your body, breath, mind and will.

II

- Set up a space to work in, with any necessary objects or endowed substitutes for those objects.

- Use your planned preparation and then immediately pursue the objective.

- Remember an exercise is neither a performance nor a rehearsal. You are playing an exercise, so repeat it many times if you want, as you explore and discover more about your role and the behaviour of your character in this scenario and relationship.

- This is like a pianist's scales or a dancer at the bar. This is a way to step towards your role and discover transformation through relationships (with an object in this case).

III

- Ask your partner for feedback on what they saw. The feedback should be simple and neither interpretative nor critical: as the observer, simply say what you saw happening in the actor's body. Don't interpret that behaviour, simply witness and reflect it.

- Allow the actor to learn from your observation; do not try and directly teach them. You might comment on breath patterns, physical tensions, vocalized breath, outer tempo-rhythms or Laban effort actions, unexpected movements or 'shadow moves' (physical actions which reveal inner life, despite a prevailing effort to disguise it).

- Allow time for private reflection afterwards, making notes or drawings in your working script on what you have discovered. Reflect on whether and how you found the preparation useful to playing the exercise.

Teaching Tip: For a more efficient process, you can have everyone doing object exercises at once, and provide ongoing feedback yourself as the actors work, guiding their transformation.
This offers less peer-learning, but can deliver a more efficient rehearsal.

Trigger events

Bring to life the key event which drives your character into the play. Provide impetus for your scripted character action. Feed rich, shared imagery into the action.

- Preparation and Part I will take around 20–30 minutes; Part II will need to be done as preparation between sessions; Part III will take 30 minutes per improvisation.

- Using the list of facts and backstory, select the key trigger event for your character, which is unseen in the action of the play. This is the defining event in your character's backstory, without which none of the action of the play could happen. For Nora, this might be the moment she signed her name to borrow the money to save Torvald's life. For Romeo it might be breaking up with Rosaline.

- Explore this moment in further detail.

I

- Work with a partner and tell the story of that moment from your character's point of view.

II

- With a partner (or partners), prepare an improvisation of this moment.
- Answer the ten questions together. Prepare the space as fully and realistically as your resources will allow. Perhaps plan an exercise to stimulate your mind, body and will before you begin the improvisation (as discussed in 'Object exercise', page 199).

III

- When you are ready, improvise this event, with the rest of the group watching to provide appropriate feedback about behaviour.
- Remember, of the ten questions, we will only see the answer to question 10: What can you do to overcome those obstacles? Do it.
- Allow yourselves the right to try it a couple of different times in different ways to uncover its potential.
- Allow time for reflection on the discoveries made through this exercise. Make notes in your working script and add any images that you have discovered to the text.

Character relations (5–10 minutes per character in the chair)

Make character transformation a product of character relationships. Explore how different physical dynamics reflect different psychological relationships. Explore different possibilities within relationships.

- Work as a full group. The exercise is non-verbal (though that doesn't mean it is silent).

I

- Sit an actor in role, in a chair in the centre of the room. This person need only be open to what is going on around them.
- The rest of the group will explore their relationships with the character in the chair, at the point they first encounter them in the play.
- Everyone find a metaphor for what you see when you look at the character who is in the chair: perhaps you see someone rotting, someone radiating sunlight and warmth, a slug, someone covered in cobwebs or a great, warm teddy bear.
- See this metaphorical image as real now.
- Move around the room, balancing the space.
- As you move through the space, let yourself see only that character and the space. Your movement through the space will be conditioned by their presence.
- Explore moving closer to them or further from them; explore being behind them or next to them. Explore how you feel when you are near them. Allow your imagination to stimulate your senses. Be aware of their smell (as you imagine it), what new detail you see as you get closer to them, how they might colour the air around them. Viscerally inhabit rich, sensory imagery.
- Allow them to affect and transform you because of how you see and experience them in your imagination. Demonstrate nothing; experience the sensations generated by proximity to this person as you see them.

II

- When you have explored this, put another character in the chair and do the same work.
- Explore the relationships at different points in the script: do the same exercise as the characters see each other at the end of the play.
- Reflect on the experience of this. How were you transformed in the chair, simply by how everyone else viewed you? How

were you transformed in the space, simply by how you saw someone? Did this experience uncover something of your role – of what and who these relationships make you?

> *Teaching Tip:* Keep actors focused on the power of the image they are working with, simply exploring different physical relationships to the character in the chair. It will really help to keep this simple. Guide actors away from demonstrating anything self-consciously – no-one needs to be shown what they are seeing, feeling or thinking. Don't let this go on too long with each character, or it can become self-indulgent.

Relationship exercise

Explore a key relationship for your character which is not explored in the text. Add dimension and depth to your characterization. Connect more vividly with the world of your character. Again, this brings all the ten questions together.

- Split this work across two sessions. Part I can be done as pre-class preparation. Allow 20–25 minutes for Part II. Part III should then be prepared as pre-class work. Allow 35–40 minutes for Part IV.

I

- Select a relationship in the play which is not directly explored in the plot, but which is crucial to your character and their story. For Nora and Torvald this might be their relationships with their fathers. For Lady Macbeth and Macbeth this might be their relationship to each other before they lost their child. For Romeo and Juliet this might be Romeo's relationship with Rosaline and Juliet's with Tybalt (we never see them together).

These relationships are implicitly or directly referred to in the play, and underpin many of the choices the characters make or avoid making in the action of the drama.

- Go through the script and write down any relevant facts and opinions on this relationship. Write them down in the order in which they appear in the play and note who gives this information/opinion (how trusted is the source?).

- What do you learn about the relationship? What key influence does this relationship have over the choices your character makes?

II

- If the relationship is with a character not in the action of the script (e.g. Rosaline), do this next. If you are working with a character in the play already (e.g. Tybalt) then you can skip this stage.

- Find a partner to play the other person in that relationship.

- Share your list of facts and opinions with that actor.

- How does that person make your character feel? How do you think your character makes them feel?

- Your partner should ask questions as you answer these two crucial questions, uncovering more detail about the relationship.

- Describe the other character as your character sees them. Use characteristics to do so (see the *Eysenck* exercise (page 187) for a list of possible characteristics if you need help here).

- If this person were an animal, what animal would they be in your character's eyes?

- Find a simile to describe the experience of being close to this person. Are they like a twin to you? Does it feel as if they are always wearing armour or carrying a deadly weapon? Are they like a source of light and warmth? Does being in a room with them feel like being with cockroaches?

- All this is about how your character sees and experiences the other person, not how you (the actor) see them.

III

- Define a scenario – either one mentioned in the text, or one which seems pertinent to the relationship. This will be a scenario you can prepare and improvise. It does not need to be a verbal exchange; it must involve you sharing a space with that other character.

- Perhaps the teenage Nora is wrapping Christmas presents while her father silently works at his desk. Perhaps Torvald is telling his father he plans to marry Nora. Perhaps Rosaline is breaking up with Romeo.

- Answer the ten questions for this scenario.

- Plan an exercise you can use to prepare your mind, body and will.

- Prepare the room so you have whatever basic furniture you need for the improvisation.

- When you are ready, begin the improvisation – play your actions. Do not divert from the objective unless you are driven to do so by something your scene partner does or says.

- Remember, as ever, that this is an exercise and not a rehearsal or a performance. You are here to learn about your role, so allow yourself the right to experiment, and repeat the exercise or moments from it, if you feel it will help.

- Reflect on this exercise. What sensations did you experience? How were you transformed? Who did you become – the person you fear you might be, or wish you could be? Something else entirely?

- Analyse your discoveries, being prepared to realize you found something completely unexpected: don't head home disappointed like Christopher Columbus because you didn't find what you expected and failed to see the potential in what you did find.

Follow-up

These deepen and extend the work of the exercises away from the rehearsal room, providing simple routes for ongoing character discovery.

- Make your journey into class or rehearsal, seeing the world as your character sees it. This is not about being fully 'in character' (e.g. Lady Macbeth doesn't need to be lost in the twenty-first century), it is about seeing through their eyes. Let a quality of seeing transform you: perhaps all Lady Macbeth will be able to see is other mothers and their children; perhaps Torvald will see how well dressed other men are. Reflect on the sensations and tensions of this quality of seeing.

- Draw your character's first drawings as a child: of their family, of their home, of their bedroom. These are naive but honest depictions of their foundational view of the world. What do family, home and a safe place look like to them at this stage of their development?

- Visualize your character's journey through the rituals of their day: waking, washing, dressing, eating, travelling, working and so on. First do so with your passive imagination: picture all this happening to someone else. Now do so with your active imagination: picture all this happening to you, engaging your sensory imagination to piece together the feelings of these experiences.

- Write your character biography. This can include detail not included in the backstory. It will be an expansion on your character's backstory and allow your imagination free reign, as you add colour and texture beyond the realms of the drama. This is not a crucial part of the process (the backstory is that); this is exploratory play which can unlock a more intimate relationship between you and the character.

- What dreams might your character have? Think of dreams as a realm in which wishes and fantasies can be fulfilled, and fears become realized. Draw images from your character's dreams (you might look at the art work of Salvador Dalí, Ann Hamilton or others for inspiration). If you don't want to draw, make a collage of pictures cut from newspapers and magazines. You might extend this into classwork by performing or telling the stories of elements of these dreams.

- Make a self-portrait as your character. This could be in any style. Will it be like a surrealist Dalí painting? Will it be cubist like a Picasso portrait? Will it be a still life of objects that make you who you are? An image of a tiny face peering out of the window of a huge mansion? This is about the process of making more than what you produce. It probably won't be worth selling, but it will be worth making.

- Answer some of the 100 questions for your character (see Appendix 1).

Further reading

Vanessa Ewan's movement workshop on Nora in *A Doll's House* using animal work and others of these techniques can be seen at www.nationaltheatre. org.uk/video/movement-direction-creating-character

Alfreds, Mike (2007), *Different Every Night.* Nick Hern Books. Part 4, 'The Work: Rehearsal, Production, Performance; Strand One – The Text; Strand Two – Character'.

Hagen, Uta (1973), *Respect for Acting.* Wiley Publishing. Part 3, 'The Play and the Role'.

Merlin, Bella (2007), *The Complete Stanislavsky Toolkit.* Nick Hern Books. Part 2, 'Rehearsal Processes: Embodying the Role'.

Stanislavski, Konstantin, trans. Jean Benedetti (2008), *An Actor's Work.* Routledge. Chapter 15, 'The Supertask, Throughaction'.

8

THE JOURNEY

Learn to truthfully inhabit and play a role within a scene with dynamic freedom.

Framework

The exercises in this chapter are not intended to form the basis of a rehearsal process; they are exercises for you to work through at specific moments of block. They are built on the premise that there are not good or bad actors, but simply actors who are more or less inhibited in their facility to play varied, whole-hearted, courageous action. Use these exercises as tools to unlock scenes from specific inhibition.

*

Let's consider why and how we rehearse, since these exercises are designed for rehearsal rooms. The objective of rehearsals is to deliver specific, clear, truthful storytelling to the stage or screen by a specific date.

We mostly serve this objective by getting up and playing about with units and scenes together, in different imaginative ways. When assessing work, look at five specific elements – each of which has been closely worked on already in this workbook. They are the coordinating forces of a rehearsal. Assess:

Given circumstances (time, environment and situation)

Relationships

Objectives (including actions)

Events (including reactions)

Tempo-rhythm.

Assess these elements for their properties of:

Clarity

Specificity

Focus

Truth.

These will define the language of rehearsal. Combine the elements to create relevant questions. Is the focus of your action specific? Is the event and its reaction clear? Is the circumstance of place specific? Is the tempo-rhythm of your action truthful?

As you assess, continue to tackle the five key skills we addressed in Part One, 'The Actor'. Is there an inhibiting personal tension you must relinquish? Is there an imaginative leap you have not made to bring you into your given circumstances? Do you lack free presence? Is there an adaptive transformation that still needs to occur? Are you playing unfulfilled action? Relinquish, imagine, arrive, adapt, play.

The rehearsal room must deliver permission for risk-taking. First establish the four rules of play: ask first, be honest, follow the rules, admit when you're wrong.

Below are seven guiding principles which can further help in rehearsal:

1 *The text is God*
    In rehearsal, what we rely on is the text. The text will be the mediator of any conflict. The text (not the imagined audience, the director's will or the actor's instinct) will explain and define our choices. It is the field we are ploughing, it is the steady focus of all our resources, it is the mediator of all action.

2 *Fear is the devil*
    Within rehearsal, the main obstacle will be fear. Shame, pride, guilt, vanity and, especially, control will rear their heads. But they are the many heads of one monster. Each of these is

an articulation of fear: fear of not being worthy of connection in some way (with a scene partner, collaborator or imagined audience). Learn to recognize and acknowledge the monster, but do not tolerate it: it will kill off play, defeat discovery and drive you to chase immediate outcomes and the reassurance of praise.

Make rehearsals infertile ground for fear. Or better still, feel the fear and do it anyway.

3 *Make time*

The higher the stakes (the value of whatever can be gained or lost in any moment), the less time we seem to have available. There is never enough time to avert a car crash.

Lower the stakes of rehearsal wherever possible, in order to make more time. Rehearsals are not somewhere for hyperbole, which raises the stakes and hurries time along. Words like: Brilliant! Amazing! Terrible! A disaster! unhelpfully raise the stakes around our work, accelerating time and intensifying pressure. Rehearsal requires specificity.

The rhythm of rehearsal is gradual and steady. Rehearsal is about carefully, confidently chipping away at our materials (body, space, time, text) to reveal scenes, like Michelangelo revealing David from his block of marble. The direction of travel is deeper, further into the material until we find life.

Patience, long-term thinking and precision of focus are rehearsal's best friends. Your precise focus need only ever be the next confident step towards sustainable, durable solutions. A rehearsal room is not usually a home for epiphany. Rehearsals are not defined by flashes of inspiration. These may happen, but they are not what we rely on or pursue.

It will take all the time you have (no matter how long you have) to reach readiness to open your work to a public audience. So make time.

4 *Facilitate don't justify*

Your choices in rehearsals are about *facilitating* the scripted actions of your characters, not justifying or defending those actions. Aim to make character action absolutely necessary. That doesn't mean psychoanalytic understanding of motive is irrelevant; it means it is useful only when it makes action vital, immediate, necessary. Understanding of character may be necessary, but it is not the goal. The aim is to inhabit and enact, as fully and richly as possible, all that your role demands.

5 *Make a friend of ignorance*
Understanding can be useful, but more important to rehearsal is ignorance. Build a rehearsal room with a healthy relationship to not-knowing. We spend our lives negotiating our ignorance, and rehearsal rooms must embrace the unending horizon line of that ignorance. 'I don't know' is a welcome phrase. Find its function through its natural ally: 'So let's explore'.

6 *Don't let the audience in too soon*
Be alert to the intrusion of the audience in rehearsals. Our work is only validated by the subjective response of our audience; but since this response is subjective it is deliciously beyond our control. Do not try and manage what you cannot control – that's fear intervening. Inviting the audience too early into the language of rehearsal will breed self-consciousness and feed fear.

The only relevant question which involves the audience is one of clarity. For an audience, the only truth is the truth they can see and hear. The physical condition of your character, the words they speak or sounds they make, will communicate everything. Anything uninhabited simply does not exist. Make it clear, and otherwise let the audience wait until you need them.

7 *Collaborate*
Rehearsals require collaboration. Be explicit about what the terms and objectives are in every rehearsal, in order to liberate collaboration. Let people know why they are in the room.

Crucially, hold onto the fact that the work is never about you. Actors exist to inhabit metaphors for our audience's lives and experiences. The work is about the audience and their potential, seen through you. They are not looking at you, they are looking through you. Work together for the benefit that is greater than any of you alone.

You cannot rehearse alone. You cannot rehearse on known territory. Find allies and go on an adventure together, in service of the text – the guardian of the story.

Exploration

These exercises are designed as possible starters for a rehearsal, encouraging collaboration and play – the basic attitudes required in rehearsal.

- Play 'Shared count' on page 83 (counting to twenty as a group in a random order, never more than one person speaking at a time) and then let this grow into Shared speech on page 84, using the text of a scene or speech you are working on. Do not get hung up on whose line is whose; speak the text all together in a random order. Your aim is to achieve an intense quality of listening and connection with the text in the circle. You can certainly do this with script in hand.

- Play 'Rounds of applause on page 65 (passing a clap around the circle in a random order, and then in a predetermined order as if it were random). You will need to know the text to play this. Pass the text of a scene between you rather than a clap. Play your own lines in the scene, sending the text across the space or circle with clear physical gestures which deliver the lines to someone else. Every line should be thrown and also received with a clear gesture. Even if you have a long speech, every line needs to be separately thrown to and received from someone specific: *one line, one breath, one thought, one action*.

- Go fishing with a speech. Speak a speech your character has, but use it to go fishing for an idea. You will need to know the text to do this. Imagine you have a fishing rod: use the first line or two of the speech, which establish its basic thesis, to cast out your line. Use the rest of the speech to slowly draw the line in. Is there a particular moment when the fish (whatever you want) bites? Draw the fish in, and finally land it on the final thought(s) of the speech. This works best with speeches like those in Shakespeare, Shaw or Restoration texts: any speech with a clear argument.

- Play tennis with a scene. You will need to know the text to do this. Whichever of you starts the scene, serve an imaginary ball across the imaginary net. Each line is a return shot to try and beat your opponent. When is a point scored and a new serve required? When is a game won? Which shots send you dashing across the court at full stretch, or leave you with an easy slam shot? This works well with quick-fire, passionate, muscular exchanges like those in David Mamet, Arthur Miller or Edward Bond.

- Physicalize the imagery in a speech or scene. Imagine you paint the images as you speak them. Let images flow onto an imaginary canvas as you speak, painting a landscape or scene of images. If you are working on a scene, you might hold your scene partner's hand and paint with their hand, guiding their listening as you go.

- Physicalize the verbs. First go through the text and pick out all the verbs in the speech or scene. Every time you reach a verb, perform it with your body. Don't demonstrate the verb (quoting its action, indicating what it means with a superficial gesture): commit to it fully in your body.

- Play the scene sitting on two chairs facing each other. There are three physical modes available to you in this exploration: you can stand on the chair, sit on it or sit on the floor at its feet. Explore status/control within the scene, by taking different positions in relation to each other on the chairs. You cannot move the chairs closer to each other: all movement is up or down in relation to your scene partner.

- Work with a simple secondary physical activity throughout the scene or speech: eat an apple through its course. This will create a focus for your physical energy which will achieve a quality you might find liberating. It will make speaking more deliberate (because you'll have a mouthful of fruit!).

Exercises

I have split these exercises into three sections. The first section, *'Actions and objectives'*, outlines exercises to unlock truthful behaviour.

The second section, *'Inner life'*, presents exercises which unlock inner life as the source of this behaviour. The third section, *'Key modes of rehearsal'*, outlines ways of working with text which can be useful throughout a process.

Actions and objectives

No, yes but, yes and ...

Open up the dramatic action of every line in a scene, exploring how each line moves the scene on and negotiates its conflict. This will be particularly useful for a scene with quick-fire exchanges like Mamet, Bond or even Miller.

- Work with your scene partner(s).
- Allow time for two iterations of the scene and reflection.
- Play the scene, but before each line say either 'No', 'Yes but' or 'Yes and'. Every line either affirms, counters or blocks.
- Specify the most basic action within each line. Don't allow yourself simply to say 'Yes': this won't move the scene forward. Every line extends the scene in a new direction.
- Now play the scene again, without adding the words, but feeling the impulse of extension or resistance within each line.

Teaching Tip: You might play the 'Yes and' exercise (page 31) as a preparation for this.

Say it and play it

Focus on line-by-line action and shifting tactics. This can form the basis of much rehearsal, putting the emphasis on specificity and targeted precision.

- Work with your scene partner(s).

- Allow 15 minutes for the set-up and evaluation of this exercise, plus 5–10 minutes per page of text. The timing for this exercise is, inevitably, rather flexible, depending on how closely you choose to interrogate. I would promote moving reasonably quickly and not getting stuck into discussion with an exercise like this. It's not about getting it right, it's about opening the scene to more specific choices.

- Before beginning the exercise, take 5 minutes to review the vocabulary of Laban effort actions, and have a reminder of active verbs: do a brief word association using only active verbs.

- An active verb is a doing word which is about changing someone else. It will be most easily differentiated from other verbs because it never needs an extra little word to make sense: so – I slap you, I charm you, I tease you, but not – I run to you, I climb on you, I spit at you. Notice how those little extra words (to, on, at – prepositions) make it about changing your own behaviour, not changing your scene partner's.

- Play the scene, but say what action you are playing and to whom, before each line. So, in *The Glass Menagerie*, Amanda's line 'Why do you go to the movies so much Tom?' could become 'I admonish you, why do you go to the movies so much Tom?', or 'I shake you, why do you go to the movies so much Tom?', or even 'I mock you, why do you go to the movies so much Tom?'

- Crucially, you are stating the action of the line, but also playing it. Do not speak coldly, speak with the ferocious energy of that action fulfilled.

- Allow yourself to search for specificity if you need to, but don't worry if your word choice doesn't quite fit in the dictionary

– why not 'I shrimp you', or 'I snuggle you', as long as everyone involved understands exactly what shrimping and snuggling are? It might not exactly fit into a dictionary, but it doesn't need to. It needs to fit into a rehearsal and make more specific truth of the line you are playing. Allow failure.

Teaching Tip: At its least helpful, this sends the actor into their head as they start thinking about this too much. It can be useful to lead this exercise into the more physical 'Effort actions on the line' (page 221) or 'Inners out' (page 234) if it starts to inhibit the actor's action rather than specify and free it.

Objective truth

Connect directly with a scene's central emotional conflict. It works very well with duologues in which one character has a strong driving objective which the other character is desperately negotiating, e.g. the final exchanges between Desdemona and Othello in Othello. *Bring the objectives to the heart of the scene, connecting language directly to this action.*

- Work with your scene partner(s).
- Allow time enough for 5 minutes of set-up and 5 minutes reflection, along with an iteration of the scene or sequence.

|

- Select a sequence of units or a scene.
- Isolate the objectives. For example, for Nora and Torvald in the final sequence of Act 3, you might say at its simplest that Torvald wants Nora to stay. Let Torvald's only words become 'No, I need you to stay'.

- Nora will play her scripted lines, Torvald will only speak the words 'No, I need you to stay' back to her (and none of his scripted lines). The actor playing Torvald need not use these new words only where he has scripted lines; they can be spoken whenever necessary within the unit or sequence.

- Let the format for this sentence always be 'no' plus objective. This is an active provocation. So other examples could be: 'No, I need you to hold me'; 'No, I need you to leave'; 'No, I forgive you'.

- Play the scene with this extreme rewrite. The actor playing Torvald shall invest fully in the range of meanings he can communicate through this simply stated need. The actor playing Nora shall make herself vulnerable to his explicitly stated objective, and its intransigence. See how far through the scene this single conflict will carry you.

II

- After you've played the scene like this, return to the original text and play the scene again. Anytime you need or want to, return to speaking the explicit need ('No, I need you to stay') to drive you to its heart. Your director or teacher might also call it in from the side, to remind you of the scene or unit's motor.

This exercise is a gift for both actors. For the actor playing Nora, her shifting tactics will gain an urgency and drive in the face of an explicit and unbending counter-objective. For the actor playing Torvald, the range of physical tactics he will play will grow as he communicates through fixed, limited language. When he returns to the original text, its vivid function and necessity will be more richly felt.

III

- Switch and play the scene the other way round – so Torvald speaks the written text, Nora speaks only her need – perhaps 'No, I need to leave'.

Effort actions on the line

Bring a dynamic and physical precision to action playing within a scene. Make language a physical act. This is particularly useful for scenes which are lacking physical animation.

- Select a unit or short sequence of units. Allow time for several (three or four) iterations of these units or the scene.
- Revise the physical vocabulary of the Laban technique. It might help to have the eight basic efforts written up on the wall, each on a separate piece of paper, for reference throughout the exercise.

I

- Play or read the scene, and physicalize different effort actions on each of your lines: one thought, one breath, one line, one action. So you might dab, press, wring, or slash with a hand, arm or leg as you play a line, and so on. Allow your physicality into the language of the unit, i.e. don't hold your breath as you do this.
- Because this is a rehearsal, allow yourself the right to try several different iterations of a unit physicalizing different effort actions. Obviously, take care not to hurt your scene partner(s) – wring the air around them or punch an object onto which you transfer that impulse.
- Discover specific effort actions for each line, which move the unit on in a useful, provocative way. But feel free to keep changing and exploring other choices.

II

- Now play the unit without explicitly physicalizing the effort action, but keeping this effort vividly within the quality of the language.

Teaching Tip: For physically confident actors, free this exercise from the confines of Laban's vocabulary. Simply ask actors to physicalize their actions on every line. For less confident actors, focus this physicalizing onto the hands only – so wring, dab, push and so on with only your hands and fingers.

A chamber opera

Play a greater range of actions, exposing moments of generalization. Bring greater expressive force to language. This will work best with a scene you have already been working on for a while, and which you know well. Refresh a scene and open up new possibilities. Make a scene sing.

- Work with your scene partner(s). Allow twice as long as it usually takes to play the sequence.

- Select a sequence of units or a scene, in which you feel you are generalizing or want to explore more vivid psychophysical choices.

- Sing the sequence or scene as a piece of musical theatre. Improvise melody, rhythm and tempo to express the thought and feeling of the need within each line.

- Don't think musical theatre has a distinct style (so don't start hamming it up and gesturing wildly, in a parody of musical theatre). Musical theatre is simply theatre in which people's emotions and needs are so extreme that they must sing to fully communicate them. Think Bjork, Jason Robert Brown or Stephen Sondheim.

- By singing, you are forced to make more definite choices about which words have value (they are rhythmically sustained, or sit apart in pitch). You can't hit every word with equal value, or if you do the line will fall into droning monotony and that generalization will be exposed.

- Singing a line forces you to locate where the thought really lies in that line (Which word is the top note? Which is most sustained?). It will also expand your physicality, as your breath goes deeper to fulfil the requirements of singing.

- If you are feeling brave, you can record this and listen back to evaluate where in the scene you are generalizing. It will soon be obvious: the musical line will flatten out in rhythm and pitch, or alternatively every word will be stressed and the line overdramatized, losing clear sense.

- Play the scene again, not singing this time, but feel the musical range available to you in spoken text, and the proximity of heartfelt speech to song.

Listen to me

Make language immediately active in the face of the simplest obstacle: people not listening. Put a simple and direct energy into text, making language urgent and transformative. Stop a speech being a speech: make it a conversation.

- Allow time for the equivalent of three iterations of the chosen speech.

- Work as a full group to explore a key speech in the script.

- One person play a speech. The rest of the group, don't listen. Give yourselves an independent activity to get on with – packing your bag to leave the class, stacking chairs, clearing up, polishing your shoes … anything which you can focus on rather than the actor playing their speech. Imagine somewhere else you need to get to (though this should not give you an objective which is more powerful than that of the actor with the speech): go if you complete your activity and the actor with the speech hasn't persuaded you to listen.

- Actor, get their attention. You cannot touch them: use your words to reach and engage them. You can move around the room, but you must be using the speech to change these people into listeners.

- Remember, they can hear you: you don't need to be louder.
  They're not listening. Make them listen to what you need
  to say.

Punctuation as action

*Alert yourself to detailed action implied by authorial
punctuation. This is particularly useful with contemporary
or twentieth-century text in which punctuation is used very
deliberately and creatively by authors.*

- Work with your scene partner(s). Allow 5 minutes to set up and
  5 minutes for evaluation, plus time 4–5 minutes per page of
  text.

- Punctuation is an author's rhythmic tool. They use it to
  suggest breath, and specific shifts in time. Different authors
  use punctuation in different and characteristic ways. Compare
  Tennessee Williams's use of the ellipsis (...) with his use of
  the dash (–); one seems to stand for a drifting, unresolved
  thought, the other for a snatched, interrupted breath. Look
  at how David Mamet uses the full stop or period: he uses it
  where others might use a semi-colon (;) or comma. It helps the
  actor understand the thought and rhythm of his speech. Carol
  Churchill uses the slash (/) where other writers would use a
  dash, to indicate interrupted speech.

- As you work on a script, notice the suggestions of rhythm and
  action in punctuation. Respect authorial punctuation as you
  respect an author's words (remembering that Shakespeare is
  probably not responsible for the punctuation of most of his
  plays – that's mostly been done later by editors; the verse line
  is the most reliable thing to look at in his plays).

- You might try using coloured pens to highlight the different
  punctuation marks to be sure you don't ignore their value.

- Physicalize the punctuation within a scene. Play the scene,
  and make a physical shift in space at each punctuation mark.
  You might turn on a comma, move somewhere new on a

full stop or period, sit or stand on an ellipsis, freeze still on a
dash, throw your arms open on an exclamation mark and so
on. Make your own decision about what each mark will be
physically, depending on authorial style, but enact every mark.
Let your physicality be punctuated by the author's directions.

- Reflect on what you have learned about the scene and the
rhythm of any particular lines that you hadn't previously
noticed. At its best, this exercise can unlock overlooked
meanings and stage directions hidden in the text.

- It is our job to make the psychological physical, and
punctuation is just as much a psychological gesture as any
word is.

Flesh and bones

*Pare text back to its most basic action and meaning,
separating intention from tactical rhetoric. This works well with
Shakespeare, or any text which is similarly densely woven with
subclauses and complex imagery.*

- Work with your scene partner(s). Allow 15 minutes to work on
a single speech.

- Select a sequence or speech, through which you struggle to
communicate or connect with the basic meaning. By way of
example, let's look at the Lord's speech from Act 3, Scene 6 of
Macbeth:

> The son of Duncan,
> From whom this tyrant holds the due of birth
> Lives in the English court, *and is* received
> Of the most pious Edward with such grace
> That the malevolence of fortune nothing
> Takes from his high respect: thither Macduff
> Is gone to pray the holy king, upon his aid
> To wake Northumberland and warlike Siward:
> That, by the help of these – with Him above
> To ratify the work – we may again

Give to our tables meat, sleep to our nights,
Free from our feasts and banquets bloody knives,
Do faithful homage and receive free honours:
All which we pine for now: and this report
Hath so exasperate the king that he
Prepares for some attempt of war.

Make your own edit of the speech or scene. Let's strip it back
to its most basic storytelling. I'll put in **bold** the stripped back
speech:

> **The son of Duncan**,
> From whom this tyrant holds the due of birth
> Lives in the English court, and **is received**
> **Of** the most pious **Edward** with such grace
> That the malevolence of fortune nothing
> Takes from his high respect: **thither Macduff**
> **Is gone to pray the** holy **king**, upon his **aid**
> **To wake Northumberland and** warlike **Siward**:
> **That, by the help of these** – with Him above
> To ratify the work – **we may again**
> Give to our tables meat, sleep to our nights,
> Free from our feasts and banquets bloody knives,
> Do faithful homage and **receive** free honours:
> **All which we pine for now:** and this report
> Hath so exasperate **the king** that he
> **Prepares for** some attempt of **war**.

- Play just the bold lines in the speech. This leaves nothing but
  the basic message this Lord is communicating:

  The son of Duncan is received of Edward: thither Macduff
  is gone to pray the king aid, to wake Northumberland and
  Siward, that by the help of these we may again receive all
  which we pine for now. The king prepares for war.

- Look at the text the Lord is adding to this message (all the
  words not in bold); what does it do? How does it affect the
  speech, and most particularly affect his audience (in this case,
  Lennox, a Scottish thane)? Why does this Lord find these

additions to his message to be necessary? What does this imply about him and his relationship to Lennox?

- Start feeding these extra elements back into the speech, bit by bit. Add the bits you think most important first.

- Reflect on what this has done for your understanding and playing of the material.

Teaching Tip: You can do the same thing with a unit or scene – paring it back to its simplest narrative exchange, and then slowly adding in the flesh to these story bones, assessing the function of each addition as you do so. This is an excellent process to go through, to underline the core action which a scene or speech communicates.

Inner life

Planting obstacles (10 minutes)

Locate the obstacles in the scene, and make them a specific and external problem to solve. This helps when you are worried about playing or demonstrating your inner obstacles (feelings which make it hard for you to get what you want – see page 171 for more on these), rather than playing actions to overcome them.

- Work with your scene partner(s).

- Define the inner obstacles within a unit of action. So for Lady Macbeth's opening speech in *Macbeth*, in which she reads Macbeth's letter detailing the prophecies of the witches, we might reasonably imagine she is battling inner obstacles including confusion, anxiety and loneliness.

- We must not play obstacles, we must play actions to solve them: don't show the audience your fear, try and manage and

control it so you can get what you want. To enable this, plant
the obstacles in other people or objects and play against them
to confirm them: solve the problem they represent.

- So plant Lady Macbeth's anxiety in the doorway to her
  chamber – let her check if anyone is coming. Let her loneliness
  be planted in the letter's words of love from her husband ('my
  dearest partner of greatness') – cherish and savour these
  words of affection.

- Romeo's fear is not inside him: it is in all the corners around
  which a Capulet could come. Juliet's grief is not inside her: it is
  in the empty bed which the banished Romeo will never again
  warm.

- Select a unit of action, locate your objective and the opposing
  inner obstacles. Plant those inner obstacles in targets around
  you, and rehearse the unit, solving the problems which
  surround you.

Secrets

*Bring rich inner life to characters who are only on stage for
short periods (messengers, servants, delivery boys). Bring
immediate weight and tension to any scene or unit which feels
rather lightweight.*

- Select a unit or sequence of units which seem to lack inner
  tension for you.

- Work with your scene partner(s). Allow time enough for one
  iteration of the scene plus 5 minutes for set-up and 5 minutes
  for evaluation.

- In childhood development, having and keeping a secret is
  a crucial stage in developing individual agency. Give your
  character a secret, and you give them agency.

- Locate or imagine a secret you are withholding from your scene
  partner(s). This could be textual (Nora's fraud, Lady Macbeth's
  lost child) or it could be imagined (an unspoken fantasy

or desire, an object of value you have hidden about you).
Whatever it is must come from within the fabric of the play.

- Play the scene and cherish your secret – long to share or even
flaunt it, though you know you can't and won't. Hold it tightly
as you play the scene. Let it focus your inner monologue.

- Connect your secret to the scene: visualize what would happen
if you told your scene partner(s) your secret. This exercise
can really help minor roles which may have little obvious inner
substance: the waiter who recognizes a guest as a school
friend, but unrecognized, won't bring their acquaintance to
light; the messenger who wants a heavy tip to help pay off a
personal debt.

- Don't demonstrate your secret: showing it exists will give it
away. Keep it just for you.

The what?

*Bring specificity of imagery, clarity of focus and depth of
meaning to both listener and speaker.*

- Work in pairs.

- Partner A play a speech. Partner B, your aim is to fully
understand the speech. Whenever you want to hear something
again with greater specificity or clarity to understand it, simply
say 'The what?'

- Partner B, listen with the intent to understand. Don't think
of 'The what?' as tripping the heels of the speaker; imagine
Partner A is leading you through the speech by the hand and
your words are simply squeezing their hand any time they go
too fast for you or you're getting lost.

Inner monologue

*Find specificity of listening. This is particularly useful for scenes
in which you don't speak much. It will stop you from doing
'generalized listening' and force you into active listening.*

- Allow time for two iterations of the scene or sequence, plus 5–10 minutes for reflection and feedback.

- Work with your scene partner(s) and one other person.

- An inner monologue is a flowing stream of speech prompted by what you are hearing and seeing. An inner monologue need not be coherent, and it can repeat one or two phrases many times. It might include repetition of other character's lines. It need not be good prose. An inner monologue will not obliterate listening: it is active listening. Follow, connect, respond.

- Run the scene, and as you do so, speak aloud your inner monologue for this sequence to the extra person in the scene – you might cast them as a character with whom you think you could share all this. In *The Glass Menagerie* Tom might speak to his absent father, in *A Doll's House* Nora might speak to her dead mother, in *Romeo and Juliet* Romeo might speak to the Friar or the dead Mercutio. Alternatively, speak to the audience as if in soliloquy. This is a detailed private commentary on your attitudes to what is happening within the scene, and how it makes you feel about yourself.

- Perhaps you need to do this work because you aren't sure on these *attitudes. Allow you*rself the privilege of rehearsal, and make *an extreme* choice to see what it uncovers.

- Reflect on *your discoveries*. Why doesn't your character say this aloud (i.e. what is the obstacle?)? Write and draw your inner monologue in your journal, or alongside your text of the scene. Remember, though, we make plans so that we have something to change.

Endowments

Ignite visceral imagination, find richer, more vivid connection with a key event or relationship.

- Work with your scene partner(s).
- Select an event or relationship with which you struggle to make an imaginative connection.

- Allow 10 minutes for preparation and 5 minutes for evaluation, plus time to run the scene.

- Uta Hagen – the brilliant actor and acting teacher – when playing Amanda in *The Glass Menagerie* famously brought vivid life to her character's precious 'Sunday dress' by endowing it as made of cobwebs. You can imagine how this endowment will have made her behave with the dress – its frail beauty, its delicacy and fine silk network catching the light, as she proudly, delicately, anxiously sashays about the room.

- Kathryn Hunter, one of Britain's finest actors, was the first woman to play King Lear. Her slow, total psychophysical collapse holding King Lear's dead daughter Cordelia was heart-wrenching. What had given life to this remarkable evocation of horror and grief? The actor endowed her body as a crisp packet dropped onto a fire, crumpling and folding in on itself with sudden pulses of implosion.

- To create your own endowments, start from metaphor or simile. What is this moment or relationship like, or what would it be in metaphor? You might endow a scene partner – they have bugs crawling out of every orifice, they are oozing filth, they are radiating warmth and sunlight, they shed petals and flowers behind them wherever they walk. Perhaps every time they smile, you lose 10 seconds from your life, or sunlight streams over your body. Perhaps they are a well-fed, sleepy tiger, or their speech sounds like nails down a chalk board.

- You could endow yourself. Perhaps you are numb and can feel nothing, or are hearing everything through bubble wrap (sometimes useful for moments of shock or grief). Perhaps your stomach has become butterflies in a paper bag, or your skin is made of tracing paper.

- Whatever you choose, be specific. These endowments will usually work for a single relationship within a single scene or even unit. An event will then occur which will change the quality of that relationship or moment.

- Play the relevant sequence with this endowment – a metaphor or simile made actual by your imagination. Try playing different

endowments that might help ignite the moment in different
ways, and be open to their full impact on your body and mind.

- As so often, the best endowments will be invisible for the
  audience: your image will be sufficiently potent and insightful to
  speak exactly of the experience your character is suffering, like
  the cobweb dress or burning crisp packet. No one wants to
  see your hard work.

Physicalize the inner tempo-rhythm

*Make inner life outer. Reveal internal dynamics within a scene
and physically explore your character's inner life.*

- Work with your scene partner(s). Allow 10 minutes for
  preparation, plus time for two or three iterations of the scene or
  units you are rehearsing.

- Select a sequence of units or scene you want to interrogate for
  a more specific and vivid sense of your character's inner life.

- Define your character's inner state within these units, using
  Laban's vocabulary (revisit Chapter 4, page 77 for more on
  Laban and to consider your own movement profile). Consider
  flow, weight, direction and time within your character. Is your
  character's inner life bound or free flow? Are they struggling
  to conceal or manage an inner wring, dab, press, float, glide,
  slash, punch or flick?

- Physicalize this inner state as you play the units or a scene. So:

    Float – open your arms and imagine you are flying through
    the scene

    Punch – find something soft, a pillow or sofa, and punch it
    through the scene (don't just punch into mid-air, since there is
    no natural resistance and you may injure your neck: better to
    punch into your own hand)

    Glide – lightly smooth over all the surfaces in the space, as if
    you are icing a cake

Slash – slash the air, cutting through it as you play the scene
Wring – wring dry a cloth or an old piece of clothing
Dab – drum your fingers and toes throughout the scene; play
the surfaces like drums
Flick – flick away a fly throughout the scene
Press – press back a wall or down onto a chair or table.

II

- Repeat the scene with the same physical sensation, but with a
more restrained, concealed physical action:

Float – let your hands and head be buoyant; floating on the air
Punch – punch a fist closed in on itself, or punch a finger into
a hand
Glide – smooth over your palms
Slash – imagine every gesture with your hand cuts as if you are
Edward Scissorhands
Wring – twist a ring on a finger
Dab – drum your thumb and fingers together
Flick – flick away at your finger nails
Press – press your hands into each other.

III

- Now play the scene, focusing all this internal slashing or
wringing or whatever within the language. Don't be afraid to be
extreme at first: this is about unlocking something, not making
the scene 'good'.

- Reflect on this. How does this alter your relationship to the
language of the unit? How does it alter your way of seeing
other people and objects within the unit? How does it condition
your actions? How does it change your body – its temperature,
your heart-rate and physical tensions?

Inners out

Make the inner life a physical reality. This is particularly helpful with scenes clogged with emotional repression, and strong but concealed passions.

- Work with your scene partner(s).

- Allow 15 minutes more than the sequence or scene usually takes to play, plus time to play it once more and review.

- Play the scene, but make manifest all your inner states. Do not conceal your inner life. The language of the scene will remain the same, which may well be trying to disguise your inner life, but physically you will make it manifest. You might be hiding behind furniture or crawling under tables, hiding in a scene partner's lap or prostrating at their feet, standing high on tables or dancing and leaping around the room. Whatever you feel will be made manifest physically in the space.

- So Benedick might be hiding under a table from Beatrice in an early exchange from *Much Ado About Nothing*; Nora might be fluttering madly about, trying to hide everything away from Torvald in the first scene of *A Doll's House*; Laura might be soothing and stroking and shushing Tom and Amanda in the first scene of *The Glass Menagerie* and so on.

- As you physicalize your inner life, be sure that you remain supported vocally: don't push or strain your voice.

- Now play the scene again, concealing all the impulses you've just released.

- Reflect on what you have learned, perhaps drawing your physical journey into your journal.

Teaching Tip: This exercise doesn't really work with scenes of aggressive, repressed violence; making this manifest is unsafe or leads to lies, as (for their own well-being) actors have to restrain exactly what you're asking them to release.

It requires physically able and confident actors, who understand the rules of contact improvisation and know how to protect their voices. Do not do this exercise unless you are sure you can do it safely.

Obviously, furniture must be secure, breakable objects should be removed and the actors must agree contact rules – if in doubt, assert a rule of absolutely no physical contact between the players. More than most exercises, this requires complete complicity from those involved: everyone must like the sound of playing this game, or it simply gets dangerous and is no fun.

Down the line

Pare a scene back to the purest intent: to get closer or farther from someone. Cut through naturalism and literalism to reveal deeper, inner dynamics. It works particularly well with naturalistic scenes – by D. H. Lawrence or August Strindberg, for example.

- Allow time enough to run the selected units or a scene slowly and carefully – allow 3 minutes per page and assume you will run the sequence at least twice.

- Select a scene or sequence of units you want to interrogate for its simplest meaning: it may just need refreshing. This works best with duologues, though you can adapt it for other scenes.

- Stand and face your scene partner.

- You can only move along one dimension: towards and away from your scene partner. There is no side-to-side/up-and-down option.

- You cannot make physical contact with your partner, though you may want to within the course of the scene.

- Play or read the scene together. Explore moving closer to or farther from your scene partner within the scene. Explore how being near or far from you partner impacts upon the text and colours its meaning. There is only one state to examine: closer to or further from the person with whom you are working. This is all the scene will be about as you read it.

- Any naturalistic staging written into the text (handing over of props, for example) should be translated into a movement either towards or away from your scene partner. This is about a simple translation of every line and every action into a movement towards or away from the other person with whom you are sharing the space. Let the lines and actions push or pull you: make yourself a passenger, not a pilot.

- Finally, this is what a scene is about: other people and your tidal movements to and from them.

- Play the scene again, within whatever space you are working, using whatever naturalistic behaviour is demanded by the scene. See how much of the deeper intent and feeling can be retained as you play.

Teaching Tip: Hold a piece of rope/string between you to make the journeys forward and back more physical, as you pull in or retreat.

This exercise works particularly well if it grows out of a 'Communion exercise' (page 68). Allow the given circumstances and objectives to become alive in the actor's imaginations as they do the silent communion, moving towards and away from each other in silence, and then step into 'Down the line'.

Key modes of rehearsal

Improvising units

This is a basic model for all work in rehearsals. Encourage an exploratory approach. Find the text out of the given circumstances and objectives – do not put the text on as if it were a hat: inhabit the language from sensory needs, don't wear it to look good. This works particularly well with realist texts – by Chekhov, Strindberg or Gorky, for example.

- Work as a full group. Some of you will watch, providing feedback.

- Select a sequence of units. You do not need to know the text of the selected sequence.

- Read the sequence. Establish the given circumstances, identify and give a title to the defining events (which begin, punctuate and end that sequence of units) and plot each character's objective within each unit of action.

- Read the unit again, speaking aloud character objectives as you read the text of each unit.

- Define a playing space in front of you (with as much or as little 'set' as you have).

- Each actor state your character's opening objective before you begin. Now improvise the scene, pursuing your character's objectives within these given circumstances.

- Play actions. Try and get what your character wants. Make yourself available to the sensations of the unit (both from imagined circumstances and as you deal with the behaviour of others). Listen and respond.

- Do not fall into acting 'character' – character will emerge from the pattern of choices you make unit by unit. Commit to the choice your character has made, and pursue what they need in that moment. Listen and respond.

- Don't play the scene. Don't try and make the scene happen by writing or directing the scene from within. Pursue your objectives truthfully, responding honestly to whatever occurs.

- Observers, notice responses or choices which take the improvisation away from the scene as written. These moments of divergence will be the focus of discussion after the exercise is complete.

- The end point is either when you have diverged a long way from the journey of the script, or when you have reached a point beyond which you cannot travel without further analysis of the script.

- Return to the script of the unit and read it again. What did you discover? The most revealing analysis is of moments when in the improvisation you made choices different to those of your character in the script. You were playing truthfully, so what did you not see that your character sees? Why didn't you see that choice as necessary? Perhaps there is an element of your given circumstances you have overlooked, a relationship that needs more interrogation, a previous circumstance by which your character is affected that you have not considered closely enough.

- Your aim is to find the necessity of the text as written through detailed active analysis and improvisation.

- Improvise through the whole play like this. It encourages play, it promotes listening and honest response, it begins the stretch towards character in the simplest way and often makes learning lines seem easy.

- Every choice, every line of text, emerges from given circumstances, events and objectives.

Repetition

This is a model which can be used throughout rehearsal. Train listening.

- Work with your scene partner(s). Allow twice as long as it usually takes to run a scene.

- Play the scene. Repeat the key words in what is said to you – the operative words which make your line necessary – before you speak your own text. So, for example, let's look at a short exchange from *A Doll's House*:

Nora Oh – are you back already?

Helmer Yes. Has anyone been here?

Nora No.

Helmer That's strange. I saw Krogstad come out of the front door.

Nora Did you? Oh yes, that's quite right – Krogstad was here for a few minutes.

Helmer Nora, I can tell from your face, he has been here and asked you to put in a good word for him.

Nora Yes.

In the exercise, this becomes:

Nora Oh – are you back already?

Helmer Back already? Yes. Has anyone been here?

Nora Here? No.

Helmer No? That's strange. I saw Krogstad come out of the front door.

Nora You saw Krogstad. Did you? Oh yes, that's quite right – Krogstad was here for a few minutes.

Helmer A few minutes! Nora, I can tell from your face, he has been here and asked you to put in a good word for him.

Nora A good word? Yes.

- As you can see, this is an exercise about listening. It can be extended, so that your scene partner repeats every word you say, until they have fully understood what it is you are saying. This slows everything down, and forces you to work the text to expose and absorb the exact and full meaning of what you are saying.

  So, for example, this unit might play something like this:

  Nora Oh – are you back already?

  Helmer Am I back already?

  Nora Are you back already?

  Helmer Am I back already? Yes. Has anyone been here?

  Nora Has anyone been here?

  Helmer Yes. Has anyone been here?

Nora Has anyone been here?
Helmer Yes. Has anyone been here?
Nora No.
Helmer No?
Nora No.
Helmer That's strange. I saw Krogstad come out of the front door.
Nora You saw Krogstad coming out of the front door.

And so on.

It affords time for precision of action and listening and allows exploration without discussion being required. The repetition is not mindless, each iteration of a line is a further examination and interrogation as it changes and grows in response to your scene partner's behaviour.

- Now return to the scene and feel how your listening has intensified and become more specific.

Line-feeding

Deliver fresh-minted scenes and free rehearsal, unrestricted by scripts in hand. Fully explore the physical life of the scene and discover the words within the given circumstances of the scene, rather than from the page of the script.

- You may not want to improvise the text (as Dustin Hoffman famously said when rehearsing Shylock in *The Merchant of Venice*, 'You can't improvise this'), if you are in a point of the process where you want absolute specificity with the lines. Here line-feeding can be helpful.

- This can be done in conjunction with almost any other exercise, or as an exercise in itself. It inevitably slows a scene down, but early on this can be helpful in the pursuit of detail and specificity of listening and response.

- Play the scene, but with a colleague at the side 'feeding' the lines of the scene in to you. The 'feeder' will read line by line, thought by thought in manageable chunks. They will read clearly, but without colouring the line with suggested tone, rhythm or stress. Their reading will be flat, monotonous and efficient: they won't weigh down the forward motion of the scene. Simply speak the right words in the right order.

- You – the actor – play the scene, making choices about the operation of the line. You, in other words, define its specific action.

- The joy of this early on is that the thought literally comes to you. The line is utterly 'fresh-minted', since you don't know exactly what to say until it comes to you from your 'feeder'. The feeder satisfies a hunger which is discovered moment by moment.

- This takes a little practice – for the feeder too – but once you have it, it can be a very valuable rehearsal tool to facilitate detailed play with text.

Paraphrasing

Free or secure the meaning and operative thoughts within a line, speech or scene. This is particularly useful when working with complex, heightened text like Shakespeare's.

- Work with your scene partner(s). Allow 5 minutes to set up and 5 minutes to evaluate, plus time for two goes at the scene or speech.

- Read through the text of the scene or speech, clarifying the meaning of any individual words or phrases of which you are unsure.

- Play the speech or scene through, paraphrasing the text into your own language. A line like 'Gallop apace you fiery footed steeds, towards Phoebus' lodging' might become 'Hurry! Come on you hot-footed horses, drive on towards the sun's home!'

- This might feel reductive, and indeed it is exactly that. But these reductions are revealing for us about what we have and haven't grasped in the text. This can really focus you in on precise meanings and uncovers holes you may have overlooked or simply not realized were there.

Radio play

Reclaim the language of the play, independent from any staging choices you have made. When you have spent a long time working on the physical life of a scene, return to its absolute heart: the text. This works well towards the end of a rehearsal process.

- Work with your scene partner(s).
- Sit around the edges of the space you are working in, and read the whole play as a radio play. Concentrate entirely on the language; you don't need to move the scenes at all. Focus all your energy and impulses – which may have become invested heavily in the scene's physicality – into the language.
- Focus on affecting your targets – so don't close your eyes throughout this exercise, though you may choose to sometimes. Really land your actions on your targets, i.e. drive right through the whole line, so it reaches across the space to change your scene partner(s).
- Words are behaviour, and very desperate behaviour. Celebrate them in this exercise.

Follow-up

These exercises are intended to offer you a few ways to re-evaluate scenes away from rehearsal, when you have been working for a long time and need a fresh way in to them.

- Imagine there are only two verbs in the world: to open and to close. What action is your character playing, unit by unit: to open or to close their target?
- Look for a moment of 'heroic tension'. This is that moment of surprise within an archetypal character, which provides rich dimension. It is the moment of generosity from the miser; the moment of loving vulnerability from the hateful murderer; the moment of self-sacrifice from the vainglorious narcissist.

- Return to a question you have asked earlier: 'Who would do that?!' Look at the moment in your role that makes you ask this question. What is your answer now? In this moment, who does your character fear they might be and wish they could be? What is the problem in their world which demands this solution? Why do they see no other, less extreme, solution?

- Tell the story of the play or the action of a scene to a friend or family member who doesn't know it, in the simplest, clearest way possible.

- Create a 4 x 4 square grid (sixteen boxes in total). Choose a scene and fill all sixteen boxes with possible targets, real or imagined, in the scene. Don't concern yourself about whether the ideas are good or bad; just fill the boxes. Now consider one of the targets to which you haven't related much in the scene. When could you draw energy and action from the problem this target presents?

- Look at Eysenck's wheel of personality traits (page 189). Where is your character within the scene in question? What would happen if you flipped to the other side of the wheel and played from there?

Further reading

Watch Fiona Shaw preparing to go on stage as Mother Courage at: www.nationaltheatre.org.uk/video/fiona-shaw-prepares

Benedetti, Jean (1998), *Stanislavski and the Actor,* Routledge. Part Three, 'The Method of Physical Action'.

Hagen, Uta (1973), *Respect for Acting,* Wiley Publishing. Part Three, 'The Play and the Role'.

Meisner, Sanford and Longwell, Dennis (1987), *Sanford Meisner on Acting.* Vintage. Chapter 7, 'Improvisation', and Chapter 8, 'More on Preparation: "Quick as Flame"'.

Merlin, Bella (2001), *Beyond Stanislavsky.* Nick Hern Books. Act 4, 'Working on Your Role'.

Stanislavski, Konstantin, trans. Jean Benedetti (2008), *An Actor's Work.* Routledge. Year Two, 'Embodiment'.

Stanislavski, Konstantin, trans. Jean Benedetti (2010), *An Actor's Work on a Role.* Routledge. Part 1, 'Drafts'. 1. 'Othello 1930–1932' and 4. 'Approach to a Role'.

PART THREE

THE STORY

Train skills to devise original theatre. Learn to deconstruct, analyse and interpret a stimulus and then collaborate as you construct a theatrical response.

We love to make up stories together. It's how we light up dark nights. From bedtime stories to *Saturday Night Live* or *Commedia dell'Arte* to *Monty Python*, collaborating with others to devise stories is a social, joyful impulse. This section of the book looks at exercises which provide creative structures for devising original theatre.

Devising is a creative process. You build new characters, new stories, new worlds. So let's consider creation.

Every culture has its creation myth: an inciting incident, for the story of all things. These beginnings mostly take one of two forms: all things come from nothing (*ex nihilo* meaning 'out of nothing'), or all things come from something (out of chaos).

In 'out of nothing' creation myths, all things come from a Great Creator's dream, breath, speech or even excreta. The Judeo-Christian story of Genesis is an 'out of nothing' myth: 'Let there be light!' The Ancient Egyptians have something similar; so does evolutionary science (the Big Bang). In one divine moment (or week) all things are formed out of nowhere, by perfect design or perfect accident.

In an 'out of chaos' creation myth, there is a pre-existing mass of stuff. Typically, a formless expanse of mud or vapour is separated into order. This is the Classical Greek story, in which Cosmos (meaning 'order') is formed from Chaos.

Devising is not creation 'out of nothing'. We are not relying on a Great Creator's spark of inspiration to generate all matter and meaning. We are creating out of chaos, relying on one of the basic principles of thermodynamics: energy cannot be created or destroyed, only trans-formed. Surrounding us is pre-existing matter, to which we bring form. Responding to the materials around us, we forge new worlds.

But we are not Dr Frankenstein. We won't be cutting parts from the carcasses of other dissected lives to vivify a new whole in our own image. All we will end with then is a jealous beast out to punish us for its creation. Mary Shelley's story warns us that our creations will only find a soul when they have a purpose for existence, independent from its creator's ego: made in God's image, but given free will.

Like Dr Frankenstein, we want to create new life. But let's not do it for our own glory, or simply because it seems it must be done. The creation must have a life of its own: an independent and social reason to exist. Work for a social purpose.

*

In some myths, creation is an act of terrible violence. Father Sky and Mother Earth tear apart their union. As things fall apart, these gods rip off limbs, tear out hair, smash teeth: from these dismembered parts our world comes into being. And so violent conflict is written into the story of creation. In other myths, our ancestors emerged on earth from a great hole in the sky, with gods as midwives. At the moment of our birth, the gods were there to ease us into the light.

Do we need to have terrible separations and battles, bloody and painful, in order to create our new worlds? Or might we be able to act as midwives to stories, together guiding them into existence as in the stories of Native American folklore? I know which I will pursue.

There is no direct path to creating original drama. There will be more blind alleys than flashes of light. The process is organic, and its growth accordingly unpredictable: it will grow wherever it finds the potential for further life, and that can only be discovered through active exploration. As Polonius puts it in *Hamlet*, we shall 'By indirections, find directions out'.

Once again, that will urge us to embrace our own ignorance in the face of chaos. We cannot pursue guaranteed outcomes, we can only broadcast into ploughed, fertile soil and farm whatever happens to grow.

9
DESIGN

Learn to deconstruct a story and understand its form, structure and content.

Framework

To devise original theatre, you must respect and understand the craft of storytelling. This chapter offers exercises which will help you to understand and manipulate the forms, structures and archetypes of storytelling.

*

Below are ten points to guide our work on story design.

1 *Give them what they want, but not how they expect to get it.* Commit to genre conventions: they give us our creative boundaries. Freedom requires structure; without it, chaos swirls. Like a muscle, your talent requires something to push against in order to strengthen and apply itself. So work against the formal obstacles of genre.

Genre conventions are for the storyteller what the formal rhythms of verse are for the poet. Knowing you are watching a tragedy is like knowing you are reading a sonnet: the genre sets audience expectations, which we match, surpass or shock.

A horror story has certain codes associated with it, and crucially, you know them already: suspense, fear, shock, big empty houses, isolation, life or death stakes, the supernatural, long silences, sudden noises and so on. We shape scenes around genre expectations, just as a poet shapes a poem around a verse form.

We learn most genre rules while sitting on our parents' laps. You learn basic codes of comedy, tragedy, adventure, thriller, suspense, mystery, romance, as you hear the stories of the Brothers Grimm, Roald Dahl or Dr Seuss, or as Dad tells tall tales of his schooldays.

2   *Make work that moves you.*
If the story doesn't move its teller, it won't move anyone else. The art form is non-intellectual: it is about passionate feelings, experienced through immediate action.

Don't worry about how clever it is, or even how original it is; don't second guess what will move other people. Make it so it moves you.

3   *Make the psychological physical.*
Everything has to be physical. If it's invisible it doesn't exist. Since the audience cannot experience what remains private, create visual or audible signs for inner conflict. It might simply be the switch of a breath pattern, or a symbolist shift in lighting, but it must be made manifest. Mother Courage needs her cart.

What if we want the physical act not just to be recognized, but remembered? As a guide, Event Theory indicates five things that make physical actions memorable:

Surprise – when an event happens unexpectedly
Intention – when we see an event has a specific purpose rooting it
Repetition – when that event recurs
Consequence – when we see that the event affects others
Objects – when a particular object is part of the event.

The more intense the surprise, intent, repetition, consequence of the act, or remarkable the object involved, the more memorable the action.

A couple sitting together at the back of a bus is not particularly memorable. But if the girl is in bridal gear? The surprise of the objects makes them memorable. And if you know (because you've seen it) that they're running away together (intention), leaving behind a furious groom and mother-in-law (consequence), while you hear Simon and Garfunkel's *The Sound of Silence* for the crucial third time (repetition), then this final act in Mike Nichols's film *The Graduate* becomes not just memorable, but iconic.

4   *Make it personal.*

Ours is not an expositional art. Ideas convert into action: narrative exposition needs to become character ammunition. Drama is not a home for political ideas. Drama is a home for political ideas revealed as personal problems.

It is through characters' dilemmas and subsequent actions that we will reveal politics. Give one woman a terrible personal choice to make – like Nora in *A Doll's House* – and you might make an enduring political symbol. Nora speaks about her own struggle against her father and husband. She does not need to speak about generations of women in order to speak for them: that's a given since she is a character in a play.

5   *Tell the truth.*

Our ethical responsibility is to truth. This doesn't mean your work has to look like life (that's a style – naturalism); the responsibility is to communicate the truth of how we experience the world: Picasso's cubist portraits did that. Nor does this mean you can only tell stories about events and worlds you directly know. Use any world or events you like, but use them to say only what you honestly feel to be true.

Truth doesn't relate to coherence or consistency. Dimension in storytelling comes from contradiction. So don't think truth is related to coherence.

We often call untruthful acting melodramatic. A melodramatic performance is defined not by over-expression, but rather by under-motivation. When the scale of the motive doesn't match the scale of the action, we see melodrama. Be sure your motive for telling this story is honest and personal, or the story will seem melodramatic. Why do you need to tell this story? For what purpose?

The only truth you know is your own, so express it
purely and selfishly with all the imaginative flourish you possess.

6 *Remember it's a lie.*
Nothing is what it seems: everything is a metaphor. Most
crucially, *your characters are not human beings*, we just
pretend they are. Characters exist only to serve the story. They
are metaphors for the audience's human experience, like any
sculpture or portrait. Everything about their existence supports
and contributes to the life of the story. Before you flood
them with life and make them seem human, recognize their
metaphorical function: they exist only to dramatize a particular
dilemma central to the story.

The story is why they have been made. The story is why you
are here.

7 *It is about the audience.*
It is not about you.

In performance, truth will relocate: truth will reside with the
audience. You will make something you believe to be true, but
the ultimate arbiter of truth is the audience.

Let this liberate you. The audience is not there for you, the
story does not finally exist because of you. It will gain its own
life – like that monster of Frankenstein's when it falls in love.
You become the story's servant, as the audience members
uncover their own potential through the story.

So respect your audience. They are more intelligent
than you. The corporate, group intelligence of an audience
surpasses that of any individual. Trust that they will see
everything and know they will spot any lie.

As a shorthand for serving that intelligence, doubt
appearances and seek the opposite of the obvious.

8 *There is only here and now.*
It all occurs in the present tense. Even a description of the
past is happening now. What we experience is the present
relationship to past events, not the past events.

Crucially in drama, there is never enough time. Even for
Vladimir and Estragon, there is urgency as they watch death
approach, waiting for Godot to arrive.

There is a simple equation in time-bound art: time delivers empathy. More time spent with a character is more opportunity to witness the choices of that character, and thereby develop empathy with that character. If you want us to care for someone, put them with us here and now, so we see them make decisions. That's why Macbeth – despite being a murderous tyrant – is pitied by the audience: we've spent so much time with him that we can't help ourselves.

Take care to place your audience *when* you want them, as you craft their experience of the present. There are three ways to connect the audience to the here and now of the action:

In Mystery, the audience knows less than the characters.
In Thriller, the audience knows as much as the characters.
In Suspense, the audience knows more than the characters.

9 *There is always conflict.*
Nothing moves forward without conflict. This is the basis for all drama, since the pressure of conflict provides opportunity for dilemma and extreme choice.

Character is expressed through choice in the face of conflicting dilemma. Greater pressure on that choice leads to deeper insight into character: we learn more about Macbeth and Nora through their final, most ferociously pressured choices than we do anywhere else in the plays. This is a woman who must walk out the door; this is a man ready to die.

Where the sculpture is defined by form and material, the character is defined by want and desire. Put your characters' desires within extreme conflict to find out who they are and reveal the story you are telling.

Your protagonist is only as compelling as the forces of antagonism make them: your story is only as compelling as the choices your characters have to make.

10 *Save the best until last.*
The rhythm of a story is the same as the rhythm of the human pulse: it alternates between tension, suspension and release.

In storytelling, the tension of that pulse will intensify as the story moves forward. A story follows the rhythm of *Jo Ha Kyu*.

Jo Ha Kyu is a fundamental human rhythm of development and fulfilment, which is the basis of traditional Japanese theatre like Noh and Kabuki. It is also used in Japanese martial arts, poetry and music: starting slowly, you gradually build and intensify, becoming more definite, stronger – more and more so – until you reach a culmination, a climax. Then you release. Then you begin again.

The rhythm of Jo Ha Kyu is recognizable in most behaviour, from running a race to love-making. In a story the climax of the narrative will be the greatest, most intense pulse in the journey, before the audience is released back into their lives.

*

These rules of storytelling are crucial when devising the story, but are important for any actor to understand: actors serve the story. Since the story is our master, we would do well to understand it – or we may lose sight of what it demands.

Exploration

The exploratory exercises in this chapter ask you to consider the importance of structure to meaning. They test how structure and form will define meaning as much, if not more than, something's content. They ask you to analyse specific ways in which structure carries meaning.

- What spaces do we tell and hear stories in? Consider the different relationships you have to different storytellers in different environments. You sat on your Mum's lap and heard a story; you go to the cinema's big dark rooms in a complex; you read a story on a bean-bag in the corner of your bedroom; you hear one on the radio in your car; you read one together in class … What are or were your favourite experiences of hearing a story? What were the key factors in making this so special? Could these be recreated in a theatre? How? Consider these questions in your journal – make notes, do sketches and stick in images of examples.

- Draw a sequence of shapes, to consider the influence of form on meaning. Try a circle, a cross, a star, a heart, a diamond, an arrow. Write your name in or next to these shapes. How does your name change? Does it seem more formal? More intimate? Stronger? Cooler? Next to the shapes, write words indicating the meaning of the shapes. So, for example, next to your circle you might write eternity, balance, union, completeness, movement, flow and so on.

- Consider how meaning is defined by structure. What does the structure of a limerick suggest (five lines, rhyming AABBA)? In what ways is it like a joke? Write your own limerick. Now take the same content and rewrite it as a haiku (three lines, no rhyme requirement, seventeen syllables spread out 5–7–5). How is it changed by the structure? I've had a quick go to show you what I mean. First I'll make up a limerick (Pwllheli is a place in North Wales – it's impossible to write phonetically, but is pronounced something a bit like Puthelly):

    There was an old girl from Pwllheli
    Who had a most troublesome belly
    She ate fruit and fibre
    To loosen inside her
    And now it all feels like jelly.

    Now let's try and turn that into a haiku (5–7–5):

    One from Pwllheli
    Had a troublesome belly
    Fruit made it jelly.

    What does the form of the limerick offer that the haiku doesn't? Have a go yourself – it made me laugh doing it. Consider how the stricture of the form liberates your creativity with language.

- Design the floor plan of your perfect home. How would its structure contribute to the meaning of your life?

Exercises

Devise a game (30 minutes)

Train basic devising skills within a group, and explore basic story structure.

Work in groups of four or five. Commit to the deadline of time: you have 10 minutes, so make confident decisions and work quickly for your shared objective.

- Each group take two standard classroom objects: for example, some string and a chair; a wastepaper basket and a ball; a bag and a roll of sticky tape.

- In your group, devise a new game to play with these two objects. A good game – like a good story – requires a clear objective, simple rules (obstacles and conventions) and a clear point of completion/success.

- Play the game.

- Reflect on how to improve it: refine the rules and objectives of the game.

- Now present and teach the game to the rest of the group. Play it together.

- Reflect on this exercise. When devising the game, what role did you take in the team? Were you comfortable in this role? What makes a good game? Consider the structure of the game.

Devise a story (30 minutes)

Train basic devising skills within a group, and begin to focus on narrative structure.

- Work in groups of four or five (perhaps the same groups as in the last exercise, to further explore the group dynamic). Commit to the deadline of time: you have 10 minutes, so make confident decisions and work quickly for your shared objective.

- Each group take three standard classroom objects: for example, some string, a chair and a wastepaper basket; a ball, a bag and a roll of sticky tape.

- In your group, devise a new 2–3 minute story involving these three objects, and one imaginary person. Rehearse the story.

- Tell the story to the rest of the group.

- Reflect on the structure of your story: its beginning, middle and end. Discuss this narrative structure, its clarity and whether it helped your devising process.

Structure of the space (40 minutes)

Explore how different physical relationships communicate different stories and meanings.

- Work as a full group. You will need a clear space and one chair each. Timing is dependent on group size, though I would allow around 20 minutes for each iteration of this exercise, including set-up and evaluation.

I

- Take a chair each and stand together at one side of the space.

- One at a time, take your chair and place it somewhere in the space. Your aim is to suggest story by your placement of the chair. Put it down, then move back and give a few moments for everyone to look at the space with the chair in it. What moment in time (what story) is suggested to you by this chair? What story could begin here? What story could end here?

- Now remove your chair from the space. The next person go in and place their chair somewhere different.

- Continue until everyone has had a turn.

II

- Take a chair each and stand together at one side of the space.

- One at a time, take your chair and place it somewhere in the space, as above. But this time, do not remove your chair after evaluating the implied story. Add the next chair to the picture, so that we have a gradually filling space. What relationships are implied? Which chair has the greatest potential for authority? Which feels warmest, most intimate to us? Which feels coldest, most distant?

- When staging end-on, consider the dynamics of space. Seeing is a cultural and learned act. Our eye first reaches to the top left corner of a picture, since we are taught from so young an age to scan a page from top left to bottom right (it's how we read Roman script).

  Up-stage right (the top left corner of the picture as you face it) will feel dynamic, dominating.
  Up-stage left (the top right corner of the picture as you face it) will feel more remote, cold, even disturbing.
  Up-stage centre (the centre and top of the picture) will feel formal, authoritative, strong.
  Down-stage right (the bottom left of the picture) is warmer, more intimate, strong.
  Down-stage centre (the bottom and centre) is hot, the most intimate and immediate point in the stage picture.
  Down-stage left (the bottom right of the picture) feels cooler, less intimate and is the weakest point.

- What happens if everyone moves, so you are no longer in an 'end-on' configuration (with everyone looking from one end of the space)? Move so you are in the round (everyone standing round in a circle) or in traverse (people looking from two facing sides of the space). What has changed?

III

- Return to the end-on configuration.

- Place one chair centre-stage and observe the different qualities it has facing in the six different directions (up-stage right and so on); what stories or relationships are implied?

Narrative structure (45 minutes)

Uncover the structure of narrative. Train yourself to use narrative forms as a basis for play and devising.

- Work as a full group.
- Select a story you all know well from your childhood – I will reference *Cinderella*.

I

- Isolate the beginning, middle and end of the story.
- By beginning let's agree we mean:

    Set-up – the scene(s) in which we meet the main characters and establish their major wants, the setting and basic conventions of the story world; and
    Inciting incident – the event that kicks the story off.

- By middle let's agree we mean:

    Crisis point – the point at which the central character seems as far as is imaginable from getting what they want.

- By end let's agree we mean:

    Climax – the final major reversal that changes everything for the central character and throws them either into a tragedy or comedy; and
    Resolution – the final moments in which we see the new world order created by this climax.

- For example, the beginning of *Cinderella*:

    Set-up – we meet Cinderella, her stepmother and stepsisters preparing for the Prince's ball. We see Cinderella's lonely life, serving the rest of her family.
    Inciting incident – the Fairy Godmother appears and offers to make Cinderella's dreams come true.

- The middle of *Cinderella*:

    Crisis point – it's midnight at the ball, and Cinderella has to flee the Prince before the magic wears off.

- The end of *Cinderella*:

  Climax – the Prince fits the glass slipper onto Cinderella's foot. Resolution – Cinderella marries the Prince and forgives her stepmother and stepsisters.

- Now locate the *rising action* and the *falling action* of the story. Rising action is the wave of plot which swells towards the crisis point, and often brings the central character closer to what they want. It may include plot complications and secondary conflicts.

- Falling action is the wave of plot which rushes from crisis to climax, as the basic conflict unravels, often very messily.

- In *Cinderella*:

  Rising action – Cinderella's Fairy Godmother turns mice into horses, pumpkins into carriages and sends Cinders to the ball.

- Falling action – the Prince desperately searches the kingdom for the woman whose foot fits the single glass slipper.

II

- Take 10 minutes to tell the story together.

- One of you start telling it, but work like a 'tag team'. Anytime you want to tag out from the telling because you are losing your way in the story, or if as a listener there is detail you want to add, then 'tag in'. Tell the story as an all-seeing narrator, in the third person and past tense ('Cinderella ran home from the ball as fast as she could, while the prince stared out into the dark night').

III

- Isolate the *protagonist* and *antagonist* in your story. The protagonist is the central character, from whose point of view the story is seen or told. The antagonist is the protagonist's main rival or opponent.

- In *Cinderella*, the protagonist is Cinderella. The antagonist is her stepmother.

- Take 10 minutes to tell the story as a tag team, from the protagonist's point of view. Use the first person and past tense ('Once upon a time, many years ago, I lived with my mean stepmother and ugly sisters …'). This will be an enjoyably unreliable narrator. How are the events of the story altered by this perspective?

IV

- Take 10 minutes to tell the story with a different protagonist. What happens to the story if the stepmother is the protagonist?
- Reflect together on what you have discovered.

Archetypal themes (40 minutes)

Uncover how themes (meaning the big ideas in stories) guide the story and its central transformation. Analyse and work with such themes in your own stories.

- As we develop our understanding of story, we will deal with archetypes a lot. A quick reminder: archetypes are not stereotypes. A stereotypical story lacks imagination, expressing a poverty of both content and form, dressed in cliché. These stories will be narrow. Archetypal stories are universal, communicating beyond specific cultures and communities. They may introduce us to foreign worlds, exotic and strange, but within them we will find ourselves: humans and experiences which are recognizable from our own lives. Archetypes are used to mould personal stories with global reach.

I

- Work individually – this can be done as pre-class work. Write down the names of three stories you know well (you will reference these in several exercises). I will reference *Macbeth*, *A Doll's House* and *Cinderella*.
- All stories are concerned with transgression and transformation. A story's themes are the key values or ideas

which arise from the specific transgression and transformation
of its protagonist.

- Tradition has it that there are only seven themes that define
transformation:

   Love
   Money
   Power
   Revenge
   Survival
   Glory
   Self-awareness.

- The quest for these makes the story.

- The end of the story will either absolutely fulfil or absolutely
disrupt the central themes: if love is a central theme, then love
will be fully realized or absolutely disrupted by the climactic
event of the drama. If the themes are fulfilled, that is comedy. If
they are absolutely disrupted, that is tragedy.

- *Macbeth*'s key themes are power, glory and survival;
Cinderella's themes are love and power; *A Doll's House*
explores money, love and self-awareness. Macbeth dies a
powerless king, a despised tyrant: the absolute disruption of
power, glory and survival. Cinderella finds true love with the
most powerful man in the kingdom: the absolute fulfilment of
love and power. Nora ends without money or the love of her
family, but self-aware for the first time: a complex disruption.

- What are the key themes in your stories? How do the endings
bring these themes to a fulfilled or disrupted climax?

II

- Come up with another version of the list of seven themes. Are
there themes that you think are missing from this list (freedom,
honour, innocence …)? What if there were only three themes in
the world; which would they be?

III

- Work in pairs. Select one of the themes. Each of you tell a true story from your own life which connects to that theme, but embellish it. Invent an ending, which provides an *absolute* disruption or fulfilment of the theme.

Four elements of story (15 minutes)

Train to work with the four basic elements of story, building your own narrative out of them.

- The psychoanalyst Carl Jung observes four elements in story. These are:

  The main character pattern (a rigid behaviour pattern affecting the protagonist: Cinderella's humility; Nora's role-play as a little girl; Macbeth's ambition)

  A key relationship (with a shared behaviour pattern or balancing behaviour patterns: Nora and Helmer balance as father and daughter; Macbeth and Lady Macbeth share ambition; Cinderella and the stepsisters balance humility and vanity)

  An adventure (defined by the protagonist's objective: Nora's freedom; Macbeth's kingship; Cinderella's love)

  A final battle (the highest stakes conclusion to the action: Macbeth fights Macduff; Nora speaks honestly to Helmer; Cinderella reveals herself to her family and the prince).

I

- Work individually – this could be done as a pre-class exercise. Locate each of these four elements in your chosen stories.

II

- Work in pairs. Give yourselves 3 minutes each. Tell the story of your journey to rehearsal today, exploring Jung's terms, with yourself as the protagonist. Locate a rigid behaviour pattern, a key relationship, an adventure and a final battle. Perhaps this is the story of you (humble) versus the bus driver (arrogant), or you (victimized) versus the rail network (evil genius) or you (anxious) and your travel partner (calm) versus the traffic, as your adventure to get to rehearsals unfolds. Feel free to embellish – particularly with the final battle!

Archetypal stories (30 minutes)

Understand the basic archetypes of stories and use them as a basis for devising new stories.

- Keep referencing the three stories you have worked on in the previous exercise.

- It is often said that there are only seven stories:

  Cinderella – in which 'good' is despised, but finally recognized as it triumphs over its enemies (*Jane Eyre*, *Dirty Dancing*)
  Achilles – in which the protagonist succumbs to a fatal flaw; this is often the basis for tragedy and also farce (*The Great Gatsby*, *The Producers*)
  Faust – in which the debt that must be paid is called in, as fate catches up with the protagonist (*The Lion King*, *Schindler's List*)
  Camelot – the eternal (love) triangle: Arthur loves Guinevere, Guinevere loves Lancelot, Lancelot loves Arthur and so on round the Round Table (*La Morte D'Arthur*, *Bridget Jones*)
  The Spider and the Fly – in which the fly is tempted and chased, possibly to its own downfall (*Blues Brothers*, *Goldilocks*)
  Romeo and Juliet – in which boy meets girl, boy loses girl, boy finds – or doesn't – girl again (*Forrest Gump*, *Titanic*, but also buddy movies like *Shawshank Redemption*)
  Orpheus – the perfect gift is taken away and either restored or not (*The Aeneid*, *The Wizard of Oz*).

- Work individually – this could be done as a pre-class exercise. Go through your three stories and locate them within these archetypes. *Macbeth* is an Achilles story; *A Doll's House* is a Faust story; *Cinderella* is, well, the Cinderella story.

- Your stories may, of course, be a blend of archetypes.

II

- Work as a full group. Agree on a story archetype. Sit in a circle. Go sequentially round the circle, speaking just one word each at a time, and build a new story based on this narrative archetype.

- No-one must say more than one word at a time, and everyone must take their responsibility to move the narrative forward (so don't excuse yourselves from storytelling by just adding redundant adjectives, thus delaying the responsibility to move the story on). If you find this particularly difficult, to begin with you might take a short sentence each.

- The first time you do this exercise you will probably stumble a lot. You will get better as you practise, and you will find its greatest value as it becomes more than a fun game. Through this exercise, you can learn a lot about story craft and taking responsibility for moving a story forward within an ensemble.

Premise (25 minutes)

Discover how a story gets moving from a premise, and devise an original premise to trigger new stories into life.

A premise is the basic 'What if …?' which gets the drama moving. For example, the premise of the film *Jaws* is: What if a man-eating shark turns up at a holiday beach?

I

- Work individually. This could be done as a pre-class exercise. Choose one of your stories and write its premise.

- The premise of *A Doll's House* might be: What if a nineteenth-century woman takes a secret loan to save her husband's life? *Macbeth's* premise is something like: What if a grief-ridden, war-ravaged Thane receives a prophecy that he will be king? *Cinderella's* premise might be: What if a poor, lonely servant-girl had a fairy godmother to make her dreams come true?

II

- Work as a full group. Allow 20 minutes.

- Take a piece of paper. In 4 minutes devise a premise and write a letter to someone, propelling this premise into action. The letter will be persuasive in some way – asking for help or imploring someone to take action (like the letter Macbeth writes to Lady Macbeth, telling her about the prophecy he has received from the witches).

- Fold this letter into an aeroplane and fly it across the room. Everyone gets a new letter that lands nearby.

- Read the letter you receive, and write a reply on the back. Your reply must in some way raise the stakes (as if Lady Macbeth wrote back to Macbeth telling him King Duncan was due at the castle and they should kill him tonight).

- Share the letters, reading them out to the group as a dialogue between characters.

Genre (25 minutes)

Use genre as a way of setting, surpassing or surprising audience expectations.

I

- Work as a full group in a circle.

- Genre defines tone, convention, form, technique and, for an audience, expectation.

- Examples of storytelling genres include: thriller, murder mystery, gothic horror, farce, action adventure, science fiction, romance, romantic comedy, documentary, historical epic, biography and so on.

- Make your own list of genres.

- Each of these genres has associated conventions, forms, tone and techniques. A farce, for example, is extraordinary things happening to ordinary people. Confusion, lots of doors with people running in and out, extraordinary and improbable situations, disguise and mistaken identity, physical gags, trousers falling down and double-takes galore are all part of the genre. Farce allows us a *deus ex machina* (literally 'the hand of god', but meaning an unexpected intervention which suddenly flips the course of events in the drama, as when, in Judea in 33 AD, Brian is saved by a passing alien spaceship in Monty Python's *Life of Brian*) and can mean we don't need to commit to poetic justice in our resolution (people can get away with immoral acts and that's fine).

- In a thriller, we expect suspense, tension, excitement. Storytelling will be fast-paced, stakes will be high – probably life or death. It will be psychological, and probably about a good person in a corrupt world. There is usually a heavily defined protagonist/antagonist relationship, in which the antagonist seems unbeatable. This usually takes place in a particular, tight community, with its own vocabulary and special rules – politics, the criminal underworld, secret intelligence, the military and the Church are all classic settings for a thriller. In common with farce, there is often the mistaken identity of an innocent involved. *Othello* is a classic thriller.

- Look at your three stories. What genre conventions do they employ? Do they subvert genre expectations?

- Great storytellers position their audience to employ and then subvert or surpass genre expectations.

II

- Tell one of your stories as a tag team, but explore it within a specific genre. One of you start telling the story, but anytime you want to tag out from the telling because you are losing your way in the story, do so. Or if as a listener there is detail you want to add, then tag in.

- Try telling the same story in several different genres. You might tell the story of *Cinderella* as a thriller, a romantic comedy, a farce or a morality drama.

- Don't alter the events of the story: structure the plot and condition the events to serve the genre.

- Reflect on how the various genres served the story and its audience.

Archetypal events (20–40 minutes depending on extensions)

Devise an original movement sequence in response to one of Jung's six archetypal events. Respond to these as central beats in any story.

- The psychoanalyst Carl Jung described six archetypal events, which punctuate our social existence:

  Birth
  Death
  Separation from parents
  Initiation (rites of passage like a baptism, confirmation, bar mitzvah, eighteenth birthday party or graduation ceremony)
  Marriage
  The union of opposites.

I

- Work individually – this can be done as pre-class preparation. With which of these events do your stories engage? *Macbeth* is focused on birth and death; *A Doll's House* is about separation from parents and marriage; *Cinderella* is about initiation and marriage. Look in magazines or newspapers and find images relevant to the event. Bring these into class and stick them on the wall.

II

- Work individually. Take a chair, and find a space. For 2 minutes just explore the chair's potential: What can you do with this object? Explore its texture, weight, balance points, test different positions it can hold and ways in which you can relate to it.

- Now choose one of Jung's archetypal events as a stimulus. Give yourself 2 minutes to create five abstract shapes using the chair, responding to this event. Be confident and instinctive in your choices. Do not be literal, but respond to the images (on the wall), emotions, sensations of the event as you understand it.

- Connect these five shapes into one short movement sequence.

- Now find a partner, ideally (but not necessarily) someone who is responding to the same event. Learn each other's five shapes.

- Find a way to combine the ten shapes together, to create one movement sequence involving both your shapes. You might do them in unison, you might perform them on different levels or on different planes, or stagger and repeat them. Explore working in close proximity and very separately; explore facing each other and not. What kind of dialogue occurs between your movements?

- Next, if you have the available time, you could find another pair and join your movement sequences together into one sequence involving all four of you.

III

- Present your sequence to another pair or four. What narrative arises for the spectators to this silent dance? What relationships are suggested? What desires are implied?

- You could extend this further by adding individual words, a relevant poem or music to the sequence.

Story politics (25 minutes)

Engage with the politics of a story's setting, and understand how it influences both the action of a story and the political message an audience takes away.

- Politics, in this case, refers to the orchestration of power within the world of a story. What do you need to be, or get more of, to become powerful? Is this a patriarchy? Is it feudal or racist?

Is it sexist? Is it democratic, an autocracy or an oligarchy? Is it capitalist?

- Cinderella lives under a patriarchal, capitalist monarchy. As a poor woman, disinherited by her family, she couldn't be further from power at the beginning of the story. This is what makes her transformation so remarkable.

- Macbeth's is a feudal, patriarchal, capitalist, sexist, tribal, militaristic society in which might is right (if you can wield a heavy broadsword with skill, you will gain more power). Nora lives under a sexist, capitalist patriarchy, which values intellect. These political arrangements define the drama in both plays, particularly *A Doll's House*: the play simply won't work set outside of these political conditions.

I

- Draw or write a status line for the opening of one of your stories, with the most socially powerful character in the story at the top, the least powerful at the bottom. So, for example, *Cinderella* opens thus:

    The Prince
    Cinderella's father
    Cinderella's stepmother
    The eldest sister
    The middle sister
    The youngest sister
    Cinderella.

- The Fairy Godmother enters the story and subverts this arrangement of power, introducing a moral dimension to the politics: goodness will be rewarded with power.

II

- Work as a full group on one story. Everyone take a role within that story (giving the same character to several people if necessary) to define the arrangement of power in the room. You don't need to work in character; work as yourself but with that character's relative social power.

- Treat your room as another character. The room is in the middle of the status line. (If the room were the Prince's palace, all but one of the characters would feel diminished not empowered by this character.) For characters with higher status than it, the room is an ally or servant. For characters with lower status than the room, it is another obstacle you must overcome.

- Working on *Cinderella*, I give the room higher status than Cinderella and the youngest sister; its status might be on a par with the middle sister's. For Cinderella and the youngest sister, the room represents an obstacle.

- Now agree on a shared objective for everyone in the room: perhaps just tidying the rehearsal room, or arranging chairs and tables for a meeting. Pursue this objective through these conditioning power arrangements. Cinderella might not want to disturb the room much; her eldest step-sister might confidently crash around in it.

- Let this be serious play: commit to the power structure.

- Once the objective is achieved, reflect on behaviours and sensations. Consider how you related to each other and the space, and how your bodies and choices were conditioned.

Culture (50 minutes)

Look at culture within the setting of a story as the source of conflict and tension. Devise your own scenarios which explore this.

- Every story world has its own culture. A culture is a system of learned – rather than biological – behaviours.

- Allow 15–20 minutes for Parts I and II combined; allow 30 minutes for Part III.

I

- Work as a full group.

- Make a list of things which define a 'culture'. Be specific to your own culture, but also try and bring in references to other cultures to help you understand your own culture and its prejudices.

- You might include: beliefs, values, knowledge, rituals, language and behaviours. These things give us what we understand to be true, good, real and normal.

II

- Education establishes and endorses cultural norms. Think of the key words written up around most schools, which teach these. At my sons' school, the following five words are written over the entrance: cooperation, perseverance, kindness, honesty and responsibility. In the United Kingdom, loyalty rarely features on these lists, but honesty almost always does. We are asked to be honest more than loyal: if my friend breaks something, I learn I should be honest and tell a teacher rather than be loyal and keep quiet.

- Storytelling does the same: it establishes and then either challenges or endorses cultural norms. *Cinderella* teaches us that kindness and humility will be rewarded. *A Doll's House* endorses equality of rights and individual freedom.

- Choose one of your stories. Ask what cultural norms this story is endorsing or challenging. Make a list of words that might be up on the walls of the protagonist's imaginary primary school (Macbeth's primary school – what a thought – might have had: Scotland, power, loyalty, honour and strength).

III

- Break into groups of four or five. Give yourselves 3 minutes to devise a scenario which puts an imagined character (not one already in the story) in conflict with their cultural values. For example, in the world of my sons' school, this might be a scene in which a pupil has to choose between being honest and being kind, but cannot be both. So a teacher is telling little Chloe off for breaking a school computer. The honest thing to do is to tell the teacher that it was actually Maia who broke it. The kind thing to do is to take the blame and protect Maia, who didn't mean to do it and is on a final warning before a detention. Crisis!

- Write down your scenario and give it to another group.

- Take the scenario you have just received, and allow 3 minutes to extend it. How could you intensify the crisis for this character, raise the stakes of that moment? Intensify the pressure on the character in that moment of choice (it's not a computer Maia accidentally broke, it's Mike's nose ...).

- Write down your intensified scenario and pass it on to another group.

- You can continue to pass round scenes, raising the stakes and testing culture against individuals – making the political personal (Mike is the teacher's son ...).

- When you feel as if you have extended the scenarios to their truthful limits, make the character at the centre choose. Stage this event and present it to the rest of the group.

Archetypal character design (60–80 minutes)

Engage with the principles of character design. Apply different models of character design to stories you know. Develop enough basic understanding to devise original characters within a story.

- Work as a full group. Take 30 minutes to discuss different types of character design.

- The first model comes from *Commedia dell'Arte* (a masked theatre form begun in sixteenth-century Italy). In *Commedia*, new work was constantly being devised in response to contemporary events. The devising process worked with stock narrative – often a comic version of the story we know as the basic *Romeo and Juliet* narrative, with a bitter father as the obstacle between witty young lovers. It also worked with a set of character archetypes.

- The character archetypes define behaviour patterns for the actors, and satisfying, balanced dynamics for the story. Every character serves a different function and plays a distinct role within the story world. This is character design.

- We see similar reliance on archetypes in contemporary television, where work is being devised and produced at a similarly hectic pace. TV shows such as *Friends* rely on designed archetypes for their success: Joey, Chandler, Monica, Rachel, Phoebe and Ross each have fixed behaviour patterns, which define our expectations of their reactions and choices. These expectations deliver emotions: we basically know what to expect when Joey picks up a copy of Anton Chekhov's *The Seagull*, and we laugh as he either satisfies or surprises that expectation.

- The archetypes of *Commedia dell'Arte* are as follows:

  Harlequin is an acrobat and a wit, childlike and amorous.
  Birghella is Harlequin's best mate, roguish and sophisticated, a cowardly villain who will do anything for money.
  The Captain is a caricature of the professional soldier – bold, swaggering and cowardly.
  The Doctor is a caricature of learning – pompous and fraudulent.
  The Pantaloon is a caricature of the merchant: rich and retired, mean and miserly, with a young wife or adventurous daughter.
  Pedrolino is a moon-struck dreamer and the forerunner of the modern clown.
  Pulcinella is the cruel and ugly bachelor who chases beautiful women.
  Scaramouche dresses in black and carries a rapier – the Errol Flynn/Robin Hood of his day.
  The lovers are eloquent, sincere young lovers.
  Columbina is the female lover's servant, and herself loved by Harlequin – Witty, bright and given to intrigue.

La Ruffiana is an old woman, either the female lover's mother or a village gossip, who thwarts the lovers.

- You can see that this collection of archetypes – like the *Friends* troupe – creates a dynamic, balanced and conflict-ready community. Everyone serves a distinct role with strongly defined behaviour patterns.

- Different character designs occur in different storytelling forms. A list of roles used in the structure of much modern cinema, for example films such as *Star Wars* and *Harry Potter*, runs as follows:

    Protagonist – the central character (Luke Skywalker, Harry Potter)

    Antagonist – the central character's main opponent (The Emperor, Voldemort)

    Sidekick – the protagonist's loyal and optimistic ally (R2D2, Ron and Hermione)

    Sceptic – the sidekick's opposite, a voice of pessimistic caution doubting the protagonist's choices (Han Solo, Ron)

    Guardian – the mentor, teacher, helper, guide and moral standard for the protagonist, who helps them onto the right path (Obi Wan Kenobi, Dumbledore)

    Contagonist – an ugly term, but meaning the guardian's opposite: a figure with shadowy motives, who hinders the protagonist by causing them to take the wrong path, wittingly or unwittingly (Darth Vader, Snape)

    Reason – the logical character who influences the protagonist towards the path of reason (Leia, Hermione)

    Emotion – the opposite to Reason, whose behaviour influences the protagonist towards the path of emotion (Chewbacca and C3PO, Hagrid and Ron).

- Take 5 minutes to apply this model to a film of your choice.

- Remember, one character can fulfil more than one role – so Woody in *Toy Story* is both protagonist and reason. Richer characterizations can come when the characters are in conflict with their archetypal behaviour patterns (as with all Woody Allen's protagonists, who long to be other than they are).

- Carl Jung located nine archetypal figures in Western storytelling:

  Hero (Luke Skywalker, Harry Potter)
  Sidekick (C3P0 and R2D2, Ron and Hermione)
  Maiden (Princess Leia, Ginny)
  Wise old man (Obi Wan Kenobi, Dumbledore)
  Nurturing mother (Luke's Aunt Beru, Professor McGonagall)
  Eternal child (Chewbacca and R2D2, Hagrid)
  Villain (The Emperor, Voldemort)
  Shapeshifter (Darth Vader, Snape)
  Trickster (Han Solo, The Weasley brothers).

- Jung does not suggest that individuals or characters conform wholly or uniformly to these archetypes (so characters need not always or only be the Trickster, say). The archetypes interchange and combine with each other.

- Take 5 minutes and try this model out on a film of your choice.

- Finally, let's look at a fourth model, which can be useful when looking for a starting point for devising characters from scratch:

Archetype	Motive	Objective
Creator	stability and control	create something of enduring value
Caregiver	stability and control	protect others from harm
Ruler	stability and control	control
Jester	belonging and enjoyment	live each moment with enjoyment
Regular guy	belonging and enjoyment	connect with others
Lover	belonging and enjoyment	achieve intimacy with others
Hero	risk and mastery	prove one's worth through courage
Outlaw	risk and mastery	revenge or revolution
Magician	risk and mastery	gather knowledge about the world
Innocent	independence and fulfilment	experience paradise
Explorer	independence and fulfilment	discover your free self
Sage	independence and fulfilment	uncover the truth

- Do you recognize any of these character archetypes within your three stories? Analyse the character design in your stories. Assign characters archetypal roles.

II

- Work as a full group. Allow 20–25 minutes to explore the impact of character archetypes on a scene.

- Take a scene from a story or play you are working on. Give each actor involved an archetype from this last model to explore through their character. So, for a scene between Nora and Helmer, for example, ask the actors to play Nora as the Jester and Helmer as the Caregiver.

- Now do the same scene, but give them quite different archetypes to explore. Nora might play the Sage, Helmer the Explorer. What does this uncover about character dimension/ contradiction? Try several iterations with different archetypes.

- If you are improvising a first scene between Cinderella and her stepmother, in which Cinderella is being ordered to clean a room, you might initially ask the actor playing Cinderella to explore the Innocent, the actor playing the stepmother to explore the Ruler. Now try again: What if Cinderella is the Outlaw, the stepmother the Explorer?

- Reflect on these archetypes and what an understanding of them might liberate in devising a character.

Follow-up

These exercises carry the work on into everyday life, to encourage reflection on what you have learned and how it reaches beyond rehearsals.

- Take it in turns to prepare and teach the group a game you loved in your childhood. Play it together as a start to ongoing classwork.

- Who are the great storytellers of our age? Can you think of politicians, journalists, business leaders or performers who construct for themselves stories with archetypes and narrative structures? Make notes in your journal on these. What archetype did Barack Obama employ to sell himself as President of the United States of America? Compare him to George W. Bush or Bill Clinton. What narrative did each of these presidents write for the story of the election?

- What is the story of your life? Have you built a narrative for yourself about your behaviour patterns and experiences? How does this limit you? How does this liberate you? What would it be like to explore other patterns? Make notes in your journal.

- Watch the storyteller and novelist Chimamanda Ngozi Adichie talk on the political power of storytelling and the social responsibility of the storyteller in her talk 'The danger of a single story': www.ted.com/talks/ chimamanda_adichie_the_danger_of_a_single_story

Further reading

For a very detailed model of story design and analysis see:
www.dramatica.com

Alfreds, Mike (2013), *Then What Happens?* Nick Hern Books. Section 5, 'From Narrative to Narration'.
Berger, John (1972), *Ways of Seeing.* Penguin.
Campbell, Joseph with Bill Moyers (1988), *The Power of Myth.* Anchor Books.
Howard, Pamel (2002), *What is Scenography?* Routledge. Part 1, 'Space'.
Johnstone, Keith (1999), *Impro for Storytellers.* Faber and Faber.
McKee, Robert (1997), *Story.* Methuen.
Oida, Yoshi and Marshall, Lorna (1997), *The Invisible Actor.* Routledge. Chapter 3, 'Performing – Jo Ha Kyu'.

10
CONSTRUCT

Learn processes and models for devising original theatre in response to different sorts of stimulus material.

Framework

All the processes outlined in this chapter have one requirement in common: sophisticated collaboration within an ensemble. All theatre processes – both in training and in rehearsal – rely on this; but none is as dependent upon it as devising.

*

Specialize and exchange

Devising original theatre as an ensemble does not mean everyone does everything. You don't all need to be director-designer-writer-actors. Specialize and share.

The human success story is one of specialized collaboration. The madly inventive expansion of our species has occurred because we live, communicate and explore in collaborative communities, each of which has specialized in different skills and shared the rewards. Together we achieve more wild and wonderful things than any of us could alone.

Who knows how to make the book you are reading? No-one. Literally no-one in the world understands every element and skill which goes into making this book. But the right group of people, working in the right order, applying their specialisms to the same objective, can chop and pulp the trees, make the chemicals to form the paper, mine the carbon and oils in the ink, source the dyes, make the solvents, write the words … This book is no more one person's work than are the exercises in it.

A book is not a single thing. Nor is an idea. An idea does not drop down, like Newton's apple, onto your head: like this book, an idea is a network. In our brains, neurones make new connections and these establish new ideas. Fortune favours the connected. To devise original work, build new networks and new outcomes will naturally occur.

What we build is a network – not a hierarchy. The ensemble of specialists is not a rising ladder; whoever takes on the role of director acts as an outside eye providing feedback, not the decision-maker sitting above the others involved. Specialists take responsibility for a particular expertise; but everyone takes equal responsibility for making decisions.

As we work, the boundaries will blur and the roles spill over – when does a designer become a director? When is a writer a designer? When is an actor a writer? Often. This is healthy: this is the magic taking place. Specialize, share and create new networks.

*

Draft, assess, adapt and decide

As you devise, you will go down plenty of blind alleys and face many choices. The first choice is:

> To try to design one perfect piece of theatre, or
> To build several prototypes, then work to remodel and improve the best of these.

The collaborative process cries out for the latter, iterative process. You make drafts and initial sketches, following hunches and curiosity. This is the playful way.

This free-flow approach does not allow for prevarication. Deadlines are liberating. Commit to directions of travel and see where they take the work. The only deadly choice is no choice.

Decision-making within a group is a discrete art of its own. You could decide:

By authority (efficient, but can isolate the majority)

By majority (efficient, but can isolate the minority)

By negative minority (vote out the worst ideas until you've only a couple to try out)

By ranking (number them 1–5: democratic but slow)

By unanimity (rare, slow)

By consensus (slow, as everyone works towards being able to say either: unequivocally yes; or, I accept this can work; or, I don't think it's best but I'll go with it for the sake of the group).

Any of these models can be part of the devising process at any time. Agree on one person who can act as final arbiter over a decision if required. This individual (and it should not always be the same person – try changing it in sequence for each rehearsal) will make decisions by authority if no unanimous, consensual or majority decision can be achieved. Remember, any decision is simply keeping you travelling. You can always revise later. *The only deadly choice is no choice.*

The sketches we make will demand a good deal of group feedback. This is another art form. Below are seven guiding points about sharing feedback:

Focus on what you see (the work, not the personality involved)

Own the feedback (say 'I saw', not 'we saw' or 'they saw')

Balance the feedback (feedback isn't pointing out all the things that didn't work; start with what you thought effective or powerful)

Be specific (don't say 'it was', say 'this moment was')

Be realistic (suggestions must be achievable)

Be timely (choose the moment when the feedback is both ripe and welcome)

Get involved (make yourself part of the solution, not simply the observer of a problem).

Above all, it must be delivered with the positive and singular intent of moving the ensemble towards its shared goal.

The art of *receiving* feedback, means: join in. Develop the feedback your work receives (not you – your work): build on it, don't deconstruct it. Fold in constructive feedback, do not reject or block it.

*

In biology, we often write the story of the survival of the fittest: in a competitive world, the roughest and toughest thrive. That is not the ecology of the devising process. To thrive, we must specialize, collaborate and share resources for a greater reward. Such collaboration is the profound privilege of our work.

Exploration

These exploratory exercises are simple starters for a devising session, which will act as basic warm-ups mobilizing your imagination and creative will.

- Write these words in the middle of a page: 'the best theatrical experience of my life'. Now mind-map things that might make this happen. For instance, good food and drink, being with friends and family, being in the open air on a sunny evening, a passionate story … Whatever would make your perfect trip to the theatre. Can you make such theatre? Don't forget these ideals as you devise.

- Bring in your favourite children's story (for ages 2–6) and read it to the rest of the group. Make a choice about the physical relationship to the audience (in the round/end on, etc.) and whether there will be any interaction with your audience (there is rich potential in many such books for everyone to join in with a line, or perform a simple physical action – all those Wild Things dancing with Max in *Where The Wild Things Are*). After you have read it, with the group isolate the set-up, inciting incident, crisis, climax and resolution. The rest of the group provides feedback on this work, using the rules of feedback (in both giving and receiving) outlined in this chapter's 'Framework'. How might you revise your work in response to this feedback?

- Many moments in our lives are conducted by the rhythm of grief: shock, denial, anger, sadness, acceptance. Think of yourself when you realized you'd double booked your evening – 'What? Oh no. I'm an *idiot*! Oh man. Oh maaaaan [sigh] … Right'. Shock, denial, anger, sadness, acceptance. Grief is the rhythm of change. Every time we experience change, we experience loss: something is sacrificed as something else is gained. Change is the currency of drama. Reflect on a moment of loss in your life, but *not* someone's death – perhaps you lost a valuable object, perhaps you had plans for your future that were changed, perhaps someone close to you moved away. Observe the pattern, the rhythm of grief that conducted your response to that loss. Now work in groups of about five. Choose one of your stories and build a frozen image from each of the stages of this grief – so five frozen images in all. Everyone in the group must be involved in each picture. Try using the different models of decision-making as you work here (see 'Framework') – or if the decision-making occurs naturally and with ease, reflect at the end of the process on how decisions were made.

- Many moments are conducted by the rhythm of unexpected success: shock, denial, relief, joy, acceptance. 'What? No way! Thank goodness! Brilliant! Right then …'. Reflect on a moment of triumph or success in your life. Perhaps you got a job, got a part in a play or won an award. Observe the pattern written into your behaviour. Now work in groups of about five. Choose one of your stories and build a frozen image from each of the stages of this success – so five frozen images in all. Everyone in the group must be involved in each picture. Try using the different models of decision-making as you work here (see 'Framework') – or if the decision-making occurs naturally and with ease, reflect at the end of the process on how decisions were made.

Exercises

The following exercises model ways to develop original material based on a specific stimulus.

I have broken these exercises into three parts. The first part, *'Beginning to devise',* models exercises which will form the basis of any devising process. The second part, 'Devising narrative drama', presents two models for devising narrative drama, one using a story as its stimulus, the other using a painting as the stimulus. The third part, 'Devising non-narrative drama', uses a poem as the stimulus for devising non-narrative drama.

Any of the ways of working could differently be applied to any stimulus. Above all, devising is an organic, hand-made process. None of the models which follow is intended to be definitive, merely suggestive. Every exercise here owes much to the work of three key practitioners central to the growth of devised theatre in the twentieth century: Joan Littlewood, Augusto Boal and Keith Johnstone.

Beginning to devise

Researching the stimulus

Stimulate and feed imagination with the specifics of relationships, events and given circumstances, which condition and affect a character's desire. Uncover the story-world and setting, as discussed in Chapter 9.

- Allow 1–2 weeks for research, or ideally do this preparatory work over a holiday before you start rehearsing.

I

- Working in groups, research the political, cultural, biographical (for the writer/artist/protagonist) and social context of your stimulus material.
- Between you, research its political, cultural, biographical (considering yourself its author) and social relevance *now*.

- Divide these research tasks evenly among the group.

- As discussed on pages 140–1, research by visiting art galleries, libraries, seeing plays, watching films, reading poetry, listening to music, gathering images, interviewing relevant people.

II

- Prepare stories to share as research presentations. Don't present facts; tell stories about the research you have done: political, historical, biographical events told to your group as a story.

- Isolate the beginning (set-up and inciting incident), middle (central conflict) and end (climax and resolution) of your research story.

- Prepare a genre for the telling of your research story, appropriate to the events (e.g. comedy, tragedy, love story).

- Choose whether you will write yourself into the events or not (first person, third person, past tense, dramatic present tense).

- You might also bring in relevant objects, images and pieces of text for the group to explore.

- After you have shared these stories, reflect on them – there may be one whose potential you want to investigate further.

Stimulus themes

Engage with the big ideas in the stimulus material.

- Work first individually and then as a full group. The first part of this exercise will be done as pre-class preparation, the second part will take 10–15 minutes at the start of a session.

- Define the key themes in your stimulus material. You might use the archetypal themes outlined on page 259 as a reference, or you might develop some of your own.

- Research the themes at the heart of your stimulus material, by finding images, poems, stories, adverts, news articles which connect to the themes of the stimulus in some way. Look in

newspapers, magazines, books you have at home. Find and
cut out or copy three to five offers each.

- Bring these in and share them at the start of a session, in a
  show-and-tell style. Make explicit the link you see between the
  stimulus and this image or text. Wallpaper your rehearsal space
  with these images and words. They connect your stimulus to
  your world.

Storyretelling on themes (20–30 minutes)

*Take those big ideas and bring them to life through your own
experiences. Connect personally to these ideas. Turn these
experiences into an act of theatre, which immediately becomes
available material to adapt and develop in your devising
process.*

- Work with a partner.
- Consider one of the themes from the stimulus material. Think
  of an experience from your own life, when you have felt or
  witnessed something which relates directly to this theme. This
  must be a story you don't mind everyone else in the group
  hearing.
- Take it in turns to tell and listen to the story of this experience.
- If you are the storyteller, take care to share detail about your
  feelings and the sensory experience: what you could see, hear
  and so on in the course of these events.
- If you are the listener, connect with these events, and do ask
  specific and compassionate questions if you want to. My
  grandpa used to remind me of the difference between listening
  and waiting to speak.

II

- Once you have both shared, switch partners and work with
  someone new. Before you begin, take time to consider the
  story you were just told, and make clear in your own mind:

Who the protagonist of this story is

What the inciting incident is in the story

What the key moment of decision for the protagonist is (the crisis point)

What the end of the story is (climax and resolution).

- Tell the story you just heard to your new partner, but in the first person as if it had happened to you. Allow the story to grow and develop if you want to add detail, or need to make changes to use the first person credibly. Make yourself the author of this story.

- If you are listening, ask compassionate and specific questions. You are not trying to catch out the storyteller; you are trying to further understand this experience.

III

- Now switch partners and work with someone new.

- In just the same way, tell the story you just heard to your new partner – in the first person and as if it had happened to you.

- Continue telling stories and moving on in this way, until the stories have spread like wildfire.

- This exercise quickly generates new stories in response to the stimulus material. This sequence of storytelling is its own valid act of theatre.

- Reflect on the stories you have heard and told: there may be some you want to expand and develop as you construct your own original piece of theatre.

Super-objective (20 minutes)

Bring your attention to the social purpose of the stimulus material. Underline the political intention within the stimulus material. Ensure whatever you devise is conscious of its social function.

I

- Work as a full group. Establish the super-objective of the stimulus material.

- What is its reason for existing? What social, political or personal objective does it strive to achieve?

- *Cinderella* is designed to communicate a clear moral message to young children: goodness and humility will be rewarded; vanity and cruelty will be punished. Some moral messages will be more complex. *A Doll's House* exposes how social duties and hierarchies deny individuals self-fulfilment. *Macbeth* celebrates the reign of King James; its simplest message is: don't kill the king. But there is clearly more meaning available in the play than just this. Contemporary productions explore the effects of blind ambition, tyrannical leadership, the effects of war and grief on soldiers' minds.

- What are you trying to achieve by staging a response to this stimulus? Will you sign up to its super-objective, or do you wish to subvert it in some way? You may not have a clue at the moment, but start asking the question: What conversation will we begin among our audience?

- It might be about a feeling you want to generate – 'to make the audience go home and call their mums and tell them they love them' – or it could espouse a specific political idea.

- Write this super-objective on a big piece of paper in big, colourful letters and stick it on the wall.

II

Now write on that paper on the wall three verbs that describe the intended impact of the piece. For example:

To shock, silence and move

To move, amuse and entertain

To entertain, tickle and delight.

- As follow-up work, find two other stories or works of art which have pursued a similar super-objective. Find images of, or sections of text from, these works to share with the group and put up on your wall next time. For *A Doll's House* you might bring in text from George Orwell's *1984*, music from Tchaikovsky's *The Nutcracker* or images of Disney's film of *Pinocchio*. Each of these works explores themes related to *A Doll's House* in very different ways. Theatre-makers are magpies: there might be something shiny worth stealing in what others have done while working towards a similar end.

Alternative titles

Consider different ways to frame the stimulus material. Develop an original creative response to that understanding.

- Come up with alternative titles for your stimulus piece. What else could *A Doll's House* have been called? How about: *Nora Helmer*; *The Tarantella*; *The Singing Bird*? How would a new title alter our relationship to the material itself?
- Why is it called what it is called?

||

- As a follow-up exercise, design a cover image for the stimulus piece, if you were to publish your own edition of it with this new title. Don't worry about your own perceived artistic limitations ('I can't draw!') – make a collage or find image references to show what you imagine.
- Share these with the rest of the class and stick them up on your wall.

Devising narrative drama

Cinderella

After the basic work outlined above, these exercises explore developing a dramatic structure for an original piece of theatre. I will model them using a non-dramatic, narrative stimulus – Cinderella. The exercises could of course be applied to any stimulus which has at its heart a story – whether song, novel, cartoon, myth or narrative poem. The exercises could as easily be applied to Coleridge's The Rime of the Ancient Mariner, *the story of Medusa or Bob Dylan's* Like a Rolling Stone.

Story (10 minutes)

Make lateral connections between your stimulus material and other stories you could tell. Any of the stories you bring in could form the basis of a new piece of theatre.

I

- Work as a full group.
- What kind of story is this? Reference the story archetypes on page 262. *Cinderella* is obviously the archetypal rags to riches tale.
- Name as many different stories as you can which also tell this same kind of story. Write them up on a big piece of paper and stick this up on the wall.

II

- As follow-up work, bring in images or sections of text from them. For example, working on *Cinderella* I might bring in images from *Pretty Woman* and *Good Will Hunting*, sections of text from *Oliver Twist* and *Charlie and the Chocolate Factory*, the sheet music for a song from *Les Misérables*, or tell the real-life story of Dhirubhai Ambani – an Indian petrol pump attendant who became a multi-billionaire yarn-trader. All would go up on the wall. I would certainly research the Dhirubhai Ambani story as a basis for further devising – it might make a wonderful narrative response to *Cinderella*.

Genre (10 minutes)

Connect with the genre of the stimulus material. Any of the related material you bring in for Part II of this exercise could form the basis for devised theatre.

I

- Work in pairs.
- What genre of storytelling is your stimulus? *Cinderella* is clearly a children's fairytale.
- Write a list of five other stories which fall into this same genre, both straightforwardly and as a revision of the genre. In the case of *Cinderella*: *Little Red Riding Hood* and *The Three Little Pigs,* but also *The Hunger Games*, *Charlie and the Chocolate Factory* and *Edward Scissorhands*.
- Write a list of five or more genre conventions/expectations which are associated with this genre. In this case:

   A child is the protagonist
   The protagonist's life is put at stake
   Death is a key theme
   It has a happy ending
   There is a strong and simple moral message
   It operates in a fantasy realm
   Adults are often antagonists
   Magic/supernatural events can occur
   It is possible to communicate with animals.

- Share these with the group, and stick them on your wall.

II

- As follow-up work, find and bring in images/sections of text from these stories, as you did in the last exercise.

Protagonists (20 minutes)

Decide whose story you are telling. Define a point of view from which to devise. Any of the stories you tell in this exercise could form the basis of further devising.

- Work as a full group, sitting in a circle.
- Who is the protagonist in the story?

I

- Tell the story from the protagonist's point of view. Tell it in the first person and past tense ('I was sweeping the floors after my eldest stepsister's birthday party, when …').
- Go round the circle, speaking a word each and building the story word by word, person by person.
- Take responsibility for moving the story on, and adding colour and the deliciously unreliable perspective which the first person offers. This is all about exploring your protagonist's point of view.

II

- Now choose another character to be your protagonist and tell the story again from their point of view. Again, use the past tense and first person, speaking a word each around the circle.
- Working on *Cinderella* we could tell the story from the eldest stepsister's point of view.
- Reflect on this. How does it affect genre? How does it alter the events of the story?

> *Teaching Tip:* If word-by-word story building is proving too tricky at first, then try it phrase by phrase and work towards doing this word by word.

Story design (15 minutes)

Outline the whole story as a dramatic presentation. Bring the story to still life.

- Work in small groups of four or five.
- Observe the narrative structure of your stimulus story.
- Arranging *Cinderella* into classical structure, it looks like this:

   Set-up – we see Cinderella held in servitude to her stepmother and stepsisters after her beloved father died. They are all preparing for the Prince's ball.
   Inciting incident – the Fairy Godmother appears to Cinderella.
   Rising action – the Fairy Godmother sends Cinderella along too, who meets the Prince.
   Crisis – Cinderella flees the ball.
   Falling action – the Prince seeks Cinderella throughout the kingdom.
   Climax – the Prince finds Cinderella.
   Resolution – Cinderella and the Prince marry.

- In 7 minutes, build a frozen image for each of these seven moments. Present them back to the full group. If you have the facility, take photographs of these and print them to stick up on your wall. If you don't have this facility, sketch them.

Act design (20 minutes)

Break the action of the story into more manageable chunks. Begin to build a dramatic structure around the story. Locate key moments of conflict for your protagonist, and begin to think of these as dramatic action.

- Work as a full group to discuss act design.

- Classical five-act structure arranges narrative events as follows:

    Act 1 includes the set-up and inciting incident
    Act 2 is the rising action
    Act 3 builds to the crisis point
    Act 4 is the falling action
    Act 5 builds to the climax and resolution.

    Not every play has five acts. Different act structures deploy the narrative events with a different rhythm. A three-act drama typically arranges the events thus:

- Act 1 – set-up, inciting incident, rising action

- Act 2 – rising action, crisis point

- Act 3 – falling action, climax and resolution.

- A two-act drama puts a single act break after the crisis.

- In a play, an act break marks a major change (for better or worse) in the fortunes of the protagonist.

- Every act has its internal structure. An act contains a crisis point for the protagonist (at which point the protagonist faces a crisis over whether or not to continue in the pursuit of their objective), and a final climax (at which point a major change occurs in the life of the protagonist).

- As the play progresses, the act's crises and climaxes grow in intensity. The major changes at the end of each act grow towards the final climax of the play, which is an un-extendable transformation of the protagonist.

- Consider *Macbeth*:

    Act 1
    Crisis: Macbeth hears Malcolm will be crowned the next king of Scotland.
    Climax: Macbeth plans to murder Duncan.

Act 2
Crisis: Macbeth hallucinates as he exits to murder Duncan ('Is this a dagger which I see before me?').
Climax: Macbeth is named King.

Act 3
Crisis: Macbeth sees Banquo's ghost.
Climax: news reaches Scotland that the English are planning to attack Macbeth.

Act 4
Crisis: Macbeth decides to kill the Macduff family ('Time thou anticipatest my dread exploits').
Climax: Macduff resolves to kill Macbeth.

Act 5
Crisis: Lady Macbeth's death is announced ('Tomorrow and tomorrow and tomorrrow …').
Climax: Macbeth is decapitated by Macduff.

- Notice that the play's most famous soliloquies occur at the moments of crisis.

- The number of acts indicates the number of major reversals. *A Doll's House* thus has three major reversals for Nora, at the conclusion of each act:

Act 1
Crisis: Krogstad tells Nora he knows about her fraud.
Climax: Torvald refuses Nora's pleas not to fire Krogstad (thus ensuring Krogstad will reveal her fraud).

Act 2
Crisis: Krogstad drops the letter revealing Nora's fraud into Torvald's locked post-box.
Climax: Nora contemplates suicide.

Act 3
Crisis: Torvald reads Krogstad's letter.
Climax: Nora leaves.

II

- Divide your stimulus story into acts. Locate the major transformations for the protagonist as a starting point for this process.

- In *Cinderella* the act divisions might look like this:

  Act 1
  Crisis: Cinderella is left alone while the rest of her family goes to the ball.
  Climax: the Fairy Godmother transforms Cinderella into a princess so she can go to the ball.

  Act 2
  Crisis: Cinderella and the Prince dance and fall in love.
  Climax: Cinderella flees the ball at midnight.

  Act 3
  Crisis: the Prince arrives at Cinderella's house, but her stepmother and step-sisters will not let Cinderella see the Prince.
  Climax: The glass slipper fits Cinderella and the Prince asks her to marry him.

- Split into as many groups as there are crises and climaxes – in this case, that would mean six groups.

- Each group work on one moment of crisis or climax.

- In 2 minutes, write a single line for the protagonist at this moment of crisis or climax.

- Share these with the rest of the group and stick them up on your wall in order.

Scene design (25 minutes)

Bring further detail to the internal structure. Take the acts and break them into scenes, finding the moments of conflict for your central character. Bring these to life.

- Work in as many equally sized groups as there are acts in your story. For *Cinderella* we would break into three groups.

- Usually a new scene marks a change in location, a leap in time or the entrance of a major new character. However, as with each act, each scene is defined by its own narrative crisis and climax events. These define the narrative function of each scene.

- The crisis point represents a challenge to the protagonist; the climax represents a change or shift in the protagonist. A sequence of scenes builds towards the major reversal which concludes an act.

- Consider scene crises and climaxes in Act 1 of *Macbeth*:

  Scene 1
  Crisis: the witches survey their future.
  Climax: the witches plan to meet with Macbeth.

  Scene 2
  Crisis: victory over the Norwegian forces is announced.
  Climax: the King announces he will make Macbeth Thane of Cawdor.

  Scene 3
  Crisis: the witches tell Macbeth he will be Thane of Cawdor and also king.
  Climax: Rosse tells Macbeth he is to be named Thane of Cawdor.

  Scene 4
  Crisis: King Duncan announces his son Malcolm will be the next king of Scotland.
  Climax: Macbeth resolves to 'o'erleap' Malcolm.

  Scene 5
  Crisis: Lady Macbeth prepares for murder ('unsex me here').
  Climax: Lady Macbeth readies Macbeth for murder ('look like the innocent flower, / But be the serpent under't').

  Scene 6
  Crisis: Lady Macbeth welcomes Duncan to her castle; the King notes Macbeth's absence.
  Climax: Lady Macbeth takes Duncan to feast with Macbeth.

Scene 7
Crisis: Macbeth decides he cannot kill Duncan.
Climax: Macbeth resolves to murder Duncan.

I

- Each group work on an act from your stimulus material.

- Break this act into scenes. At the moment, try and keep this descriptive and as simple as possible, isolating one main narrative event for each scene.

- Act 1 of *Cinderella* might have the following transformative crises and climaxes which define the scenes:

  Scene 1
  Crisis: Cinderella sits alone mourning her dead father.
  Climax: the stepsisters and stepmother force Cinderella to clear the ashes from the grate.

  Scene 2
  Crisis: Cinderella's stepmother receives an invitation to the Prince's ball.
  Climax: the stepsisters and stepmother refuse to allow Cinderella to go to the ball, and excitedly prepare themselves.

  Scene 3
  Crisis: Cinderella is left alone while the others go to the ball.
  Climax: the Fairy Godmother appears to Cinderella and turns her into a princess.

II

- Once each group has broken their act into scenes, allow 7 minutes to devise a series of tableaux (frozen images) capturing a representation of the crisis and climax from each scene.

- Share your tableaux. If possible take photographs of each image and print them out to stick on your wall. If not, roughly sketch them.

Character design (25 minutes)

Build the network of relationships which will form the basis of the characterization. Ensure a balanced character dynamic, and centre each character's existence around the story you are telling.

- Work as a full group.

I

- Write down the names of all the primary characters on separate pieces of paper. For *Cinderella* we would need seven pieces of paper:

    Cinderella
    The Fairy Godmother
    The Prince
    The stepmother
    The eldest stepsister
    The middle stepsister
    The youngest stepsister.

- Stick these names up on the wall, with plenty of space around them.

II

- Write down a list of character archetypes (choose from one of the models on pages 271–4), with one archetype per piece of paper. I will choose the following eight-figure model:

    Protagonist
    Antagonist
    Guardian/Mentor
    Contagonist
    Sidekick
    Sceptic
    Reason
    Emotion.

III

- Now stick archetypes on the wall next to character names, defining the roles of these characters in the drama. For *Cinderella*, the character design could look like this:

  Cinderella – Protagonist
  Stepmother – Antagonist
  Fairy Godmother – Guardian/Mentor
  Prince – Contagonist
  Middle stepsister – Sceptic
  Eldest stepsister – Reason
  Youngest stepsister – Emotion.

- We have no obvious sidekick for Cinderella here. Perhaps we will invent one – a pet mouse, or an imaginary friend (the broomstick that later becomes her carriage?). We could make the Fairy Godmother her sidekick (lowering this character's status) and perhaps introduce the spirit of her father as a Guardian. We could make the youngest stepsister Cinderella's sidekick, as well as Emotion: a secret ally, too scared of her mother and sisters to intervene. We could leave a sidekick out of the story.

IV

- Define an objective for each character, in relation to the protagonist's central objective, i.e. whether they help or hinder the protagonist in getting what they want. Write these next to the character names. For Cinderella (with the youngest sister as sidekick) that could be:

  Fairy Godmother – to help Cinderella find the Prince
  Prince – to find Cinderella
  Stepmother – to stop Cinderella finding the Prince
  Eldest stepsister – to stop Cinderella finding the Prince
  Middle stepsister – to help her mother stop Cinderella finding the Prince
  Youngest stepsister – to help Cinderella find the Prince without letting her mother or sisters know.

Politics (20–25 minutes)

Open up the politics of the stimulus story. Challenge these values and consider how you will handle them in your own work.

I

- Work as a full group.

- Cast yourselves (at random and against type, e.g. Cinderella might be played by a male actor for now) into roles in the story.

- Arrange yourselves into a line, with the most socially powerful and influential character (at the start of the story) at one end of the room, and the least powerful at another. For *Cinderella* the line might be arranged in the following order:

    Prince
    Stepmother
    Eldest stepsister
    Middle stepsister
    Youngest stepsister
    Cinderella.

- Where would the Fairy Godmother sit? Perhaps at the very top, since she has magical powers, or perhaps outside of the line altogether since she is not subject to its social controls.

- If you can, take a photo of this line and print it out to stick up on your wall. If you can't, commission someone in the group to draw it or write it out and stick this up.

II

- Now represent the power arrangement at the end of the story. For *Cinderella* that line might look like this:

    Prince
    Cinderella
    Stepmother
    Eldest stepsister

Middle stepsister
Youngest stepsister.

- Again, draw or print out an image of this line.

- Reflect on what it is that gives people power. In this case, marriage moves Cinderella and blood lines are important. Power is hereditary, and principally operated by men.

III

- Those of you cast in a role, play a group game of your choosing (any children's game will do: tag, stuck-in-the-mud, musical statues or any rehearsal game you particularly like). Play the game with the defined statuses conditioning your behaviour.

- Those of you in the group who are not cast in a role, observe and feedback on what behaviours you see, and how power affected people's choices.

- Question the politics of the society and challenge them. Will you want to alter the gender, class, race or social role of any of these characters? We could make the *Cinderella* story a feminist classic. What if the Prince is in fact a brilliant but poor young dance teacher at a holiday camp, and a shy Cinderella seeks freedom from her overbearing parents? *Dirty Dancing* emerges out of *Cinderella*, with its political message clear and strong.

Culture (15 minutes)

Open up the culture and values of the stimulus story. Challenge these values and consider how you will handle them in your own work.

- Work as a full group.
- Define five words that are key to your story world's culture. These are values rewarded by the story's central society. For *Cinderella* we might choose:

Beauty
Family
Strength
Honour
Loyalty.

- Write these words out on five pieces of paper, and stick them up over the door to your rehearsal room, as you might find them over the entrance to a school.

II

- Half of the group play a children's game (not in role, but as yourselves), half of the group watch. Players, allow the values of the story culture to condition your play and behaviour within the game. Observers, watch how these values condition their relationships within the game.

- Share feedback. Question the values of the society, and challenge their assumptions. Will you bring these cultural values into the original piece you are devising, or will you adapt them? Will you seek to challenge any of these values within the piece you create? Don't worry yet about how. In this case, what if you swap beauty for intelligence? What kind of story emerges now? *Cinderella* will no longer be loved at first sight for her beauty, and found because a shoe fits. What story begins to emerge now? *Good Will Hunting* does this, with the other values almost unaltered (intelligence, family, strength, honour, loyalty) – though interestingly I can't think of one in which intelligence replaces beauty and the protagonist remains female. Maybe you will make it.

Character development (25 minutes)

Build rounded, complex characters, who live within the designed dramatic structure. Use techniques you have developed in previous chapters to create a character.

I

- As a pre-class exercise, each member of the group will take responsibility for writing a list for one of the six topics listed below, based on a chosen character from the stimulus material. Choose from the following:

  Non-negotiable facts about the character (including given events in their past life)
  Everything the character says about themself
  Everything other people say about the character
  Everything the character says about the world
  Everything the character says about other people
  Everything the author says about the character.

- Share these lists at the start of this session.

II

- Work in equal sized groups. Each group take a character (or two if there are lots of characters/not many of you). You will need large pieces of paper (ideally A3) and marker pens.

- Remind yourselves of the archetype and role they serve in the character design developed on page 271 (protagonist/ antagonist/guardian and so on).

- Remind yourselves of the defined objective the character has in relation to the protagonist's objective developed on page 298 (e.g. to stop Cinderella finding the Prince).

- These are non-negotiable, and every choice you make must not derail these.

- Draw a silhouette of the character's body on the paper, with no detail.

- Around the outside of the silhouette, write down five dominant outer characteristics. These are characteristics the world often sees. Use Hans Eysenck's list of characteristics (page 187) as a basis. For the stepmother these might be: anxious, rigid, touchy, aggressive, impulsive.

- Inside the silhouette, write a list of three inner characteristics. These are characteristics the character usually conceals from the world. For the stepmother these might be: loving, maternal, thoughtful.

- Now, inside the silhouette, write a secret desire the character keeps from the world, which is important to their choices. This is something they long for, but wouldn't want anyone else to know about. For the grieving, angry stepmother this might be her longing for her dead husband to return.

- Now, outside the silhouette, write down the character's conscious super-objective. This is the thing that drives them throughout the story. For the stepmother this might be to see her daughters married to healthy, wealthy men.

- Now write inside the silhouette the character's motive: what this super-objective is for. For the stepmother this might be so she can die without fear that her daughters will end up as lonely as she is.

- This will all be glorious supposition. Be playful and light, but bold and confident. Introduce your characters to the rest of the group and stick these drawings up on the wall.

Character triggers (20 minutes)

Bring to life each character's trigger event. Conceive the immediate motive that drives each character into the action of the drama. Any of them could form the basis of another devising process, or become the centre of the story you build.

- What trigger event precedes the story, which drives your character into the events of the story? For the stepmother this is probably the death of her husband (Cinderella's father). Without this event, none of the events of the story would occur and she would be an entirely different woman.

- Work in small groups, taking a character (or two) per group.

- In 10 minutes, tell the story of the trigger event as a group, in role. Anyone can take on the role, telling the story to the rest of your group. Tell it in any tense you like (past or dramatic present or whatever), but keep it in the first person. Tag in and/or tag out when you want to take over or relinquish the storytelling. You can add detail, or rewrite events as you go to try and uncover what this moment meant to the character.

- Use this process to come to a consensus about the basic events which occurred, and your character's basic relationship to it, i.e. how it made them feel and how it changed their world view.

- Share these stories with the whole group, or devise a short improvisation to stage that scene.

Unit design (30 minutes)

Build a whole drama through improvisation. This is based on the kind of improvisation you will have done in Part One, Chapter 5 (pages 107–29) and in Part Two, Chapter 8 (pages 211–43).

- Work as a full group, or if you are a large group you might split into groups of about seven.

- Work with a deadline of say 20 minutes (though any time limit will do), and stick to that deadline. This is when the work could disappear into a quagmire as you try and make something 'right'. At this stage, just make something.

- Choose a scene from the story which you want to explore. Remind yourselves of the scene and its major events (crisis and climax).

- Cast the roles in the scene (don't worry about casting to type – and don't fix anything; try changing roles around each time you do this). Those of the group who are not cast will make the following decisions for the actors about to play the scene. The actors have no voice in this:

What are its given circumstances: specifically and in detail, where and when does it take place?

What are the previous circumstances: specifically where have each of the characters just come from, and what do they think will happen next?

What are the characters' objectives: what does each character want to achieve in this moment?

What are the character relationships? Remind the actors of their relative statuses in the scene.

II

- Set up a space in which to play the scene and then improvise it.

- The improvisation may stumble to a halt, or run away down a path that leads the story somewhere quite unexpected. Reflect on whatever outcomes occur, with the non-actors taking the lead in this reflection. It is the responsibility of the non-actor observers to make the scene; the actor's responsibility is to live it.

III

- Rehearse and then share the scene if you are working in groups, presenting the scenes in the order in which they might occur in a staging (remember this doesn't have to be chronological to the story).

- Get sketches in place for scenes quite quickly and playfully.

- Reflect on the prototype you have made. Prioritize this question: what is worth following further?

Writing a scene (20 minutes)

Write scenes, while still working as a full group in the room. Identify people in the group who particularly enjoy writing and want to do more of it. Produce lots of material which can form the basis of further improvisation or writing.

- Work as a full group.

- Break scenes into three parts: a beginning, a middle and an end.

- Write the name and section of each scene onto a piece of paper, and put them in a hat (e.g. 'the beginning of scene 1, in which Cinderella is singing and working alone'; 'the middle of scene 1, in which Cinderella mourns her dead father'; 'the end of scene 1 in which Cinderella is bullied back to work by her sisters and stepmother'). Pass the hat around and everyone pull out one piece of paper.

- Allow 10 minutes to write a draft of the section of scene you have been allotted. You will need to decide who is in that scene, if it is not already agreed. Work quickly, confidently and anonymously. Do not write more than one side of A4.

- At the end of the 10 minutes, write the title of your scene (which section you have written) onto the paper, fold it up and put it back into the hat.

- Pass the hat round and everyone take out a scene. Read it to the rest of the group, as if you had written it yourself.

- Reflect on what has been written. You might like to commission someone to extend what they have done, or could continue this exercise, enhancing the scenes anonymously by passing them on.

Woman Reading a Letter, *by Gerard Ter Borch*

This famous painting, by the Dutch artist Gerard Ter Borch, was painted around 1660–5.

The exercises which follow provide models for ways to devise original narrative drama in response to a non-narrative and non-dramatic stimulus – in this case, a painting. They assume that research projects, work on themes and work on the super-objectives of the image have already been done. Several of the exercises outlined in the last section could be useful here, but I won't repeat them.

These exercises could be applied to any non-narrative stimulus – a song, a photograph, a symphony, a poem. I would readily adapt them for Wordsworth's 'Upon Westminster Bridge' or The Beatles' Hey Jude (wonderful once research reveals it was written by Paul McCartney – and originally called Hey Jules – to comfort John Lennon's son Julian during his parents' divorce).

Image analysis (25 minutes)

Devise a creative response to the painting, which could form a part of any final piece of theatre if you think it merits further development.

- Work in small groups of three or four. Each group will need a copy of the stimulus image.

I

- Take five minutes to look carefully at the image. First, notice everything that is there. What is shown?
- Next, notice what isn't there. What do we not see? Who or what is missing?
- What are the relationships between the characters in this moment? What wants or desires can we imagine lie beneath?
- Look at the light, the atmosphere, the mood of the painting.
- Look at the dynamics of movement in the painting.

II

- Take 10 minutes to prepare a short (1 minute) abstract movement sequence responding to this painting.
- First, define a playing space: constrict or expand it in your imaginations. I would constrict it to 2–3 square metres for *Woman Reading a Letter*.
- Now perhaps add one or two objects into the space – maybe a chair and a table in this case.
- Next, agree on five dynamic words taken from action in the painting to explore in movement. These might be as simple as: look, shift, cover, gather, lean.
- Now, each group member separately devise a five-stage journey through the defined space, using each of these words as a basis for one movement choice.
- One by one, step in and put your movement sequences into the space. Keep repeating the sequence, as a new person moves into the space. Connect your sequences and balance the space.
- Share your sequence with the rest of the group. Hear from your audience what they saw, and what relationships or moments of unexpected narrative occurred for them.

Still life (30 minutes)

Bring the painting to brief dramatic life.

- Work in small groups.

- Take 5 minutes to build as exact a replica of the painting as possible, using the people in the group. Be precise.

- Define the unseen trigger event for the image. What happened the moment before this painting was captured?

- What are the given circumstances of that moment? Where and when did it occur?

- Tell the story of the moment as a group, locating the narrative event and the objectives of the characters involved.

- Allow 3 minutes to build an image of the run-up to the moment of the painting. Title this image.

- Allow 3 minutes to build an image of what follows the moment of the painting. Title this image.

- Now take 10 minutes to devise movement – naturalistic or otherwise – to connect these three images into a sequence and refine them.

- Present your work to the rest of the group. –

- Reflect on ways to connect all the sequences. Could you link them, or run them in parallel? If you want to, do so.

A protagonist (10–15 minutes)

Select a protagonist and begin to think about their characterization. Bring them to imaginative life.

I

- Work in small groups of three or four.

- Each group choose a protagonist. In *Woman Reading a Letter*, it could be the woman reading, as its title suggests, or perhaps one of the observers – the woman holding the pen and sitting at the writing table, the unseen observer, from whose point of view we are seeing this moment in time, or the artist who has captured it all.

- Your protagonist defines the point of view for your story. You can change this choice later, so don't be afraid about making a decision now. This gets you moving.

- Prepare to introduce your chosen protagonist to the group, imagining they are sitting in a chair next to you. Introduce them with the following format:

  It is obvious that … (say something that is obviously true because of what they are doing or wearing or where and when they are)

  I see that … (say something that you infer could be true because of these things)

  I believe that … (say something that you believe to be true, but which you could never prove).

- Speaking of the title figure in Gerard Ter Borch's painting, I might introduce her thus:

  It is obvious that you are educated.

  I see that you are wealthy.

  I believe that you are underestimated and more intelligent than people give you credit for.

- Reflect on your discoveries. How has the image changed for you already? What stories are you already writing in your imagination?

II

- As a follow-up exercise, bring in an image from a newspaper or magazine of someone whom you recognize as being somehow like the protagonist, if they were alive today. Share this with the group in the next session, explaining this choice and then putting it up on the wall.

A relationship (25 minutes)

*Devise and write monologues for characters in the stimulus.
Anything you produce here might lead you down another
creative path you want to follow and further explore.
Letter writing could form the centre of the whole drama, for
example.*

- Work in pairs.
- Focus on one key relationship in the image and unfold its
  narrative and dramatic potential.

I

- Find a moment of contact between two people in the image.
  This might be depicted physical or eye contact, or implied
  contact.
- In *Woman Reading a Letter*, I will consider the contact implied
  by the letter, as it is the centre of this image.
- Assume there is a desire, either fulfilled or unsatisfied, in this
  correspondence. Discuss the body or bodies involved. Look
  at their eyeline, jaw or brow tension, the line of their neck;
  observe their weight distribution, tension in their hands. Are
  they opening or closing in response to this correspondence?
  Does it warm or chill, strengthen or weaken, stabilize or
  destabilize them?
- Having observed the effect of this correspondence,
  discuss the intent within it. What desire might lie behind
  this correspondence and prompt this response? In *Woman
  Reading a Letter*, our research projects will influence this work.
  There was a fashion in the period of this painting (1630s) for
  paintings of people reading love-letters. Maybe that is what we
  are seeing here.

II

- Each of you take one person at this moment of contact.

- Allow 3 minutes to write a monologue for your character, or, in this case, perhaps the letter. Write one unbroken, unedited draft.

- Swap letters/monologues with your partner. Read what you receive and then write a reply in 3 minutes.

- Read these to the rest of the group, in role, as a first exploration. Allow yourself the right to fail.

- Reflect on this in your journal, and your discoveries about the relationship. No matter what your feelings are about your monologues/letters, keep them in your journal as your first story sketch, to revisit and reflect on later.

A middle (25 minutes)

Create potential crisis points for your story, any or all of which you might further pursue.

I

- Work as a full group.

- The event captured in the painting will become the inciting incident, crisis point, climax or resolution in a story.

- Initially, assume it is the crisis moment and the centre of the drama. This will be the simplest for a devising process, but be open to shifting it to one of the other points in the story later.

- What is the extreme decision taken at this moment? In *Woman Reading a Letter*, what does this letter communicate that changes the protagonist forever?

- Everyone write onto a piece of paper an ending to the following sentence:

  Because of this, I wished I were …

- Fold over the top of the paper to conceal what has been written. Swap with someone else in the room.

- Everyone now write an ending to the following sentence on that piece of paper:

  Because of this, I wished I could …

- Fold over the paper to conceal what you have written and swap with someone new.

- Everyone now write an ending to the following sentence on that piece of paper:

  Because of this, I feared I must …

- Swap with someone new. Read all three sentences, and then write one sentence underneath beginning:

  This is the moment I decided to …

- Read these four sentences out to the group. In the case of the love letter our protagonist is reading, it could be:

  Because of this I wished I were … able to choose my own destiny.
  Because of this I wished I could … run away and become independent.
  Because of this I feared I must … marry the man my father has chosen for me.
  This is the moment I decided to … run away, change my name and become a teacher.

II

- As follow-up work, everyone take one of these crisis decisions and write a single metaphor to describe the character's feeling at that moment. Keats had 'on the shore of the wide world I stand alone'; Romeo had 'Juliet is the sun'; for Emily Dickinson, 'Hope is the thing with feathers'.

- Share yours at the start of the next session, and stick it up on the wall. You might use this metaphor as an acting tool later, or even as a trigger for further devising (perhaps expand the image into a poem which you will perform).

A beginning (45 minutes)

Collaboratively generate multiple beginnings to a story.

I

- Break into small groups of five or six.

- Build an inciting incident for the crisis you have defined. This incident has triggered an inevitable journey to the moment of the stimulus image. Build a frozen image (tableau) of this in 10 minutes.

- In order to build the tableau, first agree a shared location for this inciting incident. Do not plan the image itself: simply define a fertile location, rich with dramatic potential (a character's bedroom, a train station, underneath an apple tree in a field on the edge of town … something provocative to your imaginations).

- One of you will not be part of the tableau, but will stay outside to describe what has been made and its impact.

- Work in silence. Step up one at a time and make a physical offer of a frozen action. The rest of the group observe this, and take it in, then the next person go in and add to it. Do not preconceive your offers: draw your idea from what is made by the person before you. Your offer is a response to someone else's offer.

- Observer, assess what has been made. Describe any narrative that you infer, or any emotions you can see.

- The observer will now write a three-word title for this image and end the following sentence:

    This is when it all began. This is the moment when …

- Share your tableau and text with the rest of the class and reflect on your ideas. For this painting and the story I am building, the sentence (describing a scene we have built in an orchard under an apple tree) might be:

This is when it all began. This is the moment when … I fell in love.

II

- Now extend these. Build moving tableaux in which each person is performing and repeating one simple physical action or sequence. Use one Laban effort action as the basis of each movement choice: wringing, pressing, slashing, flicking, floating, punching, gliding, dabbing.

- Observer, extend your writing. End one sentence in the voice of each character in the image:

    I see …
    I feel …
    I want …
    I fear …
    I hope …

- Share these among the group and reflect on what they offer your devising process.

III

- As follow-up work, use old newspapers and magazines to make a collage representing the protagonist's experience of that moment. This need not be literal: it can rely on visual metaphors. At the start of the next session, share these and put them up on your wall.

An ending (10 minutes)

Draft multiple endings. This could of course be adapted to reveal other points in the story.

I

- Work as a full group. Sit in a circle.
- Discover the key dramatic moment following the crisis point: the moment of climax.

- The moment of climax is the moment beyond which no further extension of the story is possible. It should be beyond the capacity of anyone's imagination in the group to further extend the story.

- The climax of *Romeo and Juliet* is absolute: there is no possible extension of that love story. Nora's departure destroys the doll's house forever: it cannot be extended without beginning a new play. The reunion of the twins in *The Comedy of Errors* brings to an end all possible extensions of that confusion and mistaken-identity plot: from now on, everyone knows there are twins.

- What is the absolute extension of the story you are telling?

- Allow 5 minutes as a time limit. If you have the available technology, set a countdown timer running. Try and find as many absolute endings in that time as you can.

- One of you propose a climax to the story you are constructing. Go round the circle, extending this climax by coming up with ways to further intensify or add to it. If necessary, introduce new events in the preceding story: it can turn out that Juliet has taken a magic potion that makes her only seem dead – really she's alive and is about to wake up again!

- This is a game, don't worry about making it good.

- When you find one absolute ending to the story, propose another climax, then extend that one.

- Be bold in fulfilling your story: Juliet comes 'back to life' only to kill herself; Macbeth is confronted by a walking wood and a man not 'born of woman'. You can be extreme.

- Whenever someone reaches an un-extendable climax, propose a new ending and work that one through. Go for quantity more than quality: make endings, don't worry about making perfect endings.

- At the end of your 5 minutes, review your various endings.

- For the story I am building, we might have an ending in which the protagonist has fled alone, changed her name, become a governess, been pursued by her father and circumscribed husband, met them and lied that she is pregnant with another

man's child, been disowned and paid to disappear by her
father, lost her post as governess, but has now used the
money her father gave her to set up her own school in a small
village teaching poor girls to read.

II

- As a follow-up exercise, write three simple sentences to
describe the world as it is in resolution, after your favourite
climax. Write them down and decorate the page around them
with relevant images. Bring these in to your next session, share
them and stick them up on your wall.

Hot seat (20 minutes)

Extend your story by putting a character at its centre.

I

- Work in three equal-sized groups, each working on a section of
the story – inciting incident, crisis or climax.
- Each group take 2–3 minutes to hot seat the protagonist about
the relevant moment in the story. Everyone will take a turn to
play the protagonist. Use a timer if you have one.
- After doing this once, switch round so someone else plays the
protagonist and hot seat them about the same moment. Build
on what you have already heard; try not to discard it. If you feel
stuck, repeat other people's ideas – this too is discovery. Don't
try and be original.
- Ask questions about the events, their feelings, where and when
they were, who else was present, what they were thinking, how
it changed them. Find out what they did next and what they
had been doing previously. Use this as a way to accidentally
extend the story.
- Every hot seating session is another draft; none is definitive.
- Once everyone has played the protagonist for 2–3 minutes,
reflect on your ideas and discoveries with the rest of the group.

II

- As a follow-up exercise, everyone write about the event as a diary entry for the protagonist. Bring this in to the next session, share it with the full group and stick it on the wall.

Other voices (15 minutes)

Devise character relationships which might trigger ideas for scenes or simply provide depth and subtext to your work.

It can be helpful to have built a character design (page 296) before doing this exercise.

I

- Work as a full group. Everyone will need a piece of paper and a pen.
- Cast everyone in the group as someone in the world of the story, representing some characters more than once if necessary. In the story I'm developing from *Woman Reading a Letter*, we'd have the protagonist's father, her circumscribed husband, her lover, her employer and the children she teaches in this exercise.
- Put the protagonist in a chair in the middle of the room. They must remain silent throughout this exercise.
- Imagine your characters are in the very middle of the story. Go round the room, allowing everyone to state their relationship to the protagonist.
- Explore moving around the room in relation to the protagonist on the chair. Try being close to or far from the protagonist, behind or in front of them (as in 'Character relations' on page 203).
- Find a place in the room in relation to the protagonist where you feel most comfortable. Get a pen and paper and sit either facing or not facing the protagonist.
- On one side of the paper, write down three things:

> A secret you are keeping from the protagonist
>
> Three words describing how the protagonist makes you feel
>
> One major want you feel towards the protagonist.

- On the other side, write down:

  > One thing you want to tell the protagonist
  >
  > Three words describing how you think you make the protagonist feel
  >
  > One major want you think the protagonist feels towards you.

- While this is happening, the protagonist writes down three words describing how each of the characters makes them feel.

- Read out what you have written to the protagonist.

II

- As follow-up work, write a simple super-objective for the character you have been exploring. Bring this to the next session and share it with the group, before sticking it up on the wall.

Genre (20 minutes)

Consider through which genre you will tell your story.

- Work as a full group to explore genre in your story.

- Write out as many different genres as you can think of on separate pieces of paper. Put these in a hat, or face down on the floor in the circle.

- Tell the story in the third person and past tense to the rest of the group ('She was walking down the road, when she saw …'), but do so exploring given genre conventions. As you step into the circle, take out a piece of paper from the hat and tell the story in that genre.

- Tag team the storytelling. Anytime you are running out of energy, tag a colleague in to take over the telling, or if you have an idea you are bursting to explore, tag in. As you enter the circle, take a new genre.

- All this must be in service of finding the genre to match the story and its narrative objectives. Will the story I am building be – like the English nineteenth-century novels it is aping – a gothic romance and psychological thriller? Or will it be liberated by being treated as a realist drama like the French nineteenth-century novels it is also echoing? Or how about a political thriller? Maybe I will make her father and proposed husband high-profile politicians.
- Reflect on your discoveries as a group.

Storyboard (30 minutes)

Refine your story beats.

- It can be helpful to have built an act or scene design first.
- When making a film, directors build a storyboard, sketching out key shots from each scene. This becomes a basis for all their later decision-making and planning.
- Work in groups of four or five, taking an act of your drama each to analyse and storyboard.
- Create a frozen image (tableau) for six key moments in your act. Title each image.
- In each image, each character speak aloud their key scenic objective.
- Share the frozen images among the group.
- If you have the facility, take a photograph of each image, and print them out to build a storyboard on your wall.
- For each moment, write the character objectives on strips of paper, and stick them on this storyboard.

Story rhythm (25 minutes)

Plot the detailed shape of the story. Focus on the rhythm, clarifying the story's strongest beats. This is useful towards the end of a process.

|

- Work as a full group.

- You will need lots of A3 paper, and sticky tape.

- Draw a line, showing the rising and falling rhythm and tension of the story. This will be like the outline of a mountain range, with peaks, valleys and cliffs, as the action reaches peaks of tension and intensity.

- There will be sudden rises and cliff falls at major events, as well as slowly rising or falling slopes at more gradual scenes.

- Put this up on the wall and plot the images from your storyboard onto the line where they sit in the drama.

- Discuss the story rhythm and sequencing. What is the balance of the storytelling? Where does it accelerate, where does tension rise and fall away? Are the peaks in the right places (at the end of the acts, with particular intensifications at the inciting incident, crisis and climax)?

- Crisis scenes are often long, slow and build up to an intense conclusion – the classic example is Act 3, Scene 3 in *Othello*.

- In an action film, the crisis often happens terrifyingly early in the structure, with the vast majority of the film taken up with its climax (John McClane's wife is captured right at the start of *Die Hard*, and he spends the whole film in the climax, chasing and being chased by those holding her). The challenge with such an early crisis is continuing to find imaginative and surprising ways to sustain the climax over 80 more minutes.

- Consider other films, novels and plays and their structures: *Waiting for Godot* is all set-up, never quite reaching its inciting incident. What about *Terminator* – which smuggles a love story in to sustain a classic action movie? William Golding's novel *The Lord of the Flies* never has a resolution: it ends when its climax is interrupted by the arrival of an adult, to bring the story to a sudden end without resolution. The central conflict is interrupted, not resolved.

II

- As a follow-up exercise, bring in examples of books, novels, plays or films which radically play with our expectations of narrative structure. Share these with your group at the start of the next session. Assess your growing narrative structure against these examples. Maybe my story of the young woman who frees herself from her father and husband will benefit from working from the end to the beginning, as in Pinter's *Betrayal*. Maybe we will never see the antagonist at all – as in *Godot* – and the father will only appear through his letters.

Storytelling into present-tense drama (25–30 minutes)

Bring your story to dramatic life, staging it for the first time.

- Work as a full group. You can return to this exercise many times, developing scenes as you work.

- Sit in a circle. Do the tag-team storytelling again, but now use the first person and dramatic present tense ('I am walking along the road when I see …'). This throws us into the action here and now.

- As you tell the story, call other actors into the space to playfully (this doesn't mean humorously) act out short sections of the story as you tell them. You may describe a key moment in the drama, and then bring up two other actors to play it out with you.

- Be free in applying this; step between direct address to the audience and interaction with scene partners. The scene partners themselves can add to the telling once they are in – they too have the licence for direct address, and can add detail or their own perspective on the scene. The protagonist must remain our main point of contact with the scene however, and should conduct the storytelling, moving it on when necessary.

- Do not let one actor play the protagonist all the time; keep switching it around among the group, so that it remains a group-owned story.

- You can switch protagonists, genres or rewrite scenes at any time.

Devising non-narrative drama

As the team's head-brass flashed out, by Edward Thomas

As the team's head-brass flashed out on the turn
The lovers disappeared into the wood.
I sat among the boughs of the fallen elm
That strewed the angle of the fallow, and
Watched the plough narrowing a yellow square
Of charlock. Every time the horses turned
Instead of treading me down, the ploughman leaned
Upon the handles to say or ask a word,
About the weather, next about the war.
Scraping the share he faced towards the wood,
And screwed along the furrow till the brass flashed
Once more.   The blizzard felled the elm whose crest
I sat in, by a woodpecker's round hole,
The ploughman said. 'When will they take it away?'
'When the war's over.' So the talk began –
One minute and an interval of ten,
A minute more and the same interval.
'Have you been out?' 'No.' 'And don't want to, perhaps?'
'If I could only come back again, I should.
I could spare an arm, I shouldn't want to lose
A leg. If I should lose my head, why, so,
I should want nothing more. ... Have many gone
From here?' 'Yes.' 'Many lost?' 'Yes, a good few.
Only two teams work on the farm this year.
One of my mates is dead. The second day
In France they killed him. It was back in March,
The very night of the blizzard, too. Now if

He had stayed here we should have moved the tree.'
'And I should not have sat here. Everything
Would have been different. For it would have been
Another world.' 'Ay, and a better, though
If we could see all all might seem good.' Then
The lovers came out of the wood again:
The horses started and for the last time
I watched the clods crumble and topple over
After the ploughshare and the stumbling team.

Develop an ensemble, non-narrative drama in response to a poem.

Many of the exercises I've already outlined would be relevant here, but I won't repeat them. I am again assuming the necessary research on the setting, etc., has been undertaken.

I would as readily adapt and use these exercises for a stimulus novel, biography, painting, photograph or piece of music. Da Vinci's *The Last Supper*, William Golding's *The Lord of the Flies* or Bob Marley's *Get Up, Stand Up* could all be triggers for this kind of work.

Learn the poem (10 minutes)

Ensure all your later work is founded on a proper knowledge of the stimulus poem.

- As a pre-class exercise, learn the poem.

I

- Work in pairs.
- Perform it to a partner, but with the intimacy this affords you. It is only for your partner to hear, so sit close.

II

- Do the 'Shared speech' exercise on page 84 or throw the poem between you with *'Rounds of applause'* on page 65.

- There is no better way to engage with and respond to a poem than in your own breath, fresh-minting each line.

Write the poem (10 minutes)

This asks you to really discover and understand the poem. It brings you towards a deeper connection with the poem.

- Work individually.
- Write out the poem yourself, in your own hand.
- Take your time to do this, and write it as if you were the author. Stare at the blank page for a while first: enjoy the possibility of the white space. Pretend you are coming up with these words, one by one.
- Find each thought. Find the vital words to make sense of each thought.
- Pretend you wrote he poem, and enjoy the sight of it in your own handwriting.
- Read the poem to a new partner, taking care to mark each line-break in your reading.

Write a new poem (35 minutes)

Don't treat the poem as holy. Break it and find new possibilities in it.

- Work in groups of about five.
- Cut the poem up, thought by thought, so you have a floor scattered with fragments. Make sure they are scattered randomly all around.
- Each group member now gather three phrases each, at random, from around the room. Bring these back to your group.
- The group will now have fifteen phrases from the poem, unconnected and randomly chosen. Read them out to each other and place them in the middle for the group to see.

- You now have 10 minutes to arrange the words – cutting or repeating any words, but adding none – into a new text. It needn't have a clear argument – that almost certainly won't be possible. Find images and discover new sense out of these fragments, as they connect and counterpoint.

- Allow 10 further minutes to find an appropriate way to present the text, which serves its atmosphere and mood. You might sit in a circle and read it line by line, or scatter yourselves around the space and take a word each. You might read a section each, playing to imagined targets, or face a partner and take it in turns to read a line each. Find an appropriate physical and vocal dynamic to present the text.

- Now share your new texts with the rest of the group and reflect on how these might connect to each other.

Movement responses (30 minutes)

Devise an original movement sequence in response to the poem.

- Work in small groups. You will need an even number of groups to make this work (for example, two, four or six groups).

I

- Each group select one section of text from the poem. This should be more than four lines, less than eight.
- Give these lines to another group.

II

- Each group come up with one resource: a chair, a toy, a ball of string …
- Give this resource to another group (but not the same group to which you gave the lines of text).

III

- Each group define a physical score – a set of five instructions for physical behaviour. For example:

  four people enter the space running
  two people walk in straight lines, stop, turn, look over their shoulders, walk on
  two people watch
  four people turn together and crouch
  Everyone responds to each other.

- These instructions should be simple, physical and open and should be done consecutively.

- Give these instructions to another group (but not the same group to which you gave a resource).

IV

- Each group will now have three things: some lines from the play, a physical resource and a physical score.

- Take 10 minutes to devise an original movement sequence, lasting up to 2 minutes, employing each element and at all times responding to the text.

- Present these back to the rest of the class.

- Reflect on the impact of what has been created, and how it might link to other work you have made.

Verbatim

Find material in your local community which you can bring into your devising process.

I

- Work as a full group, interviewing people you invite to come in to meet you, or work in pairs or small groups, visiting people off site.

- This work derives from asking engaging questions, not giving answers.

- As a group, decide on what theme or issue you most want to address in your work. In this case, perhaps what it means to be a victim of war.

- Who could you meet and interview? Who would be able to speak from personal experience about this issue?

- Start by looking as close to home as you can. Is there anyone in the group, or close to the group, whom you could interview? If not, is there anyone in or connected to the wider community of your school or theatre? Beyond this, what local groups or associations could help you?

- Write a letter or email, asking for permission to interview the relevant people. Be clear about what the interview will involve, and what you think you might do with the interview once you have it.

- After receiving explicit permission, arrange to record interviews with these people.

- Your aim here will be to get your interviewees to tell you stories about their lives, connected to the experience or theme on which you are centring your work.

- Plan your questions as a group. Questions should be open and encourage extended answers.

- Do not worry about the quality of the recording: this can be done on any technology, as you can work from transcripts of the interview later.

II

- In class, prepare an improvisation based on the interview: respond to it, and devise a short, edited presentation of the interview.

- If you have recordings of the interviews, you might perform a silent movement sequence while the rest of the group listen to the interview playing. Alternatively, explore performing sections of the interview as part of the presentation.

Ensemble storytelling

Establish a basic character design for an ensemble drama. Begin basic characterization.

- In an ensemble drama, there is no single protagonist.

- An ensemble plot is effectively a collection of subplots. There will be no main plot. Every character will have their own storyline, with its own discrete conflict and resolution. None of these stories will carry the whole piece, but will rather weave together to create a whole. The coherence a main plot would normally provide will be created in some other way. *The Full Monty*, *Brassed Off*, *Crash*, even *X-Men* and certainly *Downton Abbey* (or any soap opera) are famous examples of ensemble dramas.

- 'Working with As the team's head-brass flashed out, what will hold the piece together will be the village community and the focus on the war (World War I). Shared settings (as in *Crash*), focal events (as in *Babel*) or themes (*Love Actually*) are the gravity of ensemble dramas. In this instance, the coherence usually provided by a main plot will come from location and theme (as in *Downton Abbey*).

- Remind yourselves of this list of archetypes:

Archetype	*Motive*	*Objective*
Creator	stability and control	create something of enduring value
Caregiver	stability and control	protect others from harm
Ruler	stability and control	control
Jester	belonging and enjoyment	live each moment with enjoyment
Regular guy	belonging and enjoyment	connect with others
Lover	belonging and enjoyment	achieve intimacy with others

Hero	risk and mastery	prove one's worth through courage
Outlaw	risk and mastery	revenge or revolution
Magician	risk and mastery	gather knowledge about the world
Innocent	independence and fulfilment	experience paradise
Explorer	independence and fulfilment	discover your free self
Sage	independence and fulfilment	uncover the truth

- Each choose an archetype to work from, to frame a balanced and varied collection of characters in the ensemble.

- Now make a list of people you know in your own life – they don't have to be people you know well, and could even be famous faces – whom you think broadly fit into this archetype. This is the process with which Mike Leigh begins devising his work.

- Choose one of these people as a basis for your characterization. They will become unrecognizable in the end, but they will provide a human starting point.

- Now do a personation exercise, using this individual (page 195).

A binding theme (15 minutes)

Connect the characters you are building to the binding central theme.

- Every character in the piece must be connected to the central theme in some way. In this case, that means World War I is a prominent part of their life. I am assuming the necessary research has been done already.

I

- Work individually, or in pairs.

- In the middle of a large piece of paper, draw a small circle and write the binding theme/event inside it (in this case World War I).

- Now draw five other circles around that one, with a line connecting each one to the middle circle.

- Now draw two circles connected to each of those five circles.

- Now draw one circle connected to each of those outer circles.

- Inside each of the five secondary circles, write a way in which you could be connected to the theme/event.

- In each of the two circles linked to these, write a more specific way you could be connected in this way.

- In each of the circles linked to these two circles, write a reason it could be painful to be connected like this.

- So, for example:

- As you can see, I didn't manage to complete mine in 7 minutes, but there is plenty of useful material here.

II

- Choose a role and problem to develop for your character (remembering you can always change your mind later). For example, you might choose to play a teacher struggling with her pacifist principles. Further research will almost certainly be required as follow-up work.

Biography (20 minutes)

Open up possible experiences or events in the life of your character which might contribute to the drama.

- Work individually.
- It can be useful to warm up for this exercise with a free word-association game of some sort. I like to play word-association with all the actors standing on chairs facing a partner – when they lose a life, they go from standing to sitting on the chair, then sitting to kneeling, then kneeling to lying. It's game-over after that.
- Everyone take 15 minutes for free writing, exploring your character's biography.

I

- Draw a grid with twenty-five squares in it (a 5 x 5 grid).
- Across the top of the grid, write five headings: work and play, fears and desires, likes and dislikes, friends and relations, problems and hazards.
- In 5 minutes, fill it with information about your character under each heading. Anything is valid. Do not edit your ideas, just write.
- Your box will look like this:

Work and Play	Fears and Desires	Likes and Dislikes	Friends and Relations	Problems and Hazards

II

- Write down five nouns at random. The only rule is that they must be within the setting of the poem – so, in this case, tree, carrot, hedgehog, caterpillar, shoe would be fine, but not hotdog, helicopter, quark or iPad (since none of these had been discovered or invented in Britain in 1914).

- Pass these nouns to the person next to you.

- In 5 minutes, write them out on a clean page and in note form scribble down a memorable event which happened to your character involving each thing.

- Do not edit your imagination, let it lead you to surprising corners. Don't be afraid of the extreme.

III

- Draw another 5 x 5 grid.

- Across the top of the grid, write five headings: Joy, Fear, Shock, Anger, Sadness.

- In 5 minutes, fill the grid with events from your character's life which made them feel these emotions.

IV

- Draw a long, straight line running the length of an A3 piece of paper.
- At one end is your birth, at the other end is the moment the poem was spoken.
- In 5 minutes, fill the line with drawings and words of events in your life. You might put on some of the events you've already discovered (to do with that caterpillar, or when you felt joy), you may want to fill it with new things.
- Don't edit your imagination.

V

- As follow-up work, write a short biography for your character.

Object of value (20 minutes)

Generate possible relationships, experiences and events that might contribute to your final drama.

- Work in pairs.
- Everyone bring an object to class. This object should not have great personal value, but is an object that you can imagine someone could endow with value. Any trinket or item of jewellery, for example, will do.
- Give the object to your partner. You will get it safely back at the end of the session.
- How is the object you have been given valuable to your character? How is it connected to the theme(s) of the poem? Let your imagination surprise you.
- Introduce the object to a different partner and take time to ask meaningful questions of each other about the object.

Characterization

Build and develop your characterization.

- Use techniques described elsewhere to devise and discover the character. Try writing monologues, hot seating (page 186), animal work (page 193), defining super-objectives (page 184).

- Try using the Eysenck personality traits (page 187) to further define your character. Try making a list of inner and outer characteristics (page 190) or looking at your domains of self-esteem (page 181). Rehearse 'Greatest victories' (page 183).

- At every turn, enjoy the opportunity this presents to express and explore yourself through another voice. Expand and explore your human potential through this free role-play. This self-expression is what makes our craft an art.

Letters

Generate and stage original written material.

I

- As a pre-class exercise, write a letter from your character to someone important in their lives. This might be about an event conceived in your free-writing exercise, and should certainly be to do with the theme. For example, my teacher might be writing to her brother trying to persuade him not to enlist with the army.

- The letter must be:

    Persuasive
    Passionate
    Private
    Dealing with a problem.

II

- Give your letter to someone else in the group.

- Write a reply to the letter you receive, in the voice of the character to whom it was addressed. Return the letter to the person who wrote it.

III

- Work in small groups. Prepare a staged reading of the letters. Don't concern yourselves with linking the letters in narrative terms (though this may occur – 'You can be my brother!'). Find ways to stage and present them that underline their thematic and situational links. You might intercut lines or use the space in ways that make the letters echo with each other.

Personal objectives

Devise short solo improvisations.

- Work individually. Allow time to prepare beforehand, plus 15–20 minutes in class before sharing.

I

- As preparation for this, choose three characteristics that you want to explore in the character (let these be connected to the archetype). Look at Eysenck's wheel for examples (page 189) – e.g. restless, impulsive, optimistic.

- Prepare a short (5 minutes at most) improvisation for your character in which you can explore these. Define one clear physical objective, in some way connected to the theme (e.g. to pack up and give away your brother's belongings after receiving the news he's 'missing in action'). Define clear inner obstacles which make this difficult to achieve (e.g. sadness, anger). It should require at least three physical actions to achieve the objective.

- Have a clear 'Why here, why now?'. It must have immediacy. In the example I have given, the psychology creates the 'Why now?' – no-one wants to dwell on this task.

- Define your given circumstances and bring in any basic props you might need, or prepare objects to endow/substitute for others.

II

- Rehearse and then share your improvisations. Although you are on your own, these do not have to be silent. People talk to themselves, or you might want music in or underscoring the scene.

- How could this be the beginning of a story? Extend it, connecting it to other improvisations you may have done that could form other points in your character's journey.

Opposing objectives (30 minutes)

Devise short partnered improvisations with clear conflict.

- Work in pairs.

- Devise a short exchange between your characters (no longer than the stimulus poem), which will take place in the binding setting (in this case, somewhere in the village). This exchange will in some way explore the central theme (in this case World War I).

- The exchange should be built around this simple dramatic structure: you both have opposing objectives – you want different things.

- Invent an imagined relationship between you – you might be siblings, lovers, old school friends, teacher and pupil ...

- Work from the archetypal motive conceived in your character design (page 297). Ask why your character wants stability and control/belonging and enjoyment/risk and mastery/ independence and fulfilment here and now. What current fear might be the source of this particular desire? What hole is being filled? For example: a teacher encouraging a pupil to sign up with the army; a young soldier persuading his girlfriend to marry him before he leaves for war; a daughter persuading her father to let her go out to work.

- Reflect on these exercises. What relationships arose? What did you find out about your characters?

- How could this be the middle of a story? Extend it, and perhaps connect it to other improvisations you may have done which could provide more material for your character's journey.

Shared objectives (30 minutes)

Devise short partnered improvisations with strong inner tension.

- Work in pairs with someone new.

- Devise a short exchange between you (no longer than the stimulus poem), which will take place in the binding setting (in this case, somewhere in the village). This exchange will in some way explore the central theme (in this case World War I).

- The exchange should be built around this structure: you both want the same thing, but cannot get what you want because of fierce inner obstacles. Let this stricture free your imagination.

- As in the last exercise, invent an imagined relationship between you.

- Start from the archetypal motive. Ask why your character wants stability and control/belonging and enjoyment/risk and mastery/ independence and fulfilment here and now. What current fear might be the source of this particular desire? What hole is being filled? By way of example: you want to kiss each other, but are too ashamed to say so because of shared grief for a previous lover who has died at war; you both want to clean the white feathers (a brand of cowardice) from your pacifist neighbour's doorstep, but are too afraid to remove them; one of you is telling the other that a mutual friend has died.

- Reflect on these exercises. What relationships arose? What did you find out about your characters?

- How could this be the end of a story? Extend it, and perhaps link it to other material you have been improvising as part of your character's journey.

Teaching Tip: You can change the format of these exercises and continue creating new scenes for as long as you like. You might provide a scene format in which one person is asleep and the other, for some reason, has to leave without waking them up. If they wake them up, their objective will not have been achieved. Or you might present the structure that three characters have shared objectives, but each has a secret from the other. Devise basic dramatic structures within which actors devise.

Structure

Having generated material, edit, refine and create a structure for it.

- The relationship to time is altered: the piece is not bound to narrative chronology. But what will the audience's relationship to time be? Mystery, thriller or suspense (are the audience behind, with or ahead of the action in their knowledge)?

- Title all the work you have devised so far and write these titles onto pieces of paper. Scatter them out on the floor, and start arranging them into a sequence with a story structure (though it won't tell a story).

- There will still be an inciting incident, a crisis point and a final climax.

- Work to select and place the fragments of images and action into a structure.

- Having built characters, relationships and scenes in this way (using these and other processes suggested elsewhere), you can mould an ensemble piece, in which we meet and follow multiple characters on their private journeys, with their own beginnings, crisis points and endings.

Further reading

Alfreds, Mike (2013), *Then What Happens*. Nick Hern Books. Part Two, 'Workshops for Storytelling'.

Boal, Augusto (1992), *Games for Actors and Non-Actors.* Routledge.

Clements P. (1983), *The Improvised Play: The Work of Mike Leigh.* Methuen.

Johnstone, Keith (1981), *Impro.* Methuen.

Johnstone, Keith (1999), *Impro for Storytellers.* Faber and Faber.

Littlewood, Joan (2003), *Joan's Book – The Autobiography of Joan Littlewood.* Methuen.

Read, Leonard (1958), *I, Pencil,* can be read online for free at the Library of Economics and Liberty: www.econlib.org/library/Essays/rdPncl1.html. It is the essay on which I've based the 'Framework's' discussion about how collaboration serves unimaginable creativity. An excellent animated version of this essay can be seen at: www.ed.ted.com/on/8S6Mp7EP or simply search for 'I pencil animated translation'.

Swale, Jessica (2012), *Drama Games for Devising.* Nick Hern Books.

CONCLUSION

Eve reaches out her hand, takes a shiny red apple and bites into it: the sweetness of the first apple ever tasted. She breaks the rules, angers her god and gives birth to the knowing self. In a moment of glorious curiosity and hunger, she frees humanity into self-consciousness: soon we will build tree houses for our kids in that tree and bake pies to dress up that apple.

Biting the forbidden fruit, Eve achieved our greatest transgression and gave birth to our capacity to imagine new futures. In the bite of an apple we journeyed from innocence and ignorance to imagination and identity.

Because of these gifts of Eve's, we can play make-believe, share stories and rehearse new versions of ourselves. The tools of consciousness – the awareness of ourselves as agents and subjects of change – are the vital core of storytelling. Eve freed us from the Garden of Eden and we went off on our own with nothing but each other and our imaginations to save us.

Head out from the safety of the Garden. Take your work to a knowing public. The subject of this workbook has been your private work as an actor. Your work's purpose lies in a public audience, and whatever that audience takes out into the world having bitten into that apple. The work exists for the change you effect in your audience.

Don't stay in the safety of training or rehearsal: step out into the unknown. Transgress. Make change. Adam didn't dare. Follow Eve.

LINKS TO WORDBOOK VIDEO

To view a particular video, please visit its URL below, or go to https://vimeo.com/channels/theactorsworkbook

APPENDIX 1
100 CHARACTER
QUESTIONS

These questions might send you down an interesting new path. You don't need to answer them, but it might be fun to ask them.

Introductions

1   What is your birth name and what name do you use?

2   Do you have nicknames? What are they and where did you get them?

3   Do others tend to find you physically attractive?

4   How do you dress most days?

5   How do you 'dress up'?

6   How do you 'dress down'?

7   What do you wear when you go to sleep?

8   Do you wear any jewellery?

9   What is your best feature? What would you like to change about your body?

10 What is your birth date?

11 Where do you live? Describe it in detail and how it makes you feel.

12 What is your most prized mundane possession? Why do you value it so highly?

13 What is in your pockets?

Family

14 Who was your father and what did he do for you?

15 Who was your mother and what did she do for you?

16 What was your parents' marriage/partnership like?

17 Did you have any siblings? What did they do for you?

18 What's the worst thing a family member ever did to you? What's the worst thing you've ever done to a family member?

19 When was the last time you saw each member of your family? Where are they now?

20 Were you close to any members of your extended family? Who were they and what did they do for you?

Childhood

21 What is your earliest memory?

22 What was your favourite game?

23 Did any adults outside of your family have a formative influence? Who were they and what did they do for you?

24 Who was your best friend when you were growing up? What did they do for you?

25 What is your fondest childhood memory?

26 What is your worst childhood memory?

27 How did your father make you feel when you were seven?

28 How did your mother make you feel when you were seven?

Adolescence

29 How old were you when you had your first kiss? Who was it with and how was it?

30 What is your view of authority and what single event most formed it?

31 If you had a formal education, were you a good student? With what social group did you identify?

32 What were your adolescent ambitions?

33 Who was your key role model in adolescence?

34 What is your favourite memory from this period?

35 What is your worst memory from this period?

36 How did your father make you feel when you were 14? How do you think you made him feel?

37 How did your mother make you feel when you were 14? How do you think you made her feel?

Work

38 Do you have a job? What is it and who does it make you? If you have no job, how do you earn a living?

39 How does your employer or the person in charge of you make you feel? How do you try and make them feel? What do they think of you?

40 What are your co-workers like? Do you get along with them? Anyone in particular?

41 What did you have to learn recently which you found particularly difficult?

42 Do you tend to save or spend? Why?

Sexuality

43 Would you consider yourself heterosexual, homosexual, bisexual or something else?

44 Have you ever been in love?

45 If you have had sex, who did you first have sex with and what was the experience like?

46 Have you ever had a same-sex experience? Who with and what was it like?

47   What is your private sexual fantasy?

48   Do you have a current lover? How do they make you feel? Why are attracted to them?

49   How do you feel about marriage and children?

50   How and why did your last romantic relationship end?

Miscellaneous

51   Have you ever broken the law?

52   Do you drink alcohol regularly?

53   Have you ever tried other mood-altering drugs?

54   What one act in your past would you most like to change?

55   Of what are you most proud?

56   Have you ever been in a physical fight?

57   What single trait do you most deplore in yourself?

58   What single trait do you most deplore in others?

59   What physical feature would you change in yourself if you could?

60   Do you have any recurring dreams or nightmares?

61   Do you believe in God/gods?

62   When you die, what happens to you?

63   Do you think the future is hopeful for humanity?

64   To whom would you most like to say sorry and why?

65   What did you dream about last night?

66   Is it okay to cry? When did you last cry?

67   What do you fear?

68   When – if ever – was the last time you saw the sea?

69   When was the last time you laughed out loud?

70   Has anyone or anything you deeply loved died? How did you hear about their death?

71 What was the worst injury you ever received?

72 What irrational fears do you have?

73 When did you last eat a meal? What was it and with whom?

74 When did you last cook a meal?

75 What will your new year's resolutions be?

76 What keys do you have?

77 What is your morning ritual?

78 Do you carry your wealth around? How and how much?

79 If you were to suddenly gain an obscenely large sum of money, what would you do with it?

80 What would your wishes be if a genie popped out of a bottle?

81 What do you keep beside your bed?

82 What is the most frightening disfigurement or injury you can conceive?

83 What live music have you heard?

84 What secrets do you have?

85 What is your most treasured possession?

86 Can your read? What are you reading at the moment, or what was the last thing you read?

87 Would you tip a waiter?

88 How would you vote tomorrow, if at all?

89 Would you enjoy a fancy dress party? Who or what would you go as?

90 What gift do you want for your next birthday?

91 What is your favourite time of day?

92 What is your favourite time of year?

93 What is your favourite food and drink?

94 What food and drink do you dislike?

95 What do you do to relax?

96 What habits annoy you? Which habits of your own annoy someone close to you?

97 When were you last embarrassed?

98 Are you physically fit? If so, how? When was the last time you were out of breath?

99 Do you have a pet? Or would you like one?

100 How would you plan your funeral?

APPENDIX 2
GLOSSARY

Action whatever you do to get what you want (also called 'tactics' or 'activities').

Animal work using an animal as a basis for characterization and transformation.

Antagonist the person or force providing a force of opposition and central conflict in the drama (e.g. Voldemort).

Archetype a universal model recognized and understood across cultures.

Backstory all the events a character has experienced, which precede the start of the drama and are directly relevant to the action.

Biography the full story of a character's life, including much which will not be directly relevant to the drama.

Characteristics features or qualities you can attribute to a character, which reflect their behaviour (outer characteristics) or inner life (inner characteristics).

Circles of attention (sometimes called 'circles of concentration') how broad your focus is; circle 1 is personal; circle 2 is inter-personal; circle 3 is public.

Climax the peak of the drama, when the central conflict is brought to an unsurpassable end.

Crisis a major dilemma for the central character in the story, as they face a significant choice which will define the outcome of the drama.

Endowment imagining something or someone has a particular value or quality in order to stimulate a particular relationship.

Ensemble a complementary group of individuals, working together as a collective towards a shared creative objective (it's the French for 'together').

Event something which happens in a drama to change the course of the action.

Falling action the sequence of events which sees the central conflict unravelling in between the middle and the end of a story.

French scene a scene division marked by the entrance or exit of a character.

Genre a type or category of story being told (e.g. thriller, horror, fantasy).

Given circumstances all the environmental and situational conditions which influence the behaviour of a character.

Heroic tension   a moment of contradiction within an archetypal character which provides human dimension (e.g. the moment of generosity from a miser).

Inciting incident   the on-stage event which triggers all the subsequent action of the drama (e.g. when Gandalf gives Frodo the ring).

Moment of orientation   the few seconds it takes to orient yourself in new surroundings/after an *event* has occurred.

Motive   why your character is doing something; what it is all for.

Objective   what your character wants or needs (also sometimes called 'intention', 'task' or 'action').

Obstacle   whatever is stopping your character getting what they want.

Personation   using another person as a basis for characterization.

Plot   all the events which happen on-stage or on-screen within a story.

Premise   the hypothesis which sits underneath the story, beginning 'What happens if …?'

Previous circumstances   what has been happening before a scene begins or prior to an entrance.

Protagonist   the central character in a story whom we follow (e.g. Frodo or Harry Potter).

Resolution   the moments following the climax of the story which show us how the world of the drama has been changed by that finale (e.g. the Ewoks, Obi Wan, Luke and Darth Vader all have a big party).

Rising action   the sequence of events which build the central conflict in between the beginning and the middle of the story.

Setting   location, period, duration of action and level of conflict within a story.

Set-up   the action at the beginning of a story, before the *inciting incident*, within which we usually establish the central characters, setting, major themes, genre, style and conventions of the story.

Shadow play   action which reveals unconscious or concealed inner life (e.g. Prince Charles repeatedly twisting his wedding ring).

Stakes   the personal cost of what can be lost and gained by an action.

Style   conventions in performance (e.g. absurdism, naturalism, symbolism); for an actor, this is the world in which your character lives.

Super-objective   your character's main want, towards which their every action moves.

Target   the thing or person from whom you are drawing energy and whom you are trying to change.

Tempo-rhythm   the metabolic speed and regularity of strong pulses in a character or scene.

Theme   repeated ideas or values within a drama.

Through line   a character's sequence of action within a plot.

Trigger event   the unseen event which makes the rest of the story happen (e.g. the death of Cinderella's father).

Unit   a chunk of action running from one *event* to another.

APPENDIX 3
BIBLIOGRAPHY AND
RESOURCES

On acting

Adrian, Barbara (2008) *Actor Training the Laban Way*. Allworth Press.

Alfreds, Mike (2007) *Different Every Night*. Nick Hern Books.

Alfreds, Mike (2013) *Then What Happens*. Nick Hern Books. Part Two: 'Workshops for Storytelling'.

Benedetti, Jean (1998) *Stanislavski and the Actor*. Routledge.

Boal, Augusto (1992) *Games for Actors and Non-Actors*. Routledge.

Brook, Peter (1988) *The Shifting Point*. Methuen.

Caldarone, Marina and Lloyd Williams, Maggie (2004) *Actions: The Actor's Thesaurus*. Nick Hern Books.

Carey, David and Carey, Rebecca Clark (2008) *Vocal Arts Workbook*. Methuen.

Carey, David and Carey, Rebecca Clark (2010) *Verbal Arts Workbook*. Methuen.

Chekhov, Michael (2002) *To The Actor*. Routledge.

Clements, P. (1983) *The Improvised Play: The Work of Mike Leigh*. Methuen.

Donnellan, Declan (2002) *The Actor and the Target*. Nick Hern Books.

Hagen, Uta (1973) *Respect for Acting*. Wiley.

Howard, Pamela (2002) *What is Scenography?* Routledge.

Johnstone, Keith (1999) *Impro for Storytellers*. Faber & Faber.

McEvenue, Kelly (2001) *The Alexander Technique for Actors*. Methuen.

Marshall, Lorna (2008), *The Body Speaks*. Methuen Drama.

Meisner, Sanford and Longwell, Dennis (1987) *Sanford Meisner On Acting*. Vintage Books.

Merlin, Bella (2001) *Beyond Stanislavsky*. Nick Hern Books.

Merlin, Bella (2007) *The Complete Stanislavsky Toolkit*. Nick Hern Books.

Mitchell, Katie (2009) *The Director's Craft*. Routledge.

Newlove, Jean (1993) *Laban for Actors and Dancers*. Nick Hern Books.

Oida, Yoshi and Marshall, Lorna (1997) *The Invisible Actor*. Routledge.

Stanislavski, Konstantin, trans. Jean Benedetti (2008) *An Actor's Work*. Routeledge.

Stanislavski, Konstantin, trans. Jean Benedetti (2010) *An Actor's Work on a Role*. Routledge.
Swale, Jessica (2012) *Drama Games for Devising*. Nick Hern Books.

Broader interest

Berger, John (1972) *Ways of Seeing*. Penguin.
Campbell, Joseph with Bill Moyers (1988) *The Power of Myth*. Anchor Books.
Damasio, Antonio (2000) *The Feeling of What Happens*. Vintage Books.
Damasio, Antonio (2003) *Looking for Spinoza*. Vintage Books.
Gross, Richard (1997) *Psychology: The Science of Mind and Behaviour*. Hodder Education.
McKee, Robert (1997) *Story*. Methuen.

Useful websites

themappamundi.co.uk – a glorious 3D journey round the Hereford Mappa Mundi
www.dialectsarchive.com – for free online English language dialect and accent samples
www.gutenberg.org – free books and essays now out of copyright
www.nationaltheatre.org.uk – fantastic Digital Classroom
www.poemhunter.com – for great poems
www.poetryarchive.org – for great poems and educational resources
www.rsc.org.uk – remarkable access to Shakespeare resources
www.shakespearesglobe.com – its Discovery Centre is a wonderful resource for Shakespeare scholarship
www.sounds.bl.uk/Accents-and-dialects – for free online English language dialect and accent samples
www.theatrefutures.org.uk/stanislavski-centre – the best online resource for research based on the work of Stanislavski

INDEX